Risk Management for Design Professionals in a World of Change

Bringing into Focus:
Green Design, BIM, IPD, P3, International Risks, and New Contract Documents

J. Kent Holland
Editor

Ardent Publications
8596 Coral Gables La.
Vienna, VA 22182
703-623-1932

Printed in the United States of America
Signature Book Printing, www.sbpbooks.com

First Printing   November 2009

Published and Distributed in the United States by:
Ardent Publications
8596 Coral Gables Lane
Vienna, VA 22182

Library of Congress Control Number: 2009908002

ISBN 978-0-9723158-4-5

About *a/e ProNet*

a/e ProNet was formed to bring together insurance professionals whose activities in their market area had already established them as experienced, knowledgeable, and personally committed to service the design professional community. Exceptional expertise, value-added services, and independence of ties with any particular insurance company have been membership watchwords from the outset.

Since its first formal meeting in January 1988, *a/e ProNet's* membership has grown from a handful of members to more than 30 member firms that are significant independent insurance agents and brokers, located in major metropolitan areas throughout the United States and the United Kingdom. The service territories of the Association's members have grown to include 20 countries throughout the World. Geographical location is not a bar to membership, but the absence of specialized expertise is. There are currently an estimated 20,000 plus design firms served by members of *a/e ProNet*, representing a projected professional liability annual premium volume exceeding $300 million.

Evidence of *a/e ProNet's* exceptional services is available at the website, www.aepronet.org. This website endeavors to provide a comprehensive collection of specialized risk management information and resources for design professionals. Materials include an extensive collection of *Practice Notes* and Guest Essays. Your comments on this book and the website are welcome. Please feel free to contact us by email at info@aepronet.org.

This book has been registered with the American Institute of Architects (AIA) Continuing Education System as four continuing education courses. Readers who would like to use these courses for continuing education should follow the instructions with the course quizzes located at the end of the book.

The Officers, Directors, and Members of *a/e ProNet*

Disclaimer

No liability is assumed with respect to the use of the information contained herein, nor shall the publisher, distributor, editor, authors, or any employer or entity with which the editor or authors are affiliated be liable for damages or loss resulting from its use, including but not limited to actual, consequential, or incidental damages, whether foreseeable or unforeseeable. Although every precaution has been taken in the preparation of this book, the editor and authors assume no responsibility for errors or omissions.

The opinions expressed are solely those of the authors, and do not represent the views a/e ProNet, any a/e ProNet member, any individual, partnership, corporation, institution of learning, or any other entity by which the editor and authors are or have been employed or affiliated.

Any hypothetical situations and examples discussed herein are general in nature. The content and comments in the text are provided for educational purposes and general distribution, and cannot apply to any single set of specific circumstances, and should not be applied without the review and approval of your attorney.

While this book contains explanations of various legal concepts, it is not legal advice, and should not be construed or relied upon as such. It is important to remember that statutory and common law varies from state to state, and that how one court may interpret contractual and legal responsibilities may be significantly different from the interpretation of other courts and jurisdictions.

Legal advice concerning any matter presented or discussed in this book should be sought from competent counsel, knowledgeable in the law of the jurisdiction in which services will be performed and under which a professional services contract will be enforced. Likewise, advice from insurance and risk management professionals should be sought to address issues concerning insurance and risk management for individual contracts and circumstances.

Table of Contents

Detailed Table of Contents

Chapter 6:   **Introducing the ConsensusDOCS**

Brian M. Perlberg, J.D.

About the Authors and Editor

Hugh N. Anderson is an attorney in Madison, Wisconsin, where he was a member of the law firm of Wickwire Gavin, P.C. (and most recently, Akerman Senterfitt Wickwire Gavin). His practice consists primarily of construction and contract law. He regularly assists public and private project owners, architects, engineers, and contractors in the drafting of contract documents, the development of project delivery strategies, the establishment of insurance and risk management practices, and the resolution of disputes arising from bid errors, construction problems, professional errors and omissions, contractor default, and functional failures. Mr. Anderson serves as legal counsel to the Engineers Joint Contract Documents Committee. He is a member of the American Bar Association Forum on the Construction Industry, and is a graduate of Stanford Law School. Contact information: 7926 W. Hill Point Road, Cross Plains, WI 53528; phone: (608) 798-0698; hugh.anderson@aecdocuments.com.

Ricardo Aparicio is Senior Counsel and Contracts Manager with General Electric Company's Corporate Properties and Services Operation, in charge of negotiating and executing design and construction agreements for GE's capital and environmental remediation projects globally. Mr. Aparicio is a member in good standing of the Alabama and Florida bars as well as a certified Construction Law Specialist in the State of Florida. In addition, he maintains concurrent licenses as Architect, General Contractor, and Interior Designer in the State of Florida. Mr. Aparicio holds Bachelor of Architecture and Juris Doctor (Cum Laude) degrees from the University of Miami, Florida, and is a member of the American Institute of Architects, the American Bar Association's Forum on the Construction Industry, and immediate past-president of the Construction User's Round Table. Contact information: 31 Inverness Center Parkway, Suite 410, Birmingham, AL 35242; phone: (205) 991-4332; ricardo.aparicio@ge.com.

Howard W. Ashcraft is a senior partner in the law firm of Hanson, Bridgett, Marcus, Vlahos and Rudy. A graduate of Stanford University and the University of California School of Law (Boalt Hall), Mr. Ashcraft represents designers, owners and contractors in project formation, professional practice and construction disputes with a focus on public infrastructure and complex private projects. In addition, he is the firm's technology partner and has long had an interest in the application of technology to design and construction. Currently, he is a Steering Committee member, and Legal and Risk Subcommittee Chair, of the California Council AIA Integrated Project Delivery Taskforce and a contributing author of the National Institute of Building Sciences Building Information Modeling Standard. Mr. Ashcraft is also an honorary member of the American Institute of Architects, California Council, a Fellow of the American College of Construction Lawyers, a former member of the Governing Committee of the American Bar Association's Forum on the Construction Industry, and an arbitrator/mediator in the American Arbitration Association's Large and Complex Case Panel for Construction Disputes. He is a recognized construction lawyer listed by Chambers & Partners, USA, Best Lawyers in America, the Who's Who of International Construction Lawyers and was listed in 2004 as one of the top ten attorneys in Northern California. Contact information: 425 Market Street, 26th Floor, San Francisco, CA 94105; phone: (415) 777-3200; hashcraft@hansonbridgett.com.

Jerome V. Bales is a partner with the firm of Lathrop & Gage LLP in Kansas City, Missouri, and Chairman of its Construction Department. He has over 35 years of experience handling construction claims, litigation, risk management, and contract negotiation, representing design professionals, owners, contractors, sureties, and suppliers. He also frequently serves as a mediator or arbitrator in construction and other disputes and has been named to the Construction Arbitrator Master Panel of the American Arbitration Association (top 100 in the country). Mr. Bales has handled virtually every type of claim arising from a commercial project, i.e., defects in all design disciplines, delay and impact, job site safety, wrongful termination, liquidated damages, cardinal change, differing site conditions, and other contract disputes. In 1974, he received his law degree from the University of Missouri at Kansas City (J.D., with distinction), and in 1971, his undergraduate degree from Rockhurst University (B.S.B.A.). Contact information: 2345 Grand Boulevard, Kansas City, MO 64108; phone: (800) 476-4224; JBales@LathropGage.com.

John Binder, AIA, is an architect and associate principal with the architectural firm of KEPHART. He designed the first LEED-certified green apartment building in the U.S. His approach to architecture has always been, "Let's make it happen." His professional experience includes the design of high density communities by working with multi-family developers and his goals include the promotion of healthy lifestyles and healthy choices through architecture. He has received numerous prestigious awards including, in 2006 and 2007, Pillars of the Industry Award, for two separate communities, - Project Architect for Best Garden Rental Apartment Community of the Year and 2007 - Pillars of the Industry Award - Project Architect for Best Repositioning Conversion of a Multi-Family Asset. John frequently speaks on the national level on the merits of sustainability, most recently at the National Green Building Conference. Contact information: 2555 Walnut Street, Denver, CO 80205; phone: (303) 832-4474; JohnB@kephart.com.

Matthew P. Coglianese is a partner in the law firm of Peckar and Abramson. He specializes in environmental law and employment law. As part of his environmental law practice, Mr. Coglianese has broad experience with a wide range of federal and state enforcement matters, focusing on CERCLA, RCRA, the CWA and the CAA, as well as state and local environmental matters, including mold and toxic tort litigation, and his practice includes green building counseling, environmental and corporate counseling, permitting and corporate due diligence. Prior to entering the private practice of law, Mr. Coglianese served as an Assistant Regional Counsel with the United States Environmental Protection Agency in Atlanta, Georgia, where he handled enforcement of federal water and air pollution laws. As senior attorney with a major Los Angeles-based petroleum company, he was responsible for managing numerous Superfund and state hazardous waste sites throughout the country. Mr. Coglianese received his undergraduate degree from the University of Rhode Island in 1976, his Ph.D. in Biology in 1981 from Texas A&M University and his J.D. in 1984 from the University of Miami School of Law. Contact information: One Southeast Third Avenue, Suite 3100, Miami, FL 33131; phone: (305) 358-2600; mcoglianese@pecklaw.com.

Heather L. DeBlanc, an attorney with the law firm of Nossaman, LLP, has more than a decade of experience in construction law. She has represented public agency project owners as well as general contractors and subcontractors on public works projects, with a special emphasis on educational facilities. Ms. DeBlanc has experience drafting and analyzing a variety of construction contracts, investigating projects during and after construction, and litigating contract disputes. Her representative work includes: serving as a member of the legal team advising the Nevada Department of Transportation on its Public Private Partnerships (PPP) program, which is currently in a start-up; and assisting the Mississippi

Department of Transportation with procurement strategy and the development of procurement and contract documents for the design, construction, maintenance, and operation of a new, 12-mile toll road in Jackson, MS. This project represents the first privately-operated toll road in the State of Mississippi. Ms. DeBlanc received her B.A. from the University of California, Santa Barbara, 1994, and her J.D. from Pepperdine University School of Law, 1997. Contact information: 445 South Figueroa Street, 31st Floor, Los Angeles, CA 90071; phone: (213) 612-7814; hdeblanc@nossaman.com.

Mark C. Friedlander is a partner in the law firm of Schiff Hardin LLP. He concentrates his practice in construction law, both transactional and litigation, providing services to form and incorporate new businesses, to structure transactions, to draft and negotiate contracts, and to resolve and litigate disputes. He is a member of the Design Build Institute of America and the former Chairman of its Professional Practices and Contracts Committee. He is on the Board of Governors of the American College of Construction Lawyers and was the Chair of its Project Delivery Systems Committee from 2000-2005, and is a past President of the Society of Illinois Construction Attorneys. He was a member of the Committee on Outsourcing of Design and the Construction Management Services for Federal Facilities of the National Research Council, Commission of Engineering and Technical Systems, Board of Infrastructure and the Constructed Environment, National Academy of Science and Engineering. He received his B.A. from the University of Michigan in 1978 and his J.D. from Harvard Law School in 1981. Since 1985 has been an adjunct professor at the University of Illinois at Chicago School of Architecture and since 1995 a lecturer at Northwestern University's Engineering School. Contact information: 233 South Wacker Drive, Suite 6600, Chicago, IL 60606-6473; phone: (312) 258-5546; mfriedla@schiffhardin.com

Suzanne H. Harness, AIA, is President of Harness Project Solutions, LLC, a consulting practice she founded to provide procurement counseling, and other professional services as an arbitrator, mediator, project neutral, expert witness, and trainer. She provides legal services through her firm Harness Law, PLLC. In addition, as a consultant for Construction*Risk*, LLC, she provides risk management consulting services including contract reviews and risk management training. A licensed architect and construction lawyer, Suzanne Harness has worked in the design and construction industry for over thirty years, serving both the public and the private sectors. For six years concluding in December 2008, Suzanne served on the management team of the American Institute of Architects where she was responsible for the content of AIA Contract Documents. Suzanne began her career in architecture and served ten years as an architect in private firms. Subsequently, she worked an additional ten years directly for owners, first for a commercial real estate developer and then for the U.S. General Services Administration, managing the solicitation, procurement, and execution of design and construction contracts. She received her law degree from the George Washington University Law School, and Master degree in Architecture from the Catholic University of America. Contact information: 2750 North Nelson Street, Arlington, VA 22207; phone: (703) 283-8772; sharness@harnessprojects.com; www.HarnessProjects.com.

J. Kent Holland is an attorney with the firm of Construction Risk Counsel, PLLC, emphasizing construction law. He was formerly with the law firm of Wickwire Gavin, P.C (1986–2007). He provides legal representation for design professionals, contractors and project owners. He is also the principal of ConstructionRisk, LLC, a construction risk management consulting firm, through which he provides assistance with contract drafting, contract review and negotiation; change order and claims analyses, claim preparation and claim defense. Services also include risk management counseling concerning insurance coverage (particularly professional liability and environmental insurance) – including assistance with negotiating and drafting the terms and conditions of policies and endorsements, advice to insurance underwriters; guidance to those procuring insurance. From 1982 through 1986, he was an attorney in the Office of General Counsel of the U.S. Environmental Protection Agency, with responsibility for assisting the Agency in deciding wastewater treatment construction grants disputes, contractor claims, bid protests, suspension and debarment matters and minority business enterprise matters. Mr. Holland publishes a web-based construction risk management library and legal newsletter at http://www.ConstructionRisk.com. He received his J.D. in 1979 from the Villanova University School of Law. Contact information: 1950 Old Gallows Road, Suite 750, Vienna, VA 22182; phone (703) 623-1932; Kent@ConstructionRisk.com.

Frank D. Musica joined the staff of Victor O. Schinnerer & Company, Inc., in 1991to assist the Schinnerer program with CNA in identifying the transformations occurring in professional practice, the liability exposures created by contractual language, legislation, regulations and court rulings, and management processes and procedures to reduce the risk profiles of firms. Mr. Musica also served as the Schinnerer contact with the Engineers Joint Contract Documents Committee and, for 15 years, as Insurance Counsel to the Documents Committee of The American Institute of Architects. He is Schinnerer's senior risk management attorney. Before joining Schinnerer, Mr. Musica held staff positions in national professional organizations for architects and engineers for over a decade. Prior to that, he served as in-house legal counsel in the management of a West Coast A/E firm with an international practice in commercial, institutional, and residential facilities and master planning. Mr. Musica is a graduate of the School of Architecture of the University of Notre Dame and also holds a Masters in Business Administration and a law degree. Contact information: Two Wisconsin Circle, Chevy Chase, MD 20815; phone: (301) 951-6935; frank.d.musica@schinnerer.com.

Brian M. Perlberg is Senior Counsel, Construction Law & Contract Documents, at the Associated General Contractors of America (AGC) in the Washington, D.C. area. He serves as AGC's primary attorney for all contract and construction law matters. Mr. Perlberg is the lead staff attorney and executive manager for the new industry-endorsed ConsensusDOCS, the ground-breaking effort of consensus contracts which are transforming the construction industry. Mr. Perlberg also staffs AGC's participation as a sponsor of the Engineers Joint Contract Documents Committee (EJCDC), as well as commenting organization of the American Institute of Architects (AIA) documents. Mr. Perlberg serves on the American Bar Association (ABA) Forum on the Construction Industry Steering Committee for Contract Documents. Previously, Mr. Perlberg served as General Counsel and Director of Government Affairs for the Design-Build Institute of America (DBIA). He also served as a Council Member on the Maryland Green Buildings Council. He graduated from the University of Maryland School of Law and the University of Maryland Honors Program, College Park. Contact information: 2300 Wilson Boulevard, Suite 400, Arlington, VA 22201; phone: (703) 548-3118; perlbergb@agc.org.

Heidi H. Rowe is a partner in the law firm of Schiff Hardin LLP. Ms. Rowe focuses her practice primarily on construction law. She represents owners, developers, architects, engineers, contractors, subcontractors, suppliers and lenders in their construction-related disputes. She has significant experience in contract drafting, contract negotiation and contract enforcement. She has represented clients involved in both public and private construction projects and has developed an expertise in procurement law. Her expertise includes advising clients on how to implement effective processes and procedures for managing large construction projects and minimizing claims. Her education includes: Chicago-Kent College of Law (J.D., *high honors*, 2001), *Order of the Coif,* Executive Notes and Comments Editor, *Chicago-Kent Law Review; and* Valparaiso University (B.A., Political Science, *magna cum laude,* 1997), Christ College Scholar — Humanities (honors college). Contact information: 233 South Wacker Drive, Suite 6600, Chicago, IL 60606; phone: (312) 258-5534; hrowe@schiffhardin.com.

Simon J. Santiago, an attorney with the law firm of Nossaman, LLP, has worked exclusively in the field of construction law for more than a decade and has both significant transactional and litigation experience. He represents public sector clients using innovative financing, delivery, and procurement methods to develop large-scale transportation infrastructure projects. He has advised several transportation and transit agencies on risk allocation and construction management issues, including the Florida Department of Transportation on the I-595 Corridor Improvements Program, the Texas Department of Transportation on the Dallas/Fort Worth Connector Project, and the Virginia Department of Rail and Public Transportation on the Dulles Corridor Metrorail Project. Mr. Santiago received his B.A. from the University of Illinois in 1993 and his J.D. from Washington College of Law at American University, 1996, *magna cum laude*; Notes and Comments Editor, *American University Law Review.* Contact information: 666 K Street, NW, Suite 500, Washington, D.C. 20006; phone: (202) 887-1472; ssantiago@nossaman.com.

Stephen C. Taylor is Senior Vice President and Unit Manager of Lockton Companies, LLC, the world's largest, privately owned, independent insurance broker. Affiliated with Lockton since 1994, Mr. Taylor has a special emphasis on architects/engineers professional liability and contractors' needs, including contractors' liquidated damages, efficacy, force majeure, international, and other related exposures. He has gained national account expertise through his work with Arup, Black & Veatch; Brown & Caldwell; Burns & McDonnell; CB&I; Day & Zimmermann, Inc.; J.E. Dunn; Gensler; HDR; HNTB; Klienfelder; Leo A Daly; MWH Global, Inc.; SOM; and Terracon. Prior to joining Lockton, he was a Senior Account Executive for Alexander & Alexander in its Major Account Unit, which included major architect/engineering accounts. While at Alexander & Alexander, Mr.

Taylor managed the insurance program for the construction of the Seabrook Nuclear Project (valued at more than $4 billion). He is a graduate of Wake Forest University. Contact info: 444 West 47th Street, Kansas City, MO 64112, phone: (816) 960-9555; staylor@lockton.com.

Ujjval K. Vyas is the principal of Alberti Group, a Chicago-based interdisciplinary consultancy. He and his firm specialize in emerging issues in the building industry involving sustainability and high-performance buildings, building information modeling, and alternative project delivery systems. He has lectured and published extensively on the legal and business risks associated with the sustainable building marketplace including large-scale policy, insurance, legal and technical issues. Prior to becoming a practicing attorney, Dr. Vyas taught and lectured at architecture schools at both the undergraduate and graduate levels in the United States and Canada, and served as the director of the Institute for Architecture and the Humanities in Chicago. Dr. Vyas holds a Ph.D from the University of Chicago, and his J.D., with honors, from Illinois Institute of Technology/Chicago-Kent College of Law. He teaches a graduate course of Sustainability and Real Estate at the DePaul Real Estate Center in Chicago. Contact information: 233 East Wacker Drive, Suite 304, Chicago, IL 60606; phone: (312) 810-1008; uvyas@albertigroup.net.

John M. Wilson is an attorney with the law firm of Latham & Watkins where he is a member of the Environmental, Land and Resources department as well as the Litigation department. His practice focuses primarily on business litigation and insurance litigation. He has experience in matters involving unfair competition, business torts, contract disputes, health care class actions, real property disputes, fiduciary duty violations and insurance coverage disputes. From 2003 to 2004, Mr. Wilson served as a law clerk to the Hon. Cynthia Holcomb Hall, United States Court of Appeals for the Ninth Circuit. Prior to his clerkship, he attended Stanford Law School, where he served as an Executive Editor of the *Stanford Law Review*, was a member of the Inns of Court and graduated *with distinction* in 2003. Mr. Wilson received a B.A. in History from the University of Pennsylvania in 2000, which was conferred *summa cum laude*. Contact information: 600 West Broadway, Suite 1800, San Diego, CA 92101-3375; phone: (619) 236-1234; john.wilson@lw.com.

Introduction

The title to this book reflects the fact that risk management for design professionals truly is in a world of change. Changes taking place across the globe are creating a vastly different professional environment for architects and engineers as we move further into the 21st century.

Of the new risks confronting design professionals, those of going green and meeting the sustainability requirements of contracts and new laws may prove to be among the most significant. Through the insights and experiences of some of the industry's most experienced practitioners, this book offers the reader a practical perspective on how to understand and successfully address these risks. Chapter 1 is by John Binder, the architect who designed the first LEED certified apartment building. He describes his positive experience, as well as that of other architects, in designing with the goal of producing environmentally responsible projects. While there is much to commend green design, it produces risks that may impact legal liability and insurance, risks that are perhaps not well enough understood and appreciated. In Chapter 2, Frank Musica explains, in a concise and practical manner, how to recognize these risks and offers thought-provoking claim scenarios that should be considered with regard to the insurability of risks. Chapter 3, by Kent Holland, and Chapter 4, by Ujjval Vyas, pick up and expand further upon some of the problems that will likely confront design professionals and contractors in dealing with green risks.

Significant new standard form contract documents have been published in the last couple years. Chapter 5, by Mark Friedlander and Heidi Rowe, addresses the new AIA B101-2007 document that replaces AIA B141-1997 and explains many of the more significant changes in clauses that impact risks. Completely new on the scene is the ConsensusDOCS. This is a family of contract documents that represents the combined efforts and consensus of 22 organizations representing disparate interests in construction projects. These documents, and in particular their approach to Integrated Project Delivery, are explained by Brian Perlberg in Chapter 6. Following next, in Chapter 7, is a discussion by Jerome Bales and Ricardo Aparicio regarding ConsensusDOCS' Owner-Architect Agreement. Hugh Anderson, in Chapter 8, briefly describes the new EJCDC documents issued in 2008.

We then move on to the risks arising out of Integrated Project Delivery (IPD) and Building Information Modeling (BIM). In Chapter 9, Suzanne Harness explains how the AIA's new contract forms address IPD. In Chapter

10, Howard Ashcraft presents a comprehensive discussion dealing with the legal aspects of designing with BIM, and the risks arising out of BIM. He provides thought-provoking concerns that project owners, designers, and contractors should consider when using BIM, and offers practical guidance for addressing some of the key risks that will result from BIM. In Chapter 11, Kent Holland continues the IPD/BIM discussion with a focus on the insurance ramifications.

Perhaps due in large part to economic conditions making it difficult, or even impossible, for public entities to undertake the huge amount of construction needed for expensive and complex infrastructure projects, the number of public private partnership (P3) projects has grown exponentially. In Chapter 12, Simon Santiago and Heather DeBlanc address the risks unique to P3 projects. They write from the perspective of having negotiated contracts and assisted on legal and risk management issues on numerous major P3 projects.

And finally, more design professionals are merging or growing to become global firms – conducting business in countries throughout the world. In doing so, the insurance needed to protect against the risks requires a new look – especially with regard to political risks and unique risks such as strict liability and decennial liability risks in numerous countries. Chapter 13, by John Wilson, and Chapter 14, by Steve Taylor, address international risks.

This book has been registered with the AIA Continuing Education System for continuing education courses that may be taken by the reader for continuing education credit. Four quizzes are provided at the end of the book for this purpose, along with an explanation on how to register and submit the responses to receive CE credit. We believe that this added benefit will make this practical and informative book even more worthwhile for you and your colleagues.

It is our hope that you will finish this book with a better understanding of the risks associated with going green and how to address those risks. For additional information on this area, please contact a/e ProNet or the authors.

Chapter 1

Going Green is Good

John Binder, AIA

1.1　A World of Change

Coming out of a recession is a time when we all question what is important. It's not only the design professionals who are looking at our businesses and recognizing that change is necessary to avoid being left behind. We and our clients, who are mainly in the housing industry, have been re-examining values and re-examining what is needed. They are looking for value and how to sell it. A running theme has been quality versus quantity. The metric of how we value buildings is changing. We see the focus of some of our multi-family clients moving away from low upfront costs to durability and long term building performance. We are also responding to clients at the other end of the spectrum who were building single family homes in the 2500 - 3000 square foot range and are now looking to market homes of half that size. These smaller homes will be leaner, more efficient, and therefore more affordable. There is a common theme in the directions we are pursuing. The days of excess and waste are coming to a close. Whether spoken out loud or not, the word is, "green" and the direction is to be sustainable.

What is not changing is the role of the architect. We have always been the advocates of creativity and innovation. We are also the guardians of what is fad and what is trend. We are socially responsible. Going green and sustainability are highlighted in the news every day. A concern is the damage that can be caused by those that hop on the proverbial bandwagon and promote "green washing." Surprisingly, Webster's online dictionary has a definition. The roots of green washing are *green* +brain*washing* and it is defined as: "expressions of environmentalist concerns especially as a cover for products, policies or activities." The implications are that the term describes something that is not the real deal. A word of caution is for us to represent what we understand.

1.2   Define Green

At a recent National Green Building Conference, Sara Gutterman, a well known sustainability advocate and publisher of "Green Builder Media," was asked to define, "green." She explained that, "green is a decision making process. That it is hard to define. That we define green by how we spend our dollars." She believes that no green products come from a brown company. We at KEPHART also worked at defining what being green meant. We liked the sound of, "design for today while preserving for tomorrow."

We also asked two well known Denver builders what being green means to them. Gene Myers of New Town Builders explains it is being resource efficient and healthy. When Chris Achenbach of Zocalo Development is asked the same question, he responds, "Green building is constructing and developing projects that have less impact on the environment. Green building also must consider the integration of the building with those who use it, integration with the surrounding community, and regional considerations such as how materials are sourced, efficient uses of transportation and the usage of utilities (gas, electricity, water) that support a building."

Two different responses – one more elaborate than the other. The American Institute of Architects ("AIA"), The U.S. Green Building Council, and the United States Environmental Protection Agency ("EPA") each have different ways of looking at this topic. From this architect's point of view, the definition is of concern when setting an expectation between client and architect. It behooves us to determine whose definition is being used and does the definition carry over into an agreement.

1.3   Why Go Green

In 2002, I was the project architect for what turned out to be the first LEED certified apartment building - Blair Towns for the Tower Companies. The Tower Companies had just completed a LEED certified office building and were ready to move onto their next venture. When asked why pursue this route, the answer was it is the right thing to do and they feel good about coming to work each day. This was a client that we would all like to have. They had good motives and were willing to pay additional for it.

Seven years ago, sustainability was not the hot topic that it is today. Conversations about global warming and energy conservation were not as dominant as they are today. Don't get me wrong – these are not new topics. When I was in architectural studio in the 70s, I was being educated on the insulating benefits of a Trombe wall, how a composting Clivus Multrum toilet worked, and how to design a self sufficient community. Whether or not you believe the earth is heating up, there is no doubt the earth's resources are limited. As architects, we are stewards of the environment. As architects, we pride ourselves on good design. Can good design be separated from being respectful of the environment or be separated from the health and well being of our building's occupants?

Does every building we design need to be a LEED certified building? Not all of our clients can afford to go that route. There is a cost to building a better performing building and there are costs to certifying a building. Yet, we have a social responsibility to move our clients towards sustainability. And currently the public is better informed on sustainability, much more focused on energy, and expects to see results. The challenge is for us to address these concerns by integrating them into our products as cost effectively as possible.

Today when we ask our clients who are building green, why they do it – these are some of their answers:

- They do it for market differentiation and to distance themselves from their competition.
- They do it so that a governing body won't step in, make it mandatory, and tell them how to run their business.
- And they do it because it is the right thing to do.

1.4   The Process

There are many strategies to approach the process. There are many programs that set up parameters for green certification. Some of the more well known national ones are LEED (through the U.S. Green Building Council), Energy Star (from the Department of Energy), and most recently, the National Green Building Standard (which was a collaboration of the National Association of Home Builders, American National Standards Institute, and the International Code Council). We are not advocates of one program over the other – they each have their own merits.

Gene Myers of New Town, who is building single family homes, prefers Energy Star. His market recognizes the blue label. A requirement of an

Energy Star rated home is a HERS rating, which is an analysis of the energy usage of a home. As part of the rating, a field test is conducted testing the tightness of the home and the tightness of the ducts. The rating is a scale from 0 to 100, with 86 being the current minimum value to qualify for Energy Star and 0 being a zero energy home. Gene is considering the efforts it would take a production builder to get to 0 and is evaluating the market for the home.

Chris Achenbach of Zocalo, who is in the multi-family housing market, prefers the LEED system. "It is a rigorous and meaningful standard that still provides flexibility," he states. Zocalo's RiverClay project is the Rocky Mountain region's first LEED condominium project.

In Ohio, WXZ Development prefers the National Green Building Standard. They are also are building multi-family housing and find the documentation to be more builder-friendly and less costly.

As with the design of any project, the first step is to listen to the client and to confirm its priorities. Each of the programs mentioned requires third party validation – eliminating the greenwashing aspect. Your client may not want to go that far or may not want to spend the resources on the third party certification. Some would prefer to spend their funds on improvements to the building and not on documentation.

The ideal time to begin the process is at the outset of the project, with everyone establishing and buying into the goals. Everyone includes the owner, the design team, and the contractor, if possible. Going green is not just the design of the project, but the execution as well. It is best to reach shared meaning early in the process on the client's expectations.

1.5   More on the First One

What made the Blair Towns project successful was having a motivated owner and a motivated owner's representative. The message came right from the top of the organization. He assembled all of us at long tables during schematics. All of us included civil, architect, MEP, structural, LEED consultant, and the general contractor. We went through the LEED checklists, targeting which points were readily achievable, and identifying which were a bit of stretch as well as those out of reach. We tallied our results, decided which ones to pursue, and gave ourselves a cushion. As a result, we amped up the efficiency of the HVAC equipment beyond the norm and significantly improved the values of the windows.

LEED also allows for a few points to be earned for innovation. We pursued and earned one on educating the users of the apartment building. A green guide booklet was prepared for the residents, highlighting the features of the community and how to maximize their experience in this healthier, cleaner living environment. A new concept became clear with this exercise. Our responsibilities not only included the design of the community and participating in the execution of the design through construction, but also considering the future relationship of building, users, and environment.

It was a collaborative effort with the general contractor from the outset, who committed to higher standards during construction and committed to the more intensive record-keeping. Some of the points we obtained were related to percentages of materials with recycled content and to materials produced within a certain proximity to the site. Subcontractors were also on board and were held accountable for their work.

Being the first residential project through the rating system posed a few hurdles. Some of the documentation was intensive, proving compliance with the points being achieved. The guides were written more for commercial buildings, not residential, which required a fair amount of exchange with the Council. USGBC has since amended the program and added rating systems that are more in tune with housing.

1.6   Beware of the Trap

Determine in advance what will be the sustainable goals achievements and what or whom will be the guiding principles for the team. The trap is setting the goal to collect points. Using a green program checklist to design the project is not a good methodology. Tacking on a renewable energy source to a building is not the answer. Sustainable design is integral to the process and to the design. Set sights on a zero energy building or one that will be maintenance free or one that can be recycled at a later date. Those are some goals.

Most of the "green speak" centers around five or six major principles. In our office, these bullet points are:

- Site Design/Orientation
- Energy Efficiency/Building Envelope
- Resource Efficiency
- Indoor Air Quality
- Water Quality & Conservation
- Education

When meeting with our clients, we are mindful of these concepts and develop strategies that integrate the concepts. What do we mean by integrated green strategies? Here are some examples:

- Orienting the buildings on an east-west axis, to maximize the southern exposure;
- Designing overhangs at openings to the proper depth to eliminate summer solar gain yet allowing winter sun;
- Maximizing daylighted rooms based on use and use reflective surfaces to bounce light in;
- Creating walkable communities to encourage exercise; and
- Integrating green roofs, bio swales, and permeable surfaces to minimize storm sewer infrastructure.

We are the creative thinkers and planners. There's no limit to the sustainable solutions.

1.7   Green is Good

In a recent talk, Alex Steffen of Worldchanging.com confirmed that people want to know they are living the good life and are doing the right thing. We need to continue to give the public that opportunity. No doubt litigation, liability, lawyers, and losses (that's a lot of Ls) can be a damper on our enthusiasm for doing the right thing. We should continue exploring innovative ways of building, exploring the use of alternative energies, and investigating new materials. And do so in a prudent manner.

What are our clients' expectations? They haven't changed. Buildings that don't fail. We can set our clients' expectations related to building performance as well. Let's listen to counsel and promise only what we can deliver.

Remember green is good. Paul Hawken is known for saying, "You are brilliant and the earth is hiring." Sounds like a job opening and we are here to fill it.

Chapter 2

Recognizing the Risks in Green Design and Construction

Frank D. Musica, J.D.

2.1 Introduction

Though a truly "green" design is difficult to achieve, it is impossible to argue against the value of sustainability in the design and operation of our built environment. Green design minimizes hazardous environmental consequences and reduces energy use. Green building components usually have lower "encapsulated energy," are almost always environmentally benign, and are often renewable. And perhaps most appealing to clients, life cycle costs are reduced. Although green design does not create unmanageable exposure to firms, recent professional liability and contractual claims indicate that design firms may become the victims of their own zeal. Many firms seem to overlook the risks and potential consequences of their statements, contracts, and services when it comes to sustainability.

The American Institute of Architects'14th edition of *The Architect's Handbook for Professional Practice* defines sustainability as "the concept of meeting present needs without compromising the ability of future generations to meet their own needs." Designing for sustainability involves considering environmentally responsible design alternatives consistent with the client's program, schedule, and budget. Design firms need to recognize the legal and insurance implications of the "green" movement.

2.2   The Duty to be Green

The standard of care for design professionals is usually defined as the care and skill ordinarily used by members of the same profession practicing under similar circumstances at the same time and in the same locality. In other words, design professionals are held to a standard imposed on them by their own profession, rather than an outside party. But the statements of professional groups, the language of industry standard contracts, and the constraints of codes of ethics all affect the development of the applicable standard of care.

2.3   Contracts

Design firms make recommendations based on tradeoffs involving time, money, and quality. These recommendations are the nature of the design process, and clients make significant financial commitments based on them. However, contractually committing to obtain third-party certification, achieve stated energy savings, reduce construction materials and waste, or create a healthful interior environment can lead to obligations beyond the standard of care. As contractual obligations, these are not covered by professional liability insurance. Therefore, design professionals should be wary of and may want to remove contract clauses that raise the standard of care to the use of "best efforts" or that specify a result, such as a 50% reduction of material waste.

Similarly, if the design professional is using a standard contract, such as one offered by The American Institute of Architects, and has no experience with sustainability or is not offering green design services, specific provisions related to green design should be removed from the agreement.

In 2007, AIA revealed its latest changes to the AIA contract documents. One provision, new to several of the owner-architect agreements, is the contractual duty to consider green design alternatives on every project. The new core document for practice is the B101™-2007 *Standard Form of Agreement Between Owner and Architect* agreement, which contains the following language:

§ 3.2.3 The Architect shall present its preliminary evaluation to the Owner and shall discuss with the Owner alternative approaches to design and construction of the Project, including the feasibility of incorporating environmentally responsible design approaches. The Architect shall reach an understanding with the Owner regarding the requirements of the Project.

§3.2.5.1 The Architect shall consider environmentally responsible design alternatives, such as material choices and building orientation, together with other considerations based on program and aesthetics, in developing a design that is consistent with the Owner's program, schedule and budget for the Cost of the Work. The Owner may obtain other environmentally responsible design services under Article 4.

These provisions are the end product of a careful consideration by the AIA Contract Documents Committee. Responding to organizational demands that architects, through their standard contracts, take a leadership role in green design, the committee was able to balance a marketing focus with a realistic concern for contractual liability exposure. The duty is not absolute. The provisions, examined together, state that all an architect must do to meet the sustainable design requirements of the contract is to discuss the feasibility of incorporating environmentally responsible designs with the client, and "consider environmentally responsible design alternatives" which, while not limited to the choice of materials and the orientation of the building, are constrained by the project owner's program, schedule, and budget. These are not unreasonable contract obligations but they are new duties and the failure to perform them will be a breach of contract.

Evidence that the contractual duty created by an AIA standard agreement was carried out should be within the architect's documentation of communications with the project client and the recordation of the client's authorization. If the project owner feels the contractual obligation of the architect was not met, the project owner would have to show financial damages that resulted from the architect's failure to discuss and consider these design alternatives. But once that burden is met, the project owner could claim damages ranging from failure to achieve approvals or certifications, to higher energy or water usage costs, to damage to reputation, to lost public incentives such as financial considerations, permitting advantages, and even lost opportunity costs.

The creation of these contractual obligations means that firms using the B101 need to be aware of their duties and properly communicate and document green design options with their clients. The new provisions may exceed the standard of care for professional services related to the identification of green design options, but if contained and agreed to in the contract, they will be enforced in a court of law. This obligation should be shared with the client, and subsequent discussions should cover the desire and feasibility of incorporating green design elements. Those discussions should be documented, along with any green design alternatives considered by the design professional and reasons for choosing to, or choosing not to, implement them. Otherwise, the obligation may lead to a breach of contract claim or raise a firm's professional liability exposure if a client assumes that sustainability features, including reduced energy use, are intrinsic in the design solution. Similarly, users of the B103, the contract variation for a large or complex project, and the B201, the design and construction contract administration scope document, should follow the advice above, as both contain the same provisions as the B101. The B104 abbreviated contract form and the B105 short-form contract for use on a residential or small commercial project do not have a similar requirement.

2.4   Codes of Ethics

Many factors within and outside the design and construction industry can influence the standard of care for design services. Recent changes in professional society policies and codes of ethics have made it difficult to determine if the standard of care is in line with professional services being offered and client expectations. Several professional societies, including the AIA, National Society of Professional Engineers (NSPE), American Society of Civil Engineers (ASCE), and American Society of Landscape Architects (ASLA), have added sustainability to their ethical guidelines.

A revision to the NSPE *Code of Ethics* in January 2006 incorporated an ethical obligation for sustainability. The language was clarified in July 2007 to state the following in the professional obligations section of the code:

> Engineers shall at all times strive to serve the public interest. Engineers are encouraged to adhere to the principles of sustainable development in order to protect the environment for future generations.

The original 2006 language went further in establishing the obligation of NSPE members by stating that engineers "shall strive" instead of "are encouraged." The 2007 revision significantly reduces the obligations of NSPE members and modifies its impact on the developing standard of care for sustainable design.

In December 2007, the national Board of Directors of the American Institute of Architects added sustainability goals to the code of ethics governing its members' conduct. Added was "Canon VI, Obligations to the Environment," which contains three ethical standards. AIA members cannot be disciplined for violating an ethical standard since such standards are defined as goals "toward which Members should aspire in professional performance and behavior." The goals use the word "should" rather than "must." While these ethical standards place AIA members in an advocacy role, the language's effect on the standard of care will not be known until case law develops. The AIA's ethical provisions for its members state the following:

> Members should promote sustainable design and development principles in their professional activities.
>
> • E.S. 6.1 Sustainable Design: In performing work, Members should be environmentally responsible and advocate sustainable building and site design.
>
> • E.S. 6.2 Sustainable Development: In performing professional services, Members should advocate the design, construction and operation of sustainable buildings and communities.
>
> • E.S. 6.3 Sustainable Practices: Members should use sustainable practices within their firms and professional organizations, and they should encourage their clients to do the same.

Architects should be prudent in recognizing and following the "suggestions" given in these new Ethical Standards when approaching a new project. It is likely that within a few years, aggressive plaintiff lawyers will argue that an AIA Ethical Standard should be admitted as evidence of the standard of care. The argument that statements within a Code of Ethics of a voluntary professional organization should dictate how an entire profession should operate is not an easy one to justify. Still such attempts are made. The monopoly that the American Institute of Architects has in the profession makes it act as both a professional society and a trade association. Holding a member of a trade association to the rules of the association often is easier than applying rules, guidelines, or information generated by a professional society to all members of profession. But efforts to use publications or promulgations by an organization that might represent the interests of a large number of members of a profession have been attempted in the past.

In a 1988 Montana Supreme Court case, the plaintiff argued that the AIA's publication, *The Architect's Handbook for Professional Practice*, should have been admitted into evidence as controlling authority to establish the applicable standard of care. The trial court allowed the AIA publication into evidence, which was challenged on appeal by the architecture firm as an error. On appeal, the Montana Supreme Court acknowledged that, "The [AIA] handbook describes the standard of practice for architects in the United States." The plaintiff wanted a ruling that any deviation from the standards set forth in that AIA handbook should be deemed negligence without any further proof (a legal theory known as "negligence per se"). The state supreme court did not agree. It did rule the following: "While violation of a statute may be classed as negligence per se, violation of other regulations is not generally classed as negligence per se. More precisely on point, absent specific statutory incorporation, the provisions of a national code are only evidence of negligence, not conclusive proof thereof."

The Montana Supreme Court agreed with the lower court that the AIA handbook information was properly admitted into evidence to be considered as evidence as standards of a duty on the part of the architect, but rejected the premise that the violation of AIA standards constituted negligence on the part of the architect.

This ruling is consistent with how many other courts have ruled on the use of industry publications to prove negligence. An Illinois court addressed the use of industry standards and stated the following: "Evidence of standards promulgated by industry, trade, or regulatory groups or agencies may be admissible to aid the trier of fact in determining the standard of care in a negligence action." This is consistent with the concept of proving negligence rather than establishing negligence per se. And therefore, although firms will be faced with arguments that the AIA Code of Ethics requires a specific behavior, it is highly likely that such arguments to absolutely establish a duty will not be successful.

Another organization at the forefront of adding environmental concerns to its code of ethics was the American Society of Landscape Architects (ASLA). In October 2000, the ASLA adopted a *Code of Environmental Ethics* to supplement its *Code of Professional Ethics*, amended most recently in 2006. The ethical standards are based on four tenets and state that ASLA members "should make every effort" to support those ethical obligations.

The American Society of Civil Engineers (ASCE) may have been the first professional society to incorporate sustainability requirements into its code of ethics. In November 1996, the ASCE Board of Directors, instead of adding an eighth canon, chose to add sustainability principles to canons one and three of the ASCE code. ASCE's "Fundamental Canon" is slightly more stringent than the NSPE and AIA codes because it states engineers "shall strive" to perform their professional duties in accordance with sustainable development principles. The adoption of sustainability to the ASCE code seems to have done little to modify the standard of care of civil engineers, but the effect is yet to be known on other design professionals.

Design professionals need to be aware that the addition of ethical requirements related to sustainable design may have an effect on the legal standard of care applicable to design services. Although past case law indicates that industry publications and handbooks can be considered evidence of a duty (as opposed to a violation constituting negligence), the new ethical provisions could have an impact on future judicial opinions.

2.5   Related Organizations

Other organizations are at the forefront of including sustainability in their policies and guidelines. The American Society of Heating, Refrigerating and Air-Conditioning Engineers (ASHRAE) has developed a number of publications supporting sustainability, including Standards 90.1 and 90.2 for energy efficiency, Standards 62.1 and 62.2 for indoor air quality, the *Advanced Energy Design Guides*, and the ASHRAE *Green Guide*. Similarly, the Department of Transportation (DOT), the Environmental Protection Agency (EPA), and the Association of State and Territorial Solid Waste Management Officials are supporting sustainability in guides, reports, and legislation. These organizations are studying the benefits and impacts of including waste and byproduct materials in highway and commercial construction. In a 2005 joint study between the DOT and EPA, at least 34 states had laws, regulations, policies, or, at the very least, guidance on using coal combustion products (coal fly ash) in structural fill applications. It is likely that advances will continue in this area, requiring, in the future, the use of waste products and the recycling of materials left unused on jobsites.

2.6   Green Legislation

More and more states and cities are passing "green laws" that require new public buildings and, in some cases, private buildings, to achieve a certain certification level or compliance with specific state or local requirements. The growing popularity of green design among owners and developers is often not based on moral considerations of being environmentally responsible, but rather on energy or water use restrictions, tax incentives, focused building codes, and the increasing requirements of recycling and reusing buildings and building materials. Failure by a design firm to understand the applicability of a state or local statute or regulation out of ignorance can result in major additional costs or harm; failure to comply in a design solution can result in liability.

Although the total is ever increasing, at least 28 states have passed statutes or executive orders promoting green design and many others have similar legislation pending. South Carolina, for example, passed the Energy Independence and Sustainable Construction Act of 2007, which requires all state-funded construction projects to achieve LEED Silver certification or two Green Globes if they are greater than 10,000 gross square feet or if more than 50% of the facility will be replaced.

Local laws often have a significant impact on private building as well. Local laws and ordinances range from tax incentives for building owners who incorporate energy saving principles into their structures, to sustainable design considerations for new and renovated construction projects, with most mandating certain minimum LEED® certification levels. For instance, recognizing that LEED® certification can be an important catalyst for the development of environmentally responsible and sustainable design as an expectation, the Hawaii legislature passed a statute allowing for an expedited permitting process for buildings seeking LEED® certification. This type of incentive may lead developers to include sustainable design in order to save money through a faster schedule and benefit from an increased cash flow. Thus, green design is less of a choice for these project types and becomes more of a mandate.

Design firms should be aware of green legislation passed and pending in the jurisdictions where their projects are located. Design firms must comply with applicable laws, regulations, and codes that contain sustainability requirements. Knowledge of green building laws thus becomes more important to design firms that deal with clients whose projects are subject to those laws, but it is vital that all firms become aware of changing laws. It, often, will be a challenge to understand what local laws have been passed and what actual city ordinances and resolutions. Failure to comply with such applicable laws may be used as evidence of negligence and, in some states, may be deemed negligence per se.

2.7   How "Green" is Your Design?

Few design firms have the expertise to assess the "encapsulated energy" in building materials or judge the long-term impact of the use of renewable or recycled materials. Therefore, in the past, design professionals had difficulty explaining the trade-offs intrinsic to a sustainable design because no system existed to quantify that design. Now, however, with the acceptance of several rating systems in the U.S. market, the concept of sustainability can be quantified.

2.8   LEED

In 1998, the United States Green Building Council (USGBC) developed requirements for environmental sustainability and resource conservation. This system, the Leadership in Energy and Environmental Design® (LEED) program, is a point-driven certification of buildings that sets arbitrary values for design features, construction processes, and energy use. The new construction rating system is organized into six categories: sustainable sites, water efficiency, energy and atmosphere, materials and resources, indoor environmental quality, and innovation and design process. Some of the other rating systems include existing buildings, schools, healthcare, retail, and commercial interiors. Each system mandates that certain prerequisites be met for any certification level to be awarded. Once the prerequisites have been implemented, a project must achieve at least 26 points to be "Certified," 33-38 points for "Silver," 39-51 points for "Gold," and reach 52 or more points for a "Platinum" rating. In 2009, USGBC released the third version of LEED, which introduced major modifications to the four major rating systems (new construction, core and shell, commercial interiors, and existing buildings). The systems are based on a 100-point scale, where 40 points (40%) are required for building certification, 50 points for Silver, 60 Points for Gold, and 80 points for Platinum. The revamped LEED includes a number of significant changes, but one of the most important is a reweighting of credits to more accurately reflect the environmental benefits of the strategies that project teams choose to employ. Among other changes, there is a stronger emphasis on energy-efficiency and an upgrade to the ASHRAE 90.1-2007 standard.

The LEED program also offers accreditation for professionals in the design and construction industry. The Green Building Certification Institute (GBCI) is now responsible for the administration of the professional accreditation exam. No prerequisites exist to take the exam. However, knowledge of the building industry, green design, LEED credit intents and requirements, LEED documentation processes, and an understanding of life cycle costs is highly recommended.

As part of this evolution, a new process for accrediting the professionals who work on LEED projects is being rolled out. The Green Building Certification Institute is instituting a three-tier system of credentials. The most basic will be "Green Associate," which is intended for people who want to demonstrate a commitment to green building practices but may not be directly involved in LEED projects. "AP+" will indicate a higher level of expertise. And finally, "AP Fellow" will be a sort of master green authority designation.

Whether LEED Accredited Professionals are licensed design professionals or not, they will be able to maintain the credential, but as inactive professionals unless these "legacy" APs sign an ethics agreement and satisfy a biannual requirement for 30 hours of continuing education. Along with the new designations, GBCI will gradually release a new series of accreditation exams between May and August of 2009, with the old test withdrawn early in 2009.

The promulgation of this accreditation program calls into question the ability of non-accredited professionals to design environmentally sensitive projects and of non-licensed professionals to make design decisions based on the LEED certification requirements. More information on LEED is available at www.usgbc.org.

2.9   Green Globes

In the United States, the Green Globes™ program is owned and operated by the Green Building Initiative (GBI). Green Globes features two major rating systems, one for "New Construction" and another for the "Continual Improvement of Existing Buildings." A project is awarded points based on its performance in seven areas of assessment in the new construction system and six areas in the existing building system. Under new construction, the system is divided into project delivery phases, and those phases are divided into seven assessment areas: project management, energy, indoor environment, site, water, resources, and emissions. Green Globes can be used for self-assessment, or, for a fee, third-party verification can be acquired to assign the rating. The independent verification is based on a comprehensive review of documentation and a post-construction, on-site inspection. Worthy projects will be awarded a rating of one (35-54%), two (55-69%), three (70-84%), or four (85-100%) globes based on a possible cumulative 1,000 points.

The Green Globes rating system does not require extensive training or accreditation to be used by design professionals. Assessment of a project's sustainability potential is available online through a questionnaire, which can be completed by a design professional with or without green design experience. After completion of the questionnaire, a report is generated that describes a list of achievements and recommendations. Therefore, the design professional can see the impact of its design decisions on the point score, and use that information to make future improvements. The online system also allows for the addition of project updates for up to one year, with the option to extend. More information about Green Globes is available at www.theGBI.org.

2.10   Mandatory Green Design

Currently, both LEED and Green Globes are mostly voluntary programs with which a client, together with the advice of the design professional, can make a decision to use green design. But the designation as a voluntary program is slowly eroding as more and more design professionals are required to design for sustainability. This reality is accelerated by legislative endorsements and the accreditation of standards developers by the American National Standards Institute (ANSI).

Both the USGBC and GBI have been accredited by ANSI as Standards Development Organizations. This designation allows those organizations to produce environmental design and rating systems, which will then be reviewed and approved by the ANSI Board of Standards Review to become American National Standards. Once approved, it is the desire of GBI and USGBC that those standards be incorporated by government agencies into local building codes. Currently, USGBC has partnered with the ASHRAE and the Illuminating Engineering Society of North America to develop Standard 189.1P, *High-Performance Green Buildings Except Low-Rise Residential.* This standard will address site sustainability, water use efficiency, energy efficiency, indoor environment quality, and the building's impact on the atmosphere, materials, and resources. GBI is also developing a standard called *Green Globes Design Commercial Green Building Assessment Protocol,* which will include criteria and practices for environmental design and construction of commercial buildings. If and when these standards are incorporated into building codes, design professionals must proceed with caution. Knowledge of both standards will be essential since the standard passed will differ from jurisdiction to jurisdiction. Also, if the standard is a building code, the design must comply with the code or the design professional will likely be found negligent.

There is a significant difference between voluntary, commercial, certification programs, and statutory requirements.   In many states, if a statute or ordinance has a requirement for building construction, the architect is deemed to be negligent per se if the design does not comply with the law. There is no need for expert testimony on the standard of care, since the law itself sets the standard, and a violation of the law is considered negligence without more proof. Therefore, the adoption of voluntary standards as green laws can create an absolute standard for measuring the performance of a design firm.

Normally, a court will require expert testimony to establish the standard that applies to professional services in a specific case. But there are two types of negligence where expert testimony is not required to establish the standard of care. The law includes a "common knowledge" exception where the negligence is so obvious that a jury does not need an expert to tell them that conduct fell below the standard of care. This is not often used to determine negligence in a professional services situation. The second exception to the need for expert witness testimony involves situations where the design is regulated by a statute or ordinance. The written law itself establishes the standard of care and expert testimony is not required. This latter exception is called "negligence per se."

When a design fails to meet the requirements of a state or local green ordinance, the courts might consider the ordinance as establishing the standard of care. Or, as in the example of industry codes and publications, the failure to meet the requirements of a specific ordinance might be considered merely evidence of negligence. That determination depends on the state in which the project is located and on the law that governs the contract.

A violation of the building code is considered to be negligence per se when the violation results in the harm the building code was designed to prevent. The majority of American jurisdictions follow the negligence per se doctrine and find that a breach of statutory duty is a breach of standard of care for civil negligence cases.

2.11   Green Liability

Design professionals are well aware of the competition between client demands and sound design principles. Often, the client's desire to reduce initial costs, compress delivery times, and see an immediate return on investment outweighs design options and construction techniques that could reduce a project's impact on the environment. From a professional liability perspective, many exposures are generated or intensified by the advent of sustainable design. Advertising, sustainability descriptions, and even contracts can lead to exposures beyond allegations of negligently performed services.

2.12   Unfulfilled Expectations

Although design firms are encouraging employees to learn more about LEED and Green Globes, and to become LEED Accredited Professionals, firms should market and negotiate with caution. An employee who passes the LEED accreditation test and attaches LEED AP to his business card may create client expectations. The client may have hired the design professional with a belief that the designer is an expert with significant experience and knowledge of the design principles underlying the "green" system. Unfortunately, experience or competence does not necessarily accompany LEED accreditation. This challenge creates the possibility of dissatisfied clients, and dissatisfied clients bring claims. Therefore, it is vital to conduct open and thorough communication with a client concerning reasonable expectations of sustainability. Likewise, clients have to make a genuine commitment to participate in the process, to share in the responsibility for the decisions that might lead to certification, and to invest in the process as well as the design and construction measures required to achieve certification.

Scenario:
Lured by the promise of "healthier and more productive occupants" basic to LEED publicity, a tenant rented space in a LEED Silver-certified building. At the end of the year, the tenant's records indicated a greater use of sick leave, increased complaints by employees of eyestrain and drafts, and reduced output from the clerical staff. The tenant demanded a rent rebate from the project owner based on a false promise of a healthful workplace and increased productivity. The owner sued the architect for not designing a healthful workplace and the tenant sued the architect for bodily injury based on poor indoor air quality.

2.13   Cost Recovery

The broad nature of the "green" rating system can serve as a trap for design professionals attempting to design to a pre-selected certification level. Clients expect to see the financial savings that their investment is supposed to produce. Higher certification levels usually require more design effort and greater construction costs. If an anticipated benefit is not achieved, the firm may be expected to pay for its "mistake." Therefore, a design firm should never "warrant," "guarantee," "ensure," or "use its best efforts" to achieve a certain rating.

Scenario:

A design team agreed to a project consisting of three schools that would serve as examples of sustainable design and energy conservation. The architects and consulting engineers signed a contract that stated that the projects would "reduce operating costs by 50 percent" over schools of similar size. After completion, the energy usage was comparable to other schools recently designed and constructed. Newspaper coverage identified increased design and construction costs and no energy savings. The school system was publicly embarrassed, disappointed, and blamed as being "hoodwinked" by the architect and engineers. The school system brought a claim.

2.14   Implied or Express Warranties

Building certification implies energy savings and increased productivity. The design process, however, is interdependent on the actions of the client and can be later influenced by many factors. Projects seeking certification have a final review by the USGBC or Green Globes after construction. That final review may change the certification level expected. And as the certification levels increase from "silver" to "platinum" under LEED or one to four globes under Green Globes, expectations of benefits also increase. The stated goal of the LEED system, through which LEED certification is obtained, is to distinguish building projects that have demonstrated commitment to sustainability by meeting the "highest green building and performance measures." Design professionals should be aware that such language could be construed as a warranty standard on the design and on the performance of the design as constructed. Other warranties could be claimed for anything ranging from the failure to meet the certification level planned to "excessive" energy, water, or maintenance costs. Even the failure of the design to decrease employee sick leave and increase productivity could be claimed.

Scenario:

An architect agreed to design with a goal of LEED gold certification. The developer advertised the planned office building using superlatives from USGBC information about "reduced operating costs and healthier and more productive occupants" to attract tenants at higher rents. Budget and time constraints prevented certification at the gold level. The developer sued the architect for negligence and breach of warranty based on the architect's "guarantee" of gold certification.

2.15   Fraud or Misrepresentation

It is surprisingly easy for a design firm involved in sustainable design to inadvertently give clients a false representation, commonly the result of over-selling the firm and its capabilities. For example, the calculation of energy savings and life-cycle costs is not an exact science. It depends heavily upon many factors, such as building material choices, design settings, occupancy, weather, etc. Thus, the initial savings in life-cycle costs offered by the design professional may be misleading. If a client does not understand this, the design professional could be accused of deceptive practices. An overstatement of qualifications may also lead to claims of deliberate misrepresentation in order to secure the commission—or fraud in the inducement to contract—exposing the professional to risks excluded from insurance coverage.

Scenario:

A homeowner was interested in a low-cost addition that would provide a healthful interior and save on energy costs. An architect agreed to design a "state-of-the-art" green residence. He discussed expertise and how design and service would "assure" the client of satisfaction with a project that met the schedule and budget. The homeowner, unhappy with the cost, time, and result, sued the architect under consumer protection laws, alleging fraud in the inducement of the contract for services, and demanded rescission of the contract and return of the architect's fee and legal costs, even though the project was complete.

2.16   New Product Liability

With the growth of green rating systems and laws encouraging green building, the construction industry is flush with new products aimed at cashing in on the sustainable movement. Manufacturers are putting new products on the market with limited time for research and virtually no product history of performance. So who bears the risk of specifying experimental products? The architect and the engineer are certainly likely targets for claims if products do not perform as advertised. To mitigate that liability, the design professional should fully disclose to the client the risk of using an untested product, and, if possible, share that risk with the client. Furthermore, the design professional could require the informed consent of the client when using experimental products. This informed consent would require the architect or engineer to offer several green alternatives, informing the client of the risks and benefits of each, and indicating those products that are especially experimental. Then the client should consent in writing to the use of any untested products so it is clear that the client participated in the decision to take on the risk.

Scenario:

An architect made the decision to use a green product from a new manufacturer with impressive promotional information. The architect did not conduct research on the product's availability and did not warn the client of any possible problems. The client, based on the architect's opinion, agreed to the product's use. When the contractor was ready to install the product it was not readily available, which delayed the project's completion and distorted the construction schedule. The contractor demanded increased payment for overhead, lost profits, and out-of-sequence construction. The client brought suit against the architect since the architect never informed the client that the product was subject to delayed delivery.

2.17   Practice Management Precautions

Even with the public and professional enthusiasm to design for sustainability, it is vital that firms use sound practice management techniques to keep green projects from creating unmanageable exposures or creating situations where a firm is subject to uninsurable risks.

Firms need to recognize the challenges in green design that are intrinsic in every project. Certainly with most clients there exists competition between client demands. Many times, services are provided for market-driven projects which require reduced initial costs and compressed delivery times. And often on sustainability projects, the goal is less than altruistic. Many clients want the perceived marketing advantages that a "certified green" project can project or are intent on gaining regulatory advantages or tax, development, and energy incentives.

On every project – especially those in which green design is expressed as a goal – design firms should consider the following questions:

- What is the carefully defined scope?
- How are goals and expectations defined?
- Is there compensation for a continual review of integration and changes?

- Is a warranty being implied or expressed?
- How are design decisions documented?
- Who is responsible for the investigation of materials, products, and systems?
- Who provides construction oversight?
- What expectations are created?
- How is the owner/operator being trained to maintain systems and performance?
- How will performance be documented and compared to a specific standard?
- Can extended services be provided that would mitigate the likelihood of performance at less than expectations?

Design firms can meet the challenges presented by emphasizing sustainability in project design by first recognizing the risks in holding oneself out as an expert in sustainability. They then need to take proactive efforts to manage client expectations by specifying the applicable standard of care, controlling the project scope, setting reasonable contract requirements, and requiring adequate compensation for the increased level of service and risk.

Contractual obligations that are based on aspirations rather than measurable accomplishments are especially problematic. Firms should use a contract that recognizes professional judgment and defines scope and fee. Such a contract must avoid express warranties or guarantees and should limit the liability of the design firm for consequential damages related to certification, energy, or water use or other attributes of green design.

Firms should be careful to document the "buy-in" by the client to the cost and time factors of green design and the risk of using unproven products and systems. It is important that firms emphasize the requirement of client's informed consent. Firms need to document a rational selection process in which they request technical, not promotional, material; research product and manufacturer's reputation and capacity; and inform clients of risks discovered. Managing the product or system selection process includes cautioning the owner on the availability of products and making the owner aware of the danger of substitutions.

2.18   Obtaining a Mutual Understanding on Designing for Sustainability

No matter how skilled and knowledgeable design professionals may be, there are some exposures that remain beyond the control of the design firms. Clients, lenders, and brokers – as well as end-users (tenants, residents) – are likely to develop unrealistic expectations of how a building will perform and whether it will receive a certification as a "green" project. Manufacturers and suppliers of new materials and technologies may misrepresent or overstate the performance of their products. Many facets of green certification programs simply cannot be managed by the design firm, since many of the code and regulatory restraints associated with green building practices extend beyond design services. Furthermore, the performance gains and energy and water savings associated with green design rely upon very low tolerances for construction defects or laxity in the operation and maintenance building systems. But nearly all construction and operational deficiencies are beyond a design firm's control. Responding to such risks takes more than design skills.

As the standard of care evolves, clients will expect a higher level of services. As the value of "green" projects increases because of financial benefits tied to sustainable design, clients will demand contractual assurances that they will realize a commensurate return on their investment in a high-performance design. And as the measurement of performance increases, clients will look more closely at the difference between the design requirements and the actual use of energy, water, and other operational expenses.

2.19   Managing Green Design Risks through Contract Language

The most important factor in preventing claims based on the underperformance of a sustainable design or untested materials and applications is that all parties involved understand – and acknowledge in writing – the inherent risks in such a project, the many factors that make the outcome unpredictable in nature, and the limits and responsibilities of each stakeholder to manage or control those risks.

Establishing reasonable expectations at the beginning and throughout the project is vital. One way to avoid unreasonable contractual provisions or unrealistic expectations is by educating the client and having the client understand that design services are recommendations that the client has to understand and, once satisfied, accept.

When drafting the contract for professional services, provisions should be included that limit risk or that, at a minimum, express a client's acknowledgement that not all attributes of a program for sustainability are within the control of a design firm. Contractual provisions such as disclaimers and other exculpatory language need to be worded carefully. Firms should assess their risk and work with local legal counsel to craft appropriate project-specific provisions. This is especially true when the provisions include any waiver of claims, requirements for a legal defense, or the indemnification of costs.

It is essential to avoid language or actions that could be construed to establish a warranty of service or results. At the same time, including contractual provisions that are clear on the role of the design firm is critical.

The following are two examples of contractual communication tools that can lead to a client's "informed consent."

- **When Owner wants the design to meet specific sustainability criteria:**

  Owner has made Design Firm aware that Owner wants a specific level of sustainability incorporated into this Project and that Design Firm shall use the standards published by [specific design guidelines or certification standard] for this Project. Design Firm shall research the applicable sustainability requirements and design the Project with the intention of having the Project meet the requirements. Owner recognizes that a project designed to meet a specific sustainability standard might not perform as designed because of the construction, operation, and maintenance of the Project and therefore agrees that it shall bring no claim against Design Firm if the project does not perform as intended unless the negligence of the Design Firm is the sole cause of the performance deficiency.

  Owner also recognizes that during the design of the Project, Design Firm shall use professional judgment in the selection of materials, products and systems for the Project but that Design Firm cannot and does not warrant the performance of any specified material, product or system. Design Firm will identify for Owner any material, product or system that, in the Design Firm's judgment from the Design Firm's examination of available performance information, might provide Owner with a benefit on this Project but does not have adequate information on its performance in actual construction or operation. Owner acknowledges that it shall look solely to the manufacturer, supplier or installer of materials, products, or systems if their performance does not meet expectations.

- **When Owner wants third-party certification of sustainability:**

Owner has made Design Firm aware that Owner intends to pursue [specific certification standard] for this Project. Design Firm shall research the applicable certification requirements, design the Project with the intention of having the Project meet the requirements, and document the design of the Project for submission by the Owner to the certifying organization. Owner recognizes that certification is not based on design alone but also on the construction, operation and maintenance of the Project and therefore agrees that it shall bring no claim against Design Firm if the project is not certified as intended unless the negligence of the Design Firm is the sole cause of the Project not being certified.

Owner also recognizes that during the design of the Project, Design Firm shall use professional judgment in the selection of materials, products and systems for the Project with the goal of meeting certification criteria but that Design Firm cannot and does not warrant the performance of any specified material, product or system. Design Firm will identify for Owner any material, product or system that, in the Design Firm's judgment from the Design Firm's examination of available performance information, might provide Owner with a benefit on this Project but does not have adequate information on its performance in actual construction or operation. Owner acknowledges that it shall look solely to the manufacturer, supplier or installer of materials, products or systems if their performance does not meet expectations.

2.20   Design Practice Pointers

Whether firms hold themselves out as experts in sustainability or are providing services without emphasizing green design, they should consider the following reminders:

1. Stay up-to-date with green legislation and changes in standards or codes in the jurisdictions where your projects are located.

2. Know what the current standard of care is for your profession. Examine if the standard of care for a specific project type includes green design services.

3. Read your professional society code of ethics. If a dispute arises, the applicable code of ethics will be used to establish a professional duty.

4. Be familiar with the major green rating systems and state and local green design regulations.

5. Be careful that advertising and marketing staff are not overselling design professional and firm experience with green design.

6. Understand your client's green expectations early in the process. If the client's expectations are high or unattainable, explain the green process and discuss realistic outcomes. If the client expects specific results or 100% perfection in design, carefully consider whether to accept the project.

7. Examine to what extent the design contract requires services focused on sustainability. If you do not plan to offer specific green services, eliminate those provisions.

8. Do not promise, warrant, or guarantee specific results such as a certification or third-party approval, waste reduction, decreased energy use, or anything else beyond your control.

9. Document communications with the client about green design services and options related to project sustainability.

10. Use informed consent forms when offering green design services and specifying unproven or experimental materials, products, or systems.

Chapter 3

A Word of Caution about Green Design

J. Kent Holland, Esq.

3.1   Introduction

With the increasing concern about the environment, energy conservation, and potential global warming, the push for green design and construction has grown dramatically in the last couple of years. As project owners, design professionals, contractors, and suppliers are jumping on the green band wagon, some fundamental risks arising out of this movement are either being ignored or not adequately considered. This chapter is intended to supplement the other chapters included in this book that address the subject of green design and construction.   Its focus is on addressing risks and liabilities unique to green design and construction. It provides risk management strategies for addressing these new risks through managing client expectations, drafting appropriate contract language, securing available insurance coverage, and exercising construction management or administration services to control or mitigate the risks arising out of building to meet green design requirements.

3.2   Risk and Liability Arising out of Green Design

Risks associated with green design are many and varied. Some of the risks that have been raised by attorneys, design professional risk managers, insurance underwriters, and others include:

(1) uninformed and unrealistic expectations of project owners;

(2) project failing to obtain certification that was sought – resulting in owner being unable to qualify for expected tax credits and various government incentives;

(3) increased standard of care;

(4) uninsurable guarantees or warranties;

(5) problems with completed buildings due to systems or product failures that were impacted by green design decisions;

(6) construction defects blamed on design professional for failure to specify correct systems and products and failure to properly supervise the contractor.

When it comes to risk management for the design professional and contractor, it should be readily apparent that if the owner has been led to believe that it will see measurable costs savings as compared to the costs it would incur for a conventional building, and these savings fail to materialize, the owner may seek redress against the design professionals and contractors that they believe caused them to fail to obtain the desired benefits.

3.3   Certification Isn't So Certain

Certification by third party evaluators is granted only after construction of a building is complete.   During the design stage, and even while construction is being performed, it is not possible to be certain that a building will obtain the LEED certification that is being sought. Factors beyond the control of the design professional and contractor may affect the eventual award of LEED certification. Consequently, design professionals are well advised not to sign a contract that promises the project owner that the building will achieve a LEED certification. Language in contracts that may create such promises includes "guarantees," "warranties," "assures," "ensures," and "LEED certification shall be achieved or liquidated damages shall be imposed in the amount of X dollars."

Design professionals are repeatedly taught in their insurance company risk management sessions that their professional liability policy only covers them for negligent acts, errors, and omissions. Not every mistake and error is an insured one. This is because courts only impose liability on design professionals where their services fail to meet the appropriate standard of care applicable to design professionals practicing similar services in the same time and place. If a design professional agrees to liquidated damages or to a standard of care higher than that which is imposed by law, the insurance policy will not cover damages arising out of the design firm's failure to meet that higher standard. Such damages are excluded from coverage pursuant to the contractual liability exclusion of the policy.

Warranties and guarantees are expressly excluded from coverage under the design professional policy. Consequently, if liability is imposed on the design professional pursuant to the language of the contract that promised a certain level of certification would be achieved, the damages arising out of that contractual breach will be excluded from coverage pursuant to the warranties and guarantees exclusion. Later in this chapter, we provide a more detailed explanation of insurance coverage, with examples of actual policy language that may affect the coverage.

3.4   What Can the Design Professional Contractually Commit to Achieve?

As discussed in Chapter 2, the Architect accepts new responsibilities under the AIA B101 document. The standard forms for other organizations do not yet address environmental sustainable design issues in such a philosophical and detailed manner, but it is likely that they will soon follow suit. In my review of design professional contracts over the past several years, I have noticed that instead of using trade association standard forms, project owners such as hospitals, schools, large commercial enterprises, and government agencies are more typically using forms of their own creation and that many of these forms are adding sustainable design and construction requirements, including specific warranty language for LEED certification achievement.

In one contract involving a large and complex new medical center and hospital, the design contract stated that the design firm would design the facility so that LEED Gold certification would be achieved, and that "in the event that LEED certification is not granted, liquidated damages in the amount of $2 million shall be assessed."

What if the design firm that designs the project and warrants the LEED Gold in the above situation has only minimal construction phase responsibility? If its scope of service does not call for significant construction administration services, and some other firm, such as a construction management (CM) firm, is going to be performing that function instead, how can the design firm protect itself against decisions being made during construction and commissioning that are inconsistent with achieving Gold Certification?

Unlike a supplier that gives an equipment warranty, a design professional does not have anything near the same kind of control over the factors that affect a warranty that the designer gives when warranting that a building will get a LEED certification. It is unreasonable for a project owner to demand an uninsurable warranty from a design professional.

3.5 Using Contract Language to Limit Liability

The standard AIA contract documents contain a mutual waiver of liability clause stating that both the project owner and design firm waive consequential damages that they might claim from each other. Such consequential damages may include lost profits, lost rents, lost tax breaks, lost financing terms, increased operation and maintenance costs, and other economic losses, such as loss or impairment of the building value due to failure to obtain a specified LEED certification.

This waiver of consequential damages may be an important tool to limit the architect's potential liability arising out of failure to achieve the sustainability objectives intended. Engineers and other design professionals should consider adding such a waiver to their contracts as well. A project owner might not be willing to grant a broad waiver clause, but it might accept such a clause if it is limited to consequential damages related to green design. It is worth pursuing this during contract negotiation. In drafting such a waiver of consequential damages clause specific to green design, consider delineating the consequential damages items listed in the preceding paragraph, plus any others you might think of, and state that the waiver applies, "but is not limited to," each of those items.

In addition to not agreeing to any warranties or guarantees concerning green design, it may also be advisable to add a clause affirmatively stating that the design professional is making no warranty and giving no guarantee concerning LEED certification because such certification is beyond its ability to control.

It may also be prudent to add a paragraph to the contract stating that any forms or representations that the design professional or contractor might give to the project owner concerning credit submittals do not constitute representations or warranties concerning the ultimate functionality or high performance of the building, but instead are solely for the purpose of satisfying the LEED certification process documentation requirements.

In addition to exercising great caution with the language that goes into the contracts for design and construction, project parties must also give attention to the language of marketing materials, advertisements, websites, and proposals. Despite language in contracts that has carefully avoided over-promising the quality of the services to be provided or the results to be obtained, it is surprising to see the same company potentially create liability through its marketing materials, websites, and proposals.

Proposals are often incorporated by reference or attachment to the design professional agreement. The representations contained in those proposals can, consequently, become an affirmative part of the contract. But even if not actually incorporated by reference, the content of the proposals might still be relied upon by a project owner in selecting a design professional, contractor, or vendor. Owners have successfully argued that they were expected and intended to rely upon those proposals when deciding whether or not to award a contract. Some complaints have alleged fraud and negligent misrepresentation in the proposals and marketing materials, in addition to actual negligent performance of the services or work. Owners find these allegations   particularly useful as a means to avoid liability limitations they may have agreed to in the contract. By arguing that they were "fraudulently induced" into the contract, the owners might be able to avoid a summary judgment to enforce a waiver of consequential damages clause or other limitation of liability clause in the contract.

The point is: it is not safe to think that proposals and marketing materials are merely "puffing" and can't be enforced. Owners who are not satisfied with the result of services may latch onto those materials as one basis of their claim – and that one basis might be the thing that gets them past a motion to dismiss or summary judgment motion.

3.6   Problems with Construction Materials Selected

Innovation tends to create greater risks and more litigation. Green design and construction encourages innovation. Innovation is the driving force. For green design, we are encouraged to think differently. We are encouraged to try things new. We are encouraged to take risks – to see what works and what doesn't – and learn lessons from our trials and errors. The downside is that the project owner who is asking for a green design may not understand the risk he or she is assuming when embarking on green design.

When using innovative products, it must be understood that these products are new and relatively untested. They do not have a long history of use by which they can be evaluated. Design professionals are being encouraged by groups like the AIA to consider and specify sustainable products. AIA B101-2007 even creates an affirmative obligation of the architect to do so. So the architect is required by its contract to take some additional risks of specifying new green products and systems that have no proven track record. To do this, the architect may find himself or herself relying upon marketing materials and sales pitches by green product vendors and suppliers. Additional risk for the design professional results from such reliance and yet the contract requires that the architect take that risk. The problem is that the AIA contract form fails to include a strong paragraph advising the owner of the risks of using new products and that the owner, not the architect, must assume the risk of product failure that impairs the performance of the building. A prudent design professional should insert language into its contract with the owner to expressly address these increased risks.

In a paper entitled "The Hidden Risks of Green Buildings," September 1, 2008, published originally in *NCARB Magazine*, David Odom, Richard Scot, and George H. Dubose cogently explain the risks inherent in the use of new, innovative green products and materials:

> "Most new products are experiments and most experiments fail." — Stewart Brand, *How Buildings Learn: What Happens After They're Built.*

> Stewart Brand's caution in 1994 about using new products is engaging and controversial, since progress can only be made through the use of new products and innovative approaches. Brand's caution echoes what forensic building consultants and building scientists have seen for decades: anything that departs from the "tried and true method" often fails. This isn't surprising, since even traditional building materials experience some percentage of catastrophic failures from moisture and mold problems.

> The warning is especially appropriate today with the expansion of new products, many intended for Leadership in Energy and Environmental Design (LEED®) certification.

> Although many of these "green" products have been developed within the last five years, they're intended for use in buildings that should last for more than 50 years. Even a casual review of product literature indicates that some of these products appear to have had minimal on-site testing or performance verification. Additionally, many have not been marketed in a manner suggesting caution about regional or climatic restrictions in their use. Finally, we suspect that there has been even less testing of

the complex, interrelated assemblies in which these products will be asked to co-exist for 50+ years or more.

When it comes to specifying innovative products that claim to be "green," "eco-friendly," "sustainable," or "renewable," the design professional will need to document what due diligence it performed in specifying such material or in accepting such material during the contractor submission process. It will not be a sufficient defense to say that reasonable reliance was placed upon the representations of the vendors who have all suddenly become green – any more than it would be reasonable to buy "snake oil" from a slick salesman you found on the internet and actually expect it was going to make you into superman or superwoman.

Good advice to design professionals when evaluating any product or system that claims to be green is to be super cynical. Don't believe anything. Challenge everything. Make the vendor prove its claims. And before accepting any innovative product, give the project owner the information available on the green products and warn the client about the risks – have the owner accept those risks in writing.

3.7   Administering the Project Construction to Reduce Risk

3.7.1   Design Professional's Role During Construction

The design professional firm that designs the building and specifies the building systems and materials can better manage the risk from faulty products and work if it has a significant role during the construction phase, such as being the construction administrator for the owner. By being on site during construction, the design professional can determine whether the products are being installed as planned and whether the quantity and quality of the work are meeting the contract document requirements. Since the construction contractor may not be familiar with the new products that the design firm specified, it is more likely that the contractor will make an error in the installation of the product that may cause product failure. An excellent example of this is the Exterior Insulation Finish Systems ("EIFS") that have caused so much water and mold damage to buildings over the last 10 years.

If EIFS is installed the way the manufacturers intended and then carefully maintained, it may work satisfactorily without allowing water infiltration to get behind the exterior wall where it can cause rotting and molding of interiors. Unfortunately, EIFS was installed by contractors who either didn't understand the procedures or ignored them. They cut holes and failed to put caulk in the holes. They failed to waterproof around windows and doors. They drilled holes for wiring and lights. All these acts by the contractors caused water to get behind the EIFS and ruin entire buildings. Will this same thing happen with new green products which might have worked just as the vendor represented but for careless installation by contractors who didn't know any better?

3.7.2   Construction Management Services

Perhaps green projects need to have oversight by construction management that specializes in green construction management. This does not necessarily mean someone who has LEED AP after his or her name. That designation could mean nothing more than that the individual understands the documentation requirements needed for LEED certification. What may be needed is a person with hands-on experience with construction techniques and procedures that understands whether the products are being installed in accordance with vendor specifications, and whether practical considerations are being implemented during construction. This may add another layer of cost to the project.

3.7.3   LEED AP Individual's Role

In view of how relatively easy it is to obtain LEED AP certification as compared to obtaining a contractor or professional license, it is arguable that every contractor and design firm should have one or more individuals on its staff who are LEED AP. Although LEED AP designation of a design professional might arguably raise the standard of care expectations between the project owner and the design professional, that same designation when held by the contractor's staff could conceivably be a good defense for the design professional if the building fails to obtain LEED certification as a result of poor construction practices and failure of the contractor to document its LEED efforts.

A design firm could argue that it reasonably relied on the contractor's environmental expertise since that contractor was LEED AP. Likewise, if a design professional does not advise its project owner to make LEED AP a condition precedent to hiring a contractor, it is conceivable that an owner unsatisfied with the construction result might argue that its design professional was negligent in failing to advise the owner of the importance of using only a LEED AP contractor. In any event, there is certainly no downside for the design professional in recommending to its client, the project owner, that the construction contractor, as well as major artesian contractors such as those who provide HVAC, have a LEED AP individual on their staff who is assigned to the project.

Just because a contractor or vendor has a LEED certified individual, or several certified individuals, on staff does not mean they are experienced and qualified to perform the project work to accomplish the performance expectations of the owner. Since it seems everyone today is claiming to be green, it may be prudent for design professionals to establish as part of the project owner's construction bidding process certain green construction experience requirements to be satisfied by contractors. These could include experience with a minimum number of green projects, or a minimum number of years performing green construction. Or a section of the bidding documents might require bidders to list in detail their previous green building experience. If the contractor claims to have one or more green experts, it may be appropriate to require them to be assigned to the project, and to contractually forbid the contractor from removing them from the project without the prior written approval of the project owner.

If this view seems a bit cynical, we should recall other examples from the past. When Radon was the big scare of the 1980s, it seemed that everyone was suddenly a Radon remediation expert. No experience or knowledge was necessary. And the results were not always good. Then there was the mold remediation of the 1990s. Again, inexperienced contractors were suddenly mold remediation contractors. There are many horror stories of these contractors ruining entire homes in their unprofessional efforts to clean up a little mold. And then, of course, there was asbestos removal, where some of the first contractors in that field made a real mess of things by taking asbestos that was pretty well sealed off in ceiling plenums and spreading it all over a building or getting it into the HVAC system.

I have been involved in risk management for numerous types of environmental and construction projects, starting with my years working in the construction grants program at the United States Environmental Protection Agency ("EPA"). I think green design and construction is the "latest, greatest thing" that will create a lot of litigation for the unwary.

3.8   Green Roofs – Big Risks

Some risks are so obvious it seems hard to believe that any project owner could express surprise when things don't work out as planned. Green roof tops are a great example of this. Does anyone really believe that green parks with large trees and shrubs can be put onto roof tops without an increased risk of leaking? Roofs leak. Green roofs will add to the risk of leaking. This is not to say that green roofs shouldn't be designed and built. But project owners that decide to incorporate these into their building plans need to have their expectations managed by their design firms and contractors so they don't go running into courts with law suits against the designers and contractors when they have leaking problems.

Leaking from roofs may occur as a result of roots breaking through planters. It could be from watering pipes and systems bursting. It could be from failure of the building owner to properly operate and maintain the rooftop systems that are put into place. It could even occur due to larger numbers of people walking on the roofs and doing their recreation there.

Consider the fact that many leaks occur on basic, non-innovative roofs because of simple operation and maintenance issues, such as failure to maintain proper gravel/ballast on top of the weatherproof membrane, workers walking around where they are not supposed to be, installing and removing equipment without properly repairing waterproof membranes, failing to maintain caulk around various openings and connections, failing to clean downspouts and gutters, and various failures due to routine maintenance that may seem small, but have a big impact. All these issues will be magnified by installing green roofs on buildings.

How, then, can the risk of a green roof be managed? For one thing, it is advisable that the design professional be careful that its contracts contain no guarantee or warranty concerning the performance of the roof system designed. Contractors should be careful what, if any, warranties they give concerning products and workmanship so as not to warrant that a roof will be free from all leaks for a long number of years. Landscapers and building maintenance crews over whom the designers and contractors have no control will be responsible for installing and maintaining the greenery. The building owner, through what will have to be more intensive operation and maintenance, will be impacting the contractor's finished work product in a way that impacts any warranty.

Just as with warranties for equipment, an operations manual on how to operate a green roof may be appropriate – and the project owner should be required to document that it complied with the manual in maintaining the greenery of the roof so as not to damage any of the contractor's work or void any equipment warranties.

3.9   Insurance Coverage for Green Claims against Design Professionals

Professional liability insurance is intended to cover design professionals for their negligent acts, errors, and omissions. Breaches of warranty and contract are not covered except to the extent the breaches result from negligent acts, errors, and omissions of the policy holder. Coverage for liability damages caused by anything other than design professionals' negligence is expressly excluded by the contractual liability exclusion.

Language typical of design professional insurance policies is as follows:

> We will pay on behalf of the "Insured" all sums in excess of the Deductible noted in Item 6. of the Declarations that you are legally obligated to pay as "Damages" because of "Claims" first made against you during the "Policy Period" and reported to us during the "Policy Period," or the Extended "Claims" Reporting Period if applicable, provided that:
>
> A. the "Claim" arises out of an actual or alleged negligent act, error or omission with respect to "Professional Services" rendered or that should have been rendered by you or any entity for whom you are legally responsible, including your interest in joint ventures.

There are two key exclusions—the exclusion for breach of warranty and the exclusion for contractual liability— in the typical policy that may have particular applicability to claims against design professionals based on green design

It is important to note that what the professional liability policy covers is "claims" for "damages" as defined in the policy, and that only those damages arising from a *negligent* act, error, or omission are covered by the policy. Not every error and mistake is covered by insurance. In addition to not covering intentional acts, the policy does not cover the common mistake that does not rise to the level of being a breach of the applicable standard of care.

Claims based on breach of *Warranties* are excluded from coverage. This will include such matters as unconditional commitments to achieve LEED certification. Some recent contracts I have reviewed have contained commitments by the design professional to design a building that will achieve LEED Gold certification, and have stated that failure of the building to receive this certification will result in the design professional being required to pay as liquidated damages to the project owner the amount of $2 million.

What the design professional and the project owner must understand is that this $2 million liquidated damages, even if not deemed by a court to be "punitive," is nevertheless uninsurable under a design professional policy. This is an absolute guarantee or warranty even if neither of those words is expressly used in the contract. By agreeing to pay damages for failure to achieve the Gold certification, the design professional has created a warranty that is excluded pursuant to the warranty exclusion of the insurance policy.

Contractual liability is liability that arises out the terms and conditions of the contract that the design professional would not have under the law of the local jurisdiction in the absence of the contract language. For example, if the designer agrees to indemnify its client for all damages on the project regardless of whether they were caused by someone or something other than the negligence of the designer, this becomes a contractual obligation that exceeds the responsibility the courts would otherwise impose upon the designer. Or if the design professional agrees to perform to some "highest" standard of care or to a standard of care that differs materially from that which would be imposed by law, claims for breaching this increased standard may be excluded pursuant to the contractual liability exclusion of the policy.

Indemnification provisions in the Agreement between the design professional and its client (project owner or design-builder) sometimes require that the design professional indemnify the client for damages arising out of its performance regardless of whether that performance is negligent. Such indemnity by the design professional is an uninsurable risk since the E&O carrier does not consider costs incurred by the design professional as a result of such indemnification to be "damages" as defined by the policy. Instead, those costs are excluded from coverage by the "contractual liability exclusion" and by the language of the Insuring Agreement.

When a design professional sees provisions requiring contractual liability, or warranties and guarantees, it should immediately flag them as problem clauses. Some of these clauses are obvious. Others are subtle and harder to spot because they don't use language readily recognized as referring to warranties and guarantees. If, for example, a design professional agrees to the "highest" standard of care instead of the generally accepted standard, it may inadvertently warrant that its services will be the best, and will produce a perfect result.

It may also be prudent to delete a reference in the indemnity clause that would require the design professional to indemnify its client for breach of contract since this is not insurable absent negligence.

3.10   Potential Claim Scenarios and Ideas for Managing the Risk

In this next section, a number of potential claim scenarios are presented.

1. Contractual Warranty Obligation:

The design professional is asked to sign a contract that states the building will be designed to attain LEED Gold Certification, and that if it fails to achieve that certification, the design professional will pay its client as liquidated damages the sum of $2 million. This is an uninsurable damage or claim under the professional liability policy.

Solution: Delete this contract clause in its entirety. Replace it with one which states that the design professional will perform its services in a manner consistent with the generally accepted standard of care exercised by design professionals performing similar services to attain LEED Gold certification, but that factors beyond its responsibility and control will impact whether the building is granted Gold Certification, and the design professional makes no warranty or guarantee concerning Gold Certification.

Providing this written exception and revision to the client's proposed language will certainly generate an intelligent conversation with the client that enables the design professional and project owner to come to a realistic understanding of what can be expected as a result of the professional services. Negotiating the contract is one of the most critical elements of managing client expectations for the project and for the outcome of the professional services.

2. Unfulfilled Green Expectations Under the AIA B101-2007 Contract:

The design professional, by contract, might commit itself to environmental design requirements without realizing that it is doing so, or without realizing the full extent of the responsibility it is taking on. For example, the architect signs the B101 contract that contains the following new standard clauses:

> § 3.2.3 The Architect shall present its preliminary evaluation to the Owner and shall discuss with the Owner alternative approaches to design and construction of the Project, including the feasibility of incorporating environmentally responsible design approaches. The Architect shall reach an understanding with the Owner regarding the requirements of the Project.

> §3.2.5.1 The Architect shall consider environmentally responsible design alternatives, such as material choices and building orientation, together with other considerations based on program and aesthetics, in developing a design that is consistent

with the Owner's program, schedule and budget for the Cost of the Work. The Owner may obtain other environmentally responsible design services under Article 4.

Claim Possibility 1:

If the design professional fails to discuss with its client the "feasibility of incorporating environmentally responsible design approaches," it is in breach of its contractual duties? If the client later learns or decides that its building would have been better had it been designed to LEED certification standards, it may assert grounds for action against the design professional for failing to advise it of its options during the design phase of the project.   Recovery would depend, of course, on whether the owner could prove damages. But in view of the likely expert testimony the owner would present concerning the benefits (real or imagined) of green buildings, this may be a question that would make it to a jury and would not be something that would be dismissed on a summary judgment motion.

Solution: Strike these clauses from the contract if it is not the design professional's intent to perform these duties. Do not sign the form contract without carefully considering all of its provisions and determining whether the parties actually intend for those provisions to be fulfilled.

Claim Possibility 2:

The design professional discusses with its client the feasibility of incorporating "environmentally responsible design approaches, but the client decides it is not interested in green design. It is constructing a warehouse and feels that it will not matter to the people who work there whether it is green or not. Nor will it matter to the value of the building. Finally, the owner decides it will not matter to the community since the building is being constructed in an old industrial park, where few people will actually see it. No written record is made of the "discussion" between the design professional and owner. Later, the owner sells the building to a third party (or perhaps loses it at foreclosure to a lender), and that third party or lending institution learns that the building is not functioning up to the green standards that it believes should have been incorporated into the warehouse. As an example, it may cost more to operate and this reduces the resale value of the building.

Depending upon the jurisdiction, there are a number of legal theories that the third party buyer, or a lending institution that foreclosed on the property, might use to bring suit directly against the design professional for breach of its contract, or possibly even for negligence. Without the written documentation to prove that the design professional fulfilled its contractual duty to discuss green design possibilities with its client, it may be difficult for the design professional to get out of this litigation on a motion for summary judgment. The result could be long and protracted litigation resulting in a jury trial or an unfavorable settlement.

Solution: Document in writing all discussions that the design professional has with the client. If there is an oral communication, follow up with a letter, memorandum, e-mail, meeting minutes, or other appropriate written documentation to memorialize the oral communication. If the design firm gives recommendations to the project owner and those recommendations are rejected, this, too, needs be memorialized in writing.

When it comes to determining what was said, when it was said, and who decided what, the best evidence generally is written documentation. This includes correspondence, memoranda, notes, faxes, and e-mails. As discussed elsewhere in this chapter, written documentation can be particularly important to prove you complied with contract requirements. Written evidence that you met all contractual notice requirements and obtained proper and timely approvals can be vital to your success in presenting claims or defending against them.

With written documentation, you can also prove you gave sufficient information to others so they could make intelligent decisions and possibly even assume the risk of their decisions.

Many initial communications between the parties will take place orally in the ordinary course of conversation on the project. Unless these oral conversations are somehow reduced to writing in the form of meeting minutes, memoranda, or correspondence, their content and value may be lost.

There have been case examples involving equipment substitution decisions where project owners ignored the advice of the design professional and accepted inferior "or equal" equipment against which the design professional warned. When that equipment failed to function as the contractor had promised the owner it would, the owner has turned around and sued the design professional for permitting the substitution to occur. This is not necessarily because the owner is being dishonest. It may be as simple as years have passed and the original decision-makers with the project owner have moved on to other jobs or possibly even died – and there is no corporate memory concerning the advice given by the design professional. In any event, a written record in this situation is critical to the design professional being able to prevail in this litigation by showing that it provided ample information and warning to the owner not to make the equipment substitution. This type of a denial by the project owner could be avoided if a record of the memorandum proved that the communication had been made.

Even if no written record is made to confirm that the recommendation was received by the client, there may be other methods to prove that the client received the notice and acted upon it. A follow-up note to the client referencing the written recommendation can be useful. This can state something to the effect that you are sending it to confirm that you sent the earlier memo and will be taking action in accordance with any understandings that may have been reached concerning those recommendations. You could also raise the issue at a formal project meeting and have the matter, including the fact that the written recommendation was made, recorded into the meeting minutes.

Even telephone logs and notes are useful as contemporaneous business records to show that a conversation occurred concerning the recommendation contained in the memorandum that was never formally acknowledged by the client. By doing these things, you are making it more difficult for the client to later deny having received the written recommendation.

Claim Possibility 3:

The two claim possibilities discussed above both concerned clause § *3.2.3* of the AIA B101. We turn now to the possibility of claims arising out of the second B101 clause that creates environmental design responsibilities for the design professional.

Consider the duties created by §3.2.5.1: *"The Architect shall consider environmentally responsible design alternatives, such as material choices and building orientation, together with other considerations based on program and aesthetics, in developing a design that is consistent with the Owner's program..."*

The requirements of this provision go beyond having a discussion with the client. The design professional is required to consider environmentally responsible design alternatives, including material choices (and presumably equipment and systems choices as well) regardless of whether the project owner has otherwise asked for this as part of the scope of services.

Beware that this clause essentially increases the scope of service. It might potentially increase and change what is required by the normal standard of care. In the absence of the contract clause, the design professional would have no duty to consider environmentally responsible designs – unless law, codes, ordinances, or licensing statutes might otherwise impose such a duty upon the design professional. In any event, the design professional needs to be aware of this important provision of the AIA contract.

With this clause in place, if the design professional fails to consider, and possibly choose, environmentally sensitive designs and materials that could reduce energy, reduce wastes, save water, and otherwise result in a building that might achieve LEED certification, the project owner might bring a law suit alleging damages similar to those suggested in Claim Possibility 2 above, resulting from the design professional's breach of contract.

Solution: Strike this clause from the AIA contract if the design professional does not intend to perform these services. If, however, the requirements of this section must be accepted by the design professional either by virtue of the contract language or by other standards imposed, then the design professional will need to carefully document that it adhered to the requirements. This will again include documentation of communications and conversations with the client or owner. But it will also require documentation showing what environmental considerations were made – and how ultimate decisions were reached.

3. Performance Expectations for the Building are not Met:
Even if a building obtains the LEED certification level desired by the building owner, there is no assurance that the building will be more energy efficient, improve worker health and attendance, or produce other benefits that so many of the trade journals and press have been touting. An unsatisfied project owner that has paid more money to achieve a LEED certified building than it would have paid for a conventional building may be so unhappy with the result (particularly in a bad economy) that it may seek to recover damages from the design professional. Conceivable legal theories could include negligence, breach of contract, breach of warranty, and negligent misrepresentation.

Solution: Manage the owner's performance expectations by communicating at the outset that despite reasonable efforts to obtain LEED certification, this does not necessarily translate into performance benefits even if LEED certification is obtained. There are examples of buildings that have been LEED certified because they met all the documentation requirements necessary for that certification – yet they do not perform as well as conventional buildings. Perhaps give the project owner a copy of the July 2008 GSA Report titled, "Assessing Green Building Performance," that provides case study examples showing that some buildings with LEED certification perform worse than the modeled expectations.

Be careful to avoid agreeing by contract to any warranties or guarantees concerning building performance. Include a waiver of consequential damages clause in the contract so that these types of potential damages that might be claimed by the building owner are barred from recovery. Get the building owner to include language either in the contract or as an addendum, stating that they have been informed about the risks concerning building performance, especially items such as green roofs that might leak, and that the owner accepts and assumes those performance risks.

4. Indemnification Provisions Creating Uninsurable Contractual Liability:

If the indemnification provision of the design professional policy requires the design professional to indemnify the client for damages arising out of "all performance of the professional services" or out of "all acts, errors and omissions" or "out of damages caused in whole or in part by the negligence of the design professional," each of these three provisions may create indemnity obligations for the design professional to pay to the client in the event some third party was to file a claim against the client/building owner for failure to achieve LEED certification or certain building performance expectations.

Possibilities for how the indemnification requirement could be triggered include: (1) claims by a building tenant alleging that it has been harmed by the failure of the building to attain LEED certification and it is moving out and demanding damages for its move; and (2) claims by a worker in the building, asserting he or she has become ill or diseased as a result of the building performance – perhaps the HVAC system. There are as many possible third party claim scenarios as a bunch of plaintiff lawyers sitting around a bar on a Friday night can dream up.

Under the indemnification provisions quoted above, if a third party claim is made against the design professional's client, that client is entitled to seek from the design professional indemnity for the damages it must pay to the third party. Unfortunately for the design professional, the indemnity clauses described above create uninsurable liability by holding the design professional responsible for all damages even if not caused by its negligence. Remember that only negligence is covered under the professional liability policy.

By agreeing to broad form indemnity to assume responsibility for non-negligent acts, the design professional has created an uninsured contractual liability. This is precisely the type of liability that is excluded from coverage under the professional liability policy.

Solution: Carefully review the indemnification provisions of the design professional contract. Delete any "duty to defend" obligations since these are uninsurable. Delete any language that requires indemnification other than indemnification for damages caused by the design professional's negligence.

5. LEED Letter Templates:
The letter templates that LEED requires of the design professional contain language that may create unreasonable expectations of the client and others. This language also implies a warranty or guarantee by the design professional.

Solution: Add a paragraph to the certification which states that the design professional represents that it exercised the appropriate standard of care in the performance of its services and is signing the LEED certification to the best of its knowledge, information, and belief, BUT makes no warranty or guarantee concerning building performance or any other matter.

6. Selection of Systems and Equipment:
In specifying systems and products for a building that are represented by the vendors and suppliers to be "green," the design professional is potentially subject to claims against it by its client in the event that the systems and equipment fail to meet the LEED certification requirements or fail to achieve the expected green building performance. The theories could range from negligent design, negligent selection, negligent inspection or supervision of construction, breach of contract, and breach of warranty.

Solution: Don't sign a contract containing any warranties of these systems or equipment by the design professional. Require that the manufacturers of all systems, equipment, and products provide appropriate warranties.
Specify the use of manufacturers and suppliers that have been in business for a significant period of time and have a good history with their products. This is not to say that an innovative system or product cannot be specified, but rather that when such an innovative product or system is selected, it is preferable that it be from a corporation that has been in business for a significant period of time – even if producing different products.
For major systems such a curtain wall, roofs, and HVAC, a further protection would be to require performance bonds for their work. Also require that all such vendors maintain commercial general liability insurance (CGL) and builder's risk insurance. The CGL policies should be required to name the design professional and the building owner as additional insureds.

These policies may provide coverage for damages caused to the building by malfunctioning equipment.

When specifying systems and equipment, thoroughly document how the equipment was selected and evaluated. Obtain any third party information and test data that might be available on the products.   Obtain from the vendors information and proof of use on other projects, including evidence of how the product performed.

If there are risks that the design professional identifies as inherent in the equipment that is chosen, convey those risks to the client in writing. Create documentation of the communication to demonstrate that the client has been advised of the risks and understands and accepts the risks of using the equipment.

7. Owner Does Not Have Clear Understanding of Green Design or What It Wants

If the project owner/client states in its request for proposals that it expects the design professional to create a "green design" for the building but fails to articulate or specify what it means by "green design" (through reference, for example, to LEED or Green Globes), there is potential for ambiguity and confusion concerning what the client wants and what the design professional thinks is required in its services.

Even if the request for proposals states that the building is to be "LEED certified" and there is no further statement whether the building is to be just LEED certified or LEED Silver, Gold, or Platinum, it is possible that this project owner does not know what it is asking for – and might think that "LEED certified" means LEED Gold.

Solution: If the request for proposals is less than clear about what the owner expects and requires in the way of the green building certification, this needs to be clarified in writing as part of the design professional's proposal. Any decisions about whether the building will be designed with the intent to meet a certain level of certification should be stated in the contract.

If the owner has communicated, either orally, or in writing extraneous to the request for proposals or contract documents, that it desires a "green design," this, too, should be responded to in writing. It must be clarified to state exactly what the client expects and any certification level that is to be achieved. Once again, as with the solutions proposed in the other claim scenarios, the design professional will need to manage the client expectations through careful contract language and a well-defined scope of service.

Chapter 4

Sustainable Design and Construction: When Green Turns Red

Ujjval K. Vyas, Ph.D., J.D.
Matthew P. Coglianese, Ph.D., Esq.

4.1   Introduction

"Green" is everywhere and everyone is claiming to be green. Many of the largest corporations and many smaller companies, government entities, and the media are promulgating some connection to green or sustainability. The term "green" now applies to all fields and political persuasions. Like motherhood and apple pie, green is now synonymous with positive feelings.

Typically, such attitudes have little impact on the construction industry, but the current wave of green is an exception. Owners, designers, contractors, vendors, suppliers, and operators of building assets find themselves increasingly caught up in trying to deliver green buildings. Design professionals are acting as advocates of green planning and building.

An important point to remember in dealing with the risks created by this new landscape of green is that they are systemic and not easily compartmentalized. The common silos of legal practice will often prove inadequate or counterproductive. Basic terms remain undefined and each of the parties commonly has a different idea of the definition of those terms. What an architect believes to be the definition of a green, sustainable, or high-performance building usually is very different from what a developer, contractor, or lender believes is the definition. Unfortunately, no extraordinary sentences or contract provisions will minimize or eliminate risk. In many ways, this language of green and sustainability can be considered a newly invigorated rhetoric of environmentalism sweeping up from construction and real estate into a larger policy arena.   When environmental concerns first reached serious consideration in the legal profession, no magic language existed to solve the problem. One might think of green design, construction, and real estate as environmentalism trying to penetrate into the very fabric of the built environment based on a linkage to global climate change.

4.2   Why Green/Sustainability Now?

Before we go any further, it is necessary to wrestle with the definitions of terms such as green, sustainability, green design, etc. First, as may be expected, all of these terms have a rather indistinct use. A recent scholar on the topic of sustainability stated:

Sustainability and *sustainable development* are now such "motherhood and apple pie" concepts in popular debate that they are at once over- and under-defined. *Our Common Future*, the 1987 report by the United Nations' World Commission on Environment and Development, stamped the modern concept indelibly into the dictionary of debate, with its notion that sustainable development means meeting the needs of the present (for health, environmental integrity, material progress, so forth) without compromising the ability of future to meet its needs. Since then many, many writers have produced their own pet definitions; but many others avoid a detailed or even any definition, preferring to allow a meaning of sustainability to emerge from their examples or general context.[1]

If "sustainability" has rather fuzzy outlines, the outlines of a definition of "green" are even more obscure. In general, this amorphous descriptor adds an environmental sheen to whatever follows. In the legal context, this indefinite characteristic creates serious problems for contract drafting, not to mention subsequent interpretation of contract terms or the intent of the parties.

In addition and more generally, these terms connote an alternative way of approaching policy and business decision-making. In other words, business decision-making as usual is replaced by a more socially and environmentally responsible strategy. In addition to financial gain, both social responsibility and environmental responsibility are to be considered equally, or at least more assiduously, in the deployment of economic or other resources.

These business and management guidelines are often encompassed by the term "triple bottom line" or even more generally, corporate social responsibility. Sustainability is the broader term, whereas green tends to focus more closely on environmental responsibility issues. Even so, the two terms have become interchangeable primarily as a result of the new nexus of social policy, global climate change.

4.3   Rise of the USGBC and Changes in the Architectural Profession

The built environment is now seen by many as sorely needing ameliorating action, and the non-profit United States Green Building Council ("USGBC") has stepped in to fill the void. Formed in the early 1990s, the USBGC is one of the leading organizations promoting a family of proprietary green building rating system products to effectuate positive changes in the built environment. The initial success of the USGBC was founded on the adoption of the Leadership in Energy and Environmental Design (LEED®) rating system for the construction of General Services Administration's (GSA) buildings. In essence, LEED certification became a new eco-label for buildings with the imprimatur of the federal agency responsible for government building assets. The USGBC, however, may not have had any influence in reshaping how government agencies build new structures without the inclusion of a rating system focused on energy savings and efficiency options that may maximize the financial benefits to the owners.

4.4   New Approaches Bring New Risks

Architects increasingly look to sustainability or green as a special province for which they are uniquely qualified, especially if LEED certified, but they may lack the technical knowledge to create better-performing buildings. Representations being made to the public by some design professionals and other advocates are structured around insufficiently supported claims that green buildings will perform better in terms of energy, occupant health outcomes, worker productivity, and even student test score improvements. This fundamental mismatch between the possible assumptions of architects and the reasonable expectations of owners creates an additional risk for the development or construction project as a whole.

As we look at the risks in a more detailed manner below, we should remember that the relationships between the technical, policy, and risk management issues that arise and must be addressed in the growing context of green construction and development cannot be handled effectively with a myopic perspective. The causes of the risks may necessitate treading into areas where construction attorneys have not normally travelled.

While green building provides major opportunities and benefits, it also creates several undefined liability risks and litigation potential. As owners, contractors, and end-users demand green buildings and have increased expectations, construction litigation will take on a new flavor. Owners paying more for a green building may expect a significantly higher standard of construction, efficiency, and operation, and may, as a result, place a great degree of reliance on representations made by the architect, general contractor, and the trades.

If an architect or contractor makes certain representations in a contract to build a green building by using certain types of materials, certain insulation, or committing to water reuse designs and systems, etc., and the final product does not meet those commitments or expectations, the potential for litigation becomes a reality.

And, who is contractually responsible if a building fails to attain the promised green certification? While some of this may not differ from typical construction litigation over unmet contractual expectations or design defects, certainly the subject matter, and the nuances, will be somewhat different. There will be greater emphasis on more than just bricks, mortar, and delays. Experts will need to be retained to analyze whether the stormwater management system is effective and consistent with the design and contract requirements, whether the energy efficiency of the building is as promised, and so on. And who are the green experts? Can you find one? What are their qualifications? Which member of the construction team is the designated green person? Should it be an owner's representative? The architect? A contractor's representative? Numerous suppliers and vendors continue to jump on the green wagon.

As more novel materials are utilized in building construction, there will be questions as to whether such materials meet the durability standards expected as well as warranties provided by the contractors and developers. Or will using these new green materials lead to other problems that the industry thought it had solved, such as moisture intrusion, fungal growth, etc.? Further, it is likely that there will be either new types of subcontractors, or existing subcontractors that will have to quickly become familiar with the types and sources of material that are considered green. Undoubtedly, with a broad-based definition of green and the relative lack of specific performance standards or specifications, the possibility of litigation as a result of failed expectations is greatly enhanced. Some of the potential areas of concern are explored below.

4.5   Risks for Design Professionals and Attorneys

All players in the construction arena must be familiar with the risks associated with green building and the methods for reducing those risks. Many of the potential liability issues related to building green are associated with designers – architects and engineers. This is particularly true because the 2007 AIA documents *require* that the architect consider sustainability practices in designing a building. The following is from the AIA's Sustainable Architectural Practice Position Statement:

> The AIA recognizes a growing body of evidence that demonstrates current planning, design, construction, and real estate practices contribute to patterns of resource consumption that seriously jeopardize the future of the Earth's population. Architects need to accept responsibility for their role in creating the built environment and, consequently, believe we must alter our profession's actions and encourage our clients and the entire design and construction industry to join with us to change the course of the planet's future.

To achieve those goals, the AIA position statement further states that it will:

> Promote sustainable design including resource conservation to achieve a minimum 50 percent reduction from the current level of consumption of fossil fuels used to construct and operate new and renovated buildings by the year 2010, and promote further reductions of remaining fossil fuel consumption by 10 percent or more in each of the following five years.

Of course, these AIA goals and protocols dovetail nicely with the various rating system products and programs, such as the Green Building Initiative's Green Globes, the USGBC's suite of LEED products, and the EPA's ENERGY STAR program. The AIA requirement is also reflective of the current political sentiment that building green is better and sustainability practices are socially and environmentally responsible. The precautionary principle discussed above plays a significant role in the policy formation of many, if not all, of these organizations.

A legitimate question, though, is what is really "better" from a building standpoint and what standards should be applied when considering building performance, the designer, and the other project team members. Just as the architect or engineer may be held to a more rigorous professional standard when building green or making a project sustainable, others, such as the contractor and subcontractors, also have new, increased risks.

While many have jumped head first into the green field by becoming LEED Accredited Professionals through the USGBC,[2] these newly minted

LEED professionals may not be giving enough consideration to the real risks of holding themselves out as green experts, particularly if green building is only a portion of their practice and they are primarily becoming accredited for practice development reasons. It should be noted that the LEED AP designation does not deal primarily with the design, construction, performance, or building science, but rather indicates familiarity with the LEED certification process. It has become common for both design and non-design professionals who hold this designation to, either by commission or omission, suggest that the designation provides substantive technical knowledge. It may, but it may not.

Much of the current focus is on the design professionals as they are on the front line and are the ones designing the green building. These engineers and architects will be guiding the selection of materials and contractors, as well as quarterbacking the LEED or other green certification, process. Under the traditional hierarchy, the owner will look to the architect first if LEED accreditation is delayed or not achieved, or if any green design elements fail. So, it is natural that much of the current analysis and literature relate to the potential exposure of architects and engineers, whether their current malpractice insurance will cover such exposure, or if new insurance products should be developed. The following section is an overview of the potential liability of other team members.

4.6   Risks for General Contractors

While much of the focus on potential liability related to green construction has been on design professionals, it is also important for general contractors to understand the nuances of the green construction process and the differences between traditional construction and green construction. The historical attitude of general contractors has often been something like, "We don't care if the thing is green, red, blue, etc., if you tell us what to build, we will build it." As one might expect, things aren't that simple.

Green construction can be more complex than traditional commercial construction because different techniques may be required by the contractor to install green products, or at the very least, the general contractor will have to be sufficiently well-versed to retain the most well-qualified subcontractor to install new green products. Obviously, if the subcontractor fails, the general contractor will be exposed to liability. Building green may take longer and follow different paths than traditional construction, in part due to differing materials and techniques and the certification process, so the contractor has to be aware of potential delays and insulate itself from liability for such delays in his contracts. And, as discussed below, delays in green construction may result in damages that are quite different from traditional "delay damages."

The contractor should be familiar with other administrative and documentation requirements, as well as potential regulatory and code requirements and incentives that could cause delays. Unexpected change orders, as well as on-site modifications, will require more circumspection by the project team because such changes could be conceivably inconsistent with certification goals or regulatory incentives, or the integrated performance of as-built green building components and systems. The bottom line is that the contractor and its counsel should be fully educated about the risks of building green. The general contractor may not be able to successfully transfer responsibility or liability to the owner, architect, or engineer.

A case on point is *Southern Builders, Inc. v. Shaw Development*.[3] Shaw Development purchased a piece of land in Somerset County, Maryland, and hired Southern Builders as its general contractor to construct a condominium project on the land. Southern Builders ultimately filed a $54,000 lien claim against the project, a 23-unit condominium development with total construction costs approaching $7,500,000. The developer's counterclaim alleged one count for a breach of contract and another for negligence. Significantly, for our purposes here, both counts aver damages from Southern Builders in the amount of $635,000 for the contractor's failure to "construct an environmentally sound 'Green Building,' in conformance with a 'Silver Certification Level according to the U.S. Green Building Council's Leadership in Energy and Environmental Design (LEED) Rating System'" which resulted in forfeiting tax credits under a Maryland green building program (never actually identified in the pleading).[4]

There are a number of confusions present in this language regarding the LEED certification process, including that building a project in conformance to the LEED certification system assures an "environmentally sound" building. But much more importantly for our analysis, a certification and final affirmation of a rating level cannot come before the completion of the building and is usually many months after the completion of the project. Thus, a breach of the contract cannot accrue prior to completion if the contract term at issue is to build a LEED- Silver certified project. At the outset, no one knows if the project will get appropriately LEED certified or not.

The contractual basis for Southern Builders' alleged obligation does not appear to be in the AIA A101-1997 Standard Form of Agreement between Owner and Contractor sections appended to the Counter-complaint.[5] Instead, the Counter-complaint incorporates language from the Project Manual that appears to include the specifications. That Project Manual provided, in pertinent part, as follows:

> Project is designed to comply with a Silver Certification Level according to the U.S. Green Building Council's Leadership in Energy and Environmental Design (LEED) Rating System, as specified in Division I Section "LEED Requirements."[6]

There is no documentation of the Division I Section "LEED Requirements," only this reference to such requirements. Most importantly, this provision, even if interpreted as a specification of some kind, does not say that Southern Builders must take responsibility for *constructing* or obtaining the LEED certification. All it says is that the "Project is *designed* to comply" with the desired rating level (emphasis added). Thus, one could argue that a contractor following the drawings and specifications of the design prepared by the architect and provided to the contractor, with an assumed warranty of adequacy by the owner (via the *Spearin* doctrine), should result in the appropriate certification level. All the contractor has to do is what he always does—fulfill the terms of the contract as established in the drawings and specifications. If there is a failure of certification, it would be a result of the design, not of the constructor. The negligence claims are similarly structured except the averment is that a failure to construct the building to LEED silver level is an indication that Southern Builders fell below the standard of care ordinarily required of contractors.

This analysis provides us with three lessons. First, it is possible for pleadings to become confused if there is not a deeper understanding of the green building rating systems at issue and the green building regulatory requirements. As more and more regulation establishes a mandate for green rating systems, the risks become higher both for transactional and litigation activity. This doesn't even account for a growing body of legislation or regulatory activity that lacks careful drafting or policy basis such as the Washington, D.C., council example discussed below.

Second, it appears that the underlying contractual documents did not address the risk issues associated with the tax credits dependent on the green building rating product involved.

Third, a waiver of consequential damages provision in the construction contract might serve as a defense against this type of claim. This line of attack would have to deal with the issues of direct versus consequential damages. In our situation, the AIA A101-1997 standard contract has a specific inclusion by reference of the AIA A201 General Conditions of

Contract, which in turn has a mutual waiver of consequential damages clause.[7]

Finally, we should note that a general contractor or a sub-contractor will have a major role to play in the actual acquisition of a LEED certification unless specifically eliminated from the scope of work in the contractual documents. Contractors must provide detailed documentation as well as obtain documentation from subcontractors; assure proper green material supply; address fundamental site control issues; and, often engage in collaborative activity to deliver the certification. This begs the question as to what level of specifications should be contractually required of the design professional on projects involving green rating systems. We leave aside for the moment the differentiation between a design specification, prescriptive specification, and a performance specification that can easily become confused when delivering a green project.

4.7   Direct vs. Consequential Damages and the Waiver of Consequential Damages Provision

Although the *Southern Builders* case settled, an issue over the classification of damages could have become a major contention in this case. Many construction contracts contain a waiver or mutual waiver of consequential damages, such as the A201-1997 General Conditions of the Contract of Construction that provides:

> The Contractor and Owner waive Claims against each other for consequential damages arising out of or relating to this Contract. This mutual waiver includes:
>
> 1.   damages incurred by the Owner for rental expenses, for losses of use, income, profit, financing, business and reputation, and for loss of management and employee productivity or of the services of such persons; and
>
> 2.   damages incurred by the Contractor for principal office expenses including the compensation of personnel stationed there, for losses of financing, business and reputation, and for loss of profit except anticipated profit arising directly from the Work.

The inquiry into which damages qualify under this definition of consequential damages can be difficult and may seem imprecise because such damages are the outcome of events further down the causation chain than direct damages. According to black letter law, direct damages are those which are the natural and proximate result of the breach, whereas consequential damages are those which, in the ordinary sense of events, would naturally result from a breach and can reasonably be said to have been foreseen or contemplated by the parties at the time when they made the contract as a probable result of the breach.[8]

For example, is the failure to obtain tax incentives offered by a state program a direct or consequential damage? In applying the direct versus consequential damages analysis to loss of tax incentives from failing to achieve LEED certification in the face of a waiver of consequential damages provision, a developer may argue that tax incentives were contemplated by the contract and known by the contractor at contract formation. Therefore, the failure to receive said incentives would be argued to be a *direct* result of the contractor's failure to meet the contracted LEED certification level and thus, a recoverable direct damage.

In opposition, a contractor may argue that the loss of such tax incentives constitutes consequential damages, thereby precluding recovery pursuant to contract language waiving recovery of same. While this type of analysis is not unique to green construction, the types of damages that may arise as a result of a green construction disputes may be unique, including tax credits, green grants, future development rights, or new categories of lost profits. As developers and contractors commence green building projects, failed expectations may lead to new litigation that varies from traditional construction disputes. Those in the construction industry must plan ahead and protect themselves at contract formation by explicitly delineating each party's obligations, responsibilities, and liabilities in the green construction process. Additionally, construction players must perform due diligence in advance in order to understand the specific criteria of the green building incentive programs and directives that apply in their states, counties, or municipalities.

The *Southern Builders* case, and the developing area of case law, raises several types of risks that a contractor may unknowingly assume when entering into a contract to build a green building. First, the contractor should become fully educated about the unique risks on the project. Second, the contract documents must have sufficient risk-transfer mechanisms so that there is a clear understanding of liability on behalf of all parties. Great danger exists where standard form contracts are used without specific language or liability-shifting provisions that address green building. To avoid unanticipated liability, the contractor should be hesitant to guarantee the delivery of a building that matches a certain level of certification.

A contractor should try to avoid guaranteeing the delivery of a certified building without fully understanding the implications of the contract into which it is entering with respect to green building liability. It is suggested that a contractor only agree to perform in accordance with the terms and specifications of the approved design of the building while using only the approved materials outlined therein. That way, if the contractor performs in accordance with owner-approved plans and specifications, the contractor should be shielded from liability if the plans fail to deliver a green building that meets the owner's anticipated certification or sustainability.

Moreover, a contractor should make sure that any liability incurred flows down to subcontractors. Lastly, a contractor should be aware of the potential damages being agreed to when entering into a green construction contract. Consequential damages may include, among other things, loss of funding, loss of revenues, loss of grant eligibility, rescission of tax credits, liquidated damages, breach of the lease by tenant, increased maintenance costs, and adverse marketing perception.[9]

A contractor could also become a defendant in a construction defects suit coupled with a claim for negligence. Because a contractor has a duty to homeowners, the owner of a home or condominium with a construction defect related to green elements of the home or condominium may have a valid cause of action against all parties in the construction process, including contractors.[10] Such negligence lawsuits against contractors may stem from the use of improper materials or poor workmanship.[11] However, unlike typical construction defect claims which establish a certain standard of care to which a contractor is held, the standard of care with respect to green construction defects is vague due to the fact that green construction is in its initial stages.[12] The standard of care with which a contractor must operate is currently undefined and that ambiguity will remain until more performance data has been developed and more green construction cases have been litigated.[13]

A contractor must also be wary of negligence per se claims if a particular method of construction or construction defect violated a federal, state, or local statute or ordinance.[14] A negligence *per se* claim is valid if: (1) there is an apparent violation of a statute or ordinance; (2) the persons harmed by the negligence are the class of individuals that the statute is designed to protect; and (3) the injury suffered was the type that the statute aims to prevent.[15] Negligence per se claims may provide a prima facie claim for breach of contract as well. In the event that a contractor is liable for defective construction, the party seeking damages is generally entitled to the cost of repair or diminution in value of the building, whichever is less.[16]

Obviously, project team members should only agree to assume risks that they can control. Many aspects of green certification and entitlement processes may be beyond the control of project team members. Because of this, the parties should contractually spell out the respective responsibilities to insulate themselves from potential liability. For example, from a general contractor's standpoint, it would be worthwhile to develop a policy that requires the company's contracts to explain clearly who is responsible for the green certification process and the specific role of the general contractor in that process as well as the specific duties and requirements of the general contractor.

Furthermore, the general contractor should have procedures in place to ensure that its performance during the project does not jeopardize the LEED certification process. Since compliance with the LEED certification process is documentation intensive, it is especially critical that the design professional and the general contractor communicate the pertinent documents required from the general contractor and when those documents should be provided.

These prophylactic considerations for the general contractor are reminiscent of the "mold protocols" that were developed by and for general contractors and homebuilders several years ago when the next wave of construction defect litigation was thought to be mold litigation. Many builders and contractors developed written procedures that would reduce, or eliminate, the risk of mold appearing during the construction process, or thereafter.

Other issues that could result in delays caused by the LEED certification process should be of concern to contractors. For example, flushing air from a new building, as well as additional commissioning, may be required for LEED certification points and can present problems where there is a specific completion date attached to liquidated damages for late completion. Further, as mentioned above, the parties should determine the entity that bears the risks of delays related to the acquisition of "green" products. General contractors have to contractually ensure, perhaps through broadly worded force majeure provisions, that they are not responsible for delays that are beyond their control.

Changing the mindset is a challenge as it is tough to break old habits. Perhaps with the evolution of green construction, as well as design/build projects, clear communication and contractual definition of team members' responsibilities and allocation of risks may yet become the norm rather than the exception.

4.8 Professional Liability Insurance

The common theme running through the current literature on potentially expanding liability related to green construction is whether professional liability insurance for design professionals will need to be changed to reflect increasing responsibilities for insured professionals, and whether a different standard of care is evolving for architects and others related to green construction. So far, insurers have not adversely changed their malpractice policies.

When it comes to the many design professionals who are becoming LEED accredited professionals, insurers are concerned about a voluntary and involuntary increase in the standard-of-care. It may soon be the case that the number of LEED APs, as they are referred to, will outnumber licensed architects. In addition, the new AIA Owner-Architect agreements added language that requires the architect to advocate for sustainable options. How this clause will be interpreted remains to be seen. Other potential design-related risks include:

- Liability for increased costs for certain types of damages, such as lost profits, lost business opportunities, increased tax burdens, and energy costs.
- Liability for warranty and outcome without having complete control over things such as construction means and methods, operation, and maintenance.
- Liability for structural problems and leaks associated with green roofs.
- Lack of proper green experience and qualifications on the part of the design team.
- Lack of control over materials, specifications, and substitutions on the part of contractors, including incomplete knowledge about new products, difficulties working with or installing such products, and potential performance problems related to failures and secondary effects.[17]

There are other risks unique to green construction. They include the following:

- Checking warranty and guaranty language to confirm that new green construction procedures and installation materials and/or techniques do not void the warranty or guaranty for products;

- Dealing with long-term performance goals and length of warranty issues;
- Determining if any intellectual property infringements will result from using new green techniques or equipment and who is responsible for dealing with any infringement;
- Investigating the availability of green construction material and the replacement price for such material, as well as who is responsible if material is available but is not actually obtained for the project.[18]

However, insurers may also recognize that green building and the certification process require a more collaborative and communicative working environment which, theoretically, should reduce the traditional risks that lead to construction litigation after a project has commenced. Though a common refrain, this often ignores the very small number of buildings completed and certified, in addition to the disproportionate number of mission driven building projects involved in obtaining LEED certifications.

Insurance markets apparently believe that the terms and conditions of current professional liability policies already provide a significant amount of coverage for the negligent performance of the A/E providing green services. However, the general consensus among underwriters is that a key difference between traditional design and green design is *enhanced performance expectations*, such as energy savings, employee productivity, etc. Currently, insurance companies and others are focusing on risk analysis counseling and are telling their insureds not to make promises about increased productivity, decreased absenteeism, vague unsubstantiated health benefits, increased absorption rates for commercial leasing, or increased student performance as components of their professional design services.

4.9   "Green Insurance"

Commercial General Liability Insurance

General liability insurers have not yet begun to create any significant new coverage for risks unique to green construction.[19] Perceived risks may include:

- Lack of experienced contractors and subcontractors performing the work, which could potentially result in shoddy workmanship or construction defect claims;

- Use of new and untested "green" products and materials which may not have the same lifespan as their corresponding "non-green" products or materials;
- Use of new roofing systems, which may lead to a multitude of structural and water damage claims;
- Use of unusual or high-performing HVAC systems, which may pose problems for both design professionals and constructors resulting in quality issues and claims;
- Lack of maintenance, which could lead to increased claims.

Because of these risk concerns, insurers may continue to sit on the sidelines, tracking and compiling loss data prior to issuing any new policies, coverage enhancements, coverage restrictions, or premium credits or debits.

Insuring against these risks is nearly uncharted territory. While the few policies offered by insurance carriers are a step towards insuring against the risks associated with green building, no carrier to date offers any insurance coverage, absent a replacement cost coverage policy or an endorsement offering to replace, repair, and/or update a building to green standards following a loss. The currently available policies offer to insure against losses, but are not geared to provide coverage to many of the growing risks linked to green construction, including but not limited to failing to meet contracted certification levels, failing to meet guaranteed energy savings criteria, failing to meet specified indoor air quality expectations, nonperformance of sustainable and recycled products, and many other risk concerns.

The problem with insuring against such new risks is that they are difficult to quantify and many carriers have not taken the time to analyze objectively the proclaimed efficiency and safety benefits of green buildings against their potential pitfalls. Furthermore, many insurance brokers are simply not familiar with these types of projects and the unique challenges and risks posed by them. Thus, they are not in the best position to evaluate the risks associated with green developments and projects and the potential problems that can arise. Nevertheless, the rise in green building indicates a desire for change in the manner in which the insurance industry covers and addresses these risks.

One underwriter, Victor O. Schinnerer and Company, Inc., has stated that its policies issued though CNA still provide coverage for landscape architects for things such as green roofs. For that coverage and other developing coverage, the understanding of risk and the development of well thought out practices will be critical components of maintaining such coverage. As pointed out by Schinnerer, the professional liability exposure of firms involved in projects with green roofs or rooftop gardens can be managed by acquiring design expertise, understanding, and matching client expectations, and satisfying approved products and contractor duties.[20]

From the contractor's perspective, another issue is whether builders' risk insurance will cover the risks associated with green construction. Builders' risk is a form of insurance coverage that provides protection for damage to buildings or structures during construction, renovation, or repair. Builders' risk insurers are hesitant to provide new coverage because of the perception of potential problems associated with green building materials, supplies, and fixtures. Obtaining these green materials, supplies, and fixtures brings new and unique costs and creates unknown risks for insurers. Risks may involve delays in opening (due perhaps to certification), time to procure special equipment, or flushing out HVAC systems.

One insurer has developed a green builders' risk product, called "The Delay of Occupancy or Green Amendment" endorsement. That product is an enhancement to Fireman's Fund's builders' risk/owner's risk product. This endorsement is designed to provide coverage for green soft costs[21] for additional expenses that result after a covered loss, including diverting debris to recycling, flushing out the HVAC system of the reconstructed space with fresh air, commissioning the repaired building systems, and re-registering with the USGBC.

The endorsement also covers items such as: (1) additional interest expenses on money borrowed to finance construction or repair; (2) additional real estate taxes and other assessments incurred for the period of time that construction was extended; (3) additional advertising or promotional expenses that arise; and (4) additional reasonable and necessary legal, accounting, architectural, and other expenses incurred because of a covered loss; and several other items.[22] It should be noted that these policies typically have a cap on the amount the insurer will disburse for these additional expenses.

One green environmental insurance product by AIG Environmental creates a discount for green buildings. Purchasing this product affords clients the ability to receive discounts of up to ten percent on their premiums for any properties certified under USGBC's LEED ratings. While this product is not developed specifically for green construction, it may provide some guidance in assessing another area of risk for green buildings. But what additional risk does this create for the design professionals and contractors that designed and built those buildings if the LEED ratings are not achieved and the building owner, therefore, loses the premium discount?

4.10   Conclusion

While green construction holds significant promise and opportunities in many ways, it is clear that there is a downside to, and risk in, "going green." As explained above, some of this risk is obvious while some risk is not as obvious. Many on the green bandwagon are not fully cognizant of all of the risks, risks that continue to evolve qualitatively and quantitatively. Most of the burden of identifying and evaluating the nuances of "building green" will fall on the transactional partners who are involved at the beginning of a deal. It is incumbent upon those people to proactively ensure, up-front, that the project team consists of people who can fully comprehend all of the project construction and financing details as well as understand the complete spectrum of project related green risks.

Acknowledgement: This chapter is based on a paper by the authors presented at the ABA Forum on the Construction Industry program, "Coverages, Disputes and Tactics for Survival," January 15, 2009, in Bonita Springs, Florida.

---

[1]   John Pezzey and Michael Toman, "Making Sense of 'Sustainability,'" (Resources for the Future, Issue Brief 02-25, August 2002). See also, Peter P. Rogers, Kazi F. Jalal and John A. Boyd, *An Introduction to Sustainable Development*, (Harvard Univ. Press 2006).

[2]   Though this is now handled through a subsidiary entity created by the USGBC named the Green Building Certification Institute (http://www.gbci.org/).

[3]   *See* Southern Builders, Inc. v. Shaw Development LLC, No. 19-C-07-11405, (Somerset Co. Cir. Ct. Filed, Feb. 7, 2007 [Counter-complaint]).

[4]   *Southern Builders, Inc.*, No. 19-C-07-11405 [Counter-complaint at paragraph 10, and with slight variations at paragraphs 24, 25(b), and 31(b).

[5]   The AIA 101-1997 form is a short form contract. The fact that this was used for a project that was almost 7 million dollars may indicate that little attention was paid to front-end risk management.

[6]   *Southern Builders, Inc.*, No. 19-C-07-11405 at Exhibit B at section 1.2(D)(2).

[7]   *Southern Builders, Inc.*, No. 19-C-07-11405, at paragraph 8.1.2 of AIA A101-1997 appended as Exhibit A to the Counter-complaint

[8]   Hadley v. Baxendale, 9 Exch. 341, 156 Eng.Rep. 145 (1854).

[9] Pacific Northwest Design Professional Legal Update; Special Green Edition, Skellenger Bender (Sept. 2008). Consequential damages are mutually waived in the form General Conditions contracts.

[10] Masters & Musitano, *supra* note 23, at 18.

[11] *Id.*

[12] *Id.*

[13] *Id.*

[14] *Id.*

[15] Masters & Musitano, *supra* note 23, at 18.

[16] *Id.*

[17] *Id.*

[18] J.R. Steele, *Green Construction: Initiatives and Legal Issues Surrounding the Trend*, Business Law Today, Vol. 17, No. 2 (Nov./Dec. 2007).

[19] Press Release, *Insurers Cautious in Underwriting Green Building Exposures*, *available at* http://global.marsh.com/news/press/pr20080729.php?pv=1 [last visited Nov. 6, 2008].

[20] Kevin J. Collins, Senior Vice President, Victor O' Schinnerer and Co., ASLA Business Quarterly (2004).

[21] The endorsement defines "soft costs" to mean "additional expenses over and above the projected cost of the covered construction project which occur because of a covered loss which delays the project." Fireman's Fund Insurance Company, Delay of Occupancy or Use Endorsement – Green Amendment – 145475 06 07.

[22] Fireman's Fund Insurance Company, Delay of Occupancy or Use Endorsement – Green Amendment – 145475 06 07.

Chapter 5

A Practical Guide to New and Controversial Issues in AIA B101 – 2007

Mark C. Friedlander, Esq.
Heidi H. Rowe, Esq.

5.1   Introduction

This chapter focuses on the new issues and some of the less well-known "holdover" controversial issues in the new AIA Document B101-2007 Standard Form of Agreement Between Owner and Architect, which was released in November 2007. There are numerous new provisions in the 2007 version of the AIA B101 contract (also referred to as the B101-2007) not found in prior editions of the AIA Owner/Architect agreements such as the 1997 editions of the AIA B141 or the AIA B151 (also referred to as the B141-1997 and the B151-1997, respectively). Many of these issues were treated differently in prior versions of the AIA Owner-Architect agreements, and the language has been changed in the B101-2007. Other issues are novel, never having been included in prior editions of the B141 or B151 contracts.

5.2   AIA B101 - §2.2 Standard of Care

For the first time the B101 Owner-Architect Agreement explicitly states the standard of care to which the architect must perform. Section 2.2 reads as follows:

> The Architect shall perform its services consistent with the professional skill and care ordinarily provided by architects

practicing in the same or similar locality under the same or similar circumstances. The Architect shall perform its services as expeditiously as is consistent with such professional skill and care and the orderly progress of the Project.

The first sentence, which describes the standard of care, is the formulation most commonly applied by the courts.[1] Even though it has not previously appeared as an explicit term in AIA Owner-Architect contract forms, it nevertheless would be considered an implied term in any contract for professional design services.[2]

5.3   AIA B101 - §2.5 Insurance

Previous editions of the AIA Owner-Architects Agreements did not identify or quantify the types and amounts of insurance that the Architect would be required to maintain. This has always been a major weakness in the documents and has often resulted in the creation of Insurance Riders prepared by lawyers who represent owners, developers or architects.

The new provision is a step in the right direction toward ameliorating this confusion but is far too general to be effective in doing so. Section 2.5 of B101 provides:

The Architect shall maintain the following insurance for the duration of this Agreement. If any of the requirements set forth below exceed the types and limits the Architect normally maintains, the Owner shall reimburse the Architect for any additional costs:
(Identify types and limits of insurance coverage, and other insurance requirements applicable to the Agreement, if any.)
    .1   General Liability
    .2   Automobile Liability
    .3   Workers' Compensation
    .4   Professional Liability

This provision lists the four common categories of architectural insurance (although it does not mention valuable papers insurance), but it provides no further detail. It contemplates that the Architect will insert the necessary detail in the subparagraphs. However, when an Architect submits a B101 form to its client prior to a project for review and approval, it is unlikely to have added the necessary detail at that time. Thus, the parties will probably still resort to an Insurance Rider to provide the missing the information. The

AIA could have avoided this problem by creating a standard form insurance exhibit for the B101 with blanks to be filled in for the specifics of coverage limits, durations, and other relevant information.

The phrase, "for the duration of this Agreement," at the end of the first sentence will typically need to be modified to require an Architect to maintain such insurance in full force and effect for at least a year or two after project completion.

5.4   AIA B101 - §3.1.4 Owner Decisions

A new sentence has been added that renders the Owner responsible for decisions made by the Owner without the involvement of the Architect or made by the Owner over the objection of the Architect. Section 3.1.4 reads:

> The Architect shall not be responsible for an Owner's directive or substitution made without the Architect's approval.

5.5   AIA B101 - §3.1.5 Government and Utility Requirements

This provision requires the Architect to contact any permit-issuing governmental authority and any utility servicing the project. Section 3.1.5 states:

> The Architect shall, at appropriate times, contact any governmental authorities required to approve the Construction Documents and the entities providing utility services to the Project. In designing the Project, the Architect shall respond to applicable design requirements imposed by such governmental authorities and by such entities providing utility services.

This provision merely requires an Architect to "respond" to the applicable design requirements, not to comply with them. The requirement that the Architect actually comply with these requirements is found in Section 3.4.2 (previously 1.2.3.6 of the B141-1997), but it applies only to governmental requirements, not to utility requirements. Nevertheless, Section 3.4.2 is stronger than its predecessor provision in the B141-1997 in that it actually obligates the Architect to incorporate the requirements into the Construction Documents, rather than merely allowing the Architect to "respond in the design of the Project" to the governmental requirements.

5.6   AIA B101 - §3.2.3 Preliminary Evaluation

This provision is an expansion of Section 2.2.3 of the B151-1997 pursuant to which the Architect and Owner discuss alternative approaches to design and construction. New Section 3.2.3 states:

> The Architect shall present its preliminary evaluation to the Owner and shall discuss with the Owner alternative approaches to design and construction of the Project, including the feasibility of incorporating environmentally responsible design approaches. The Architect shall reach an understanding with the Owner regarding the requirements of the Project.

Two concepts in this paragraph are new: environmentally responsible design and the requirement to reach an understanding.

Awareness of environmental issues and, in particular, "green design," is a theme that runs throughout the 2007 edition of the AIA Documents. This is likely a result of the greater understanding of climatic change and other environmental issues that have become prevalent over the last ten years. Rather than being merely one of many implicit program elements, the AIA deemed environmental issues sufficiently important to list them explicitly as an element of discussion at the various stages of the Project. Although Section 3.2.3 does not bind an Owner to include environmentally responsible approaches in the design, it functions to raise owners' awareness of environmental issues.

The last sentence requires that the Architect and Owner reach "an understanding" regarding the Project requirements. This is likely the AIA's response to the present tendency of Project participants to postpone reaching a firm agreement as to the program elements until more information and parameters are known. Postponing reaching such an agreement often complicates the efforts of the Architect by requiring re-design to accommodate agreements on Project scope and program that are reached relatively late in the design phase. However, despite being located in a paragraph discussing preliminary evaluation, the final sentence of Section 3.2.3 does not set a time limit on when the understanding regarding Project requirements must be obtained.

5.7   AIA B101 - §3.2.5.1 Basic Environmental Design

This provision requires the Architect to consider environmental issues as part of its Basic Services for design. Section 3.2.5.1 states:

> The Architect shall consider environmentally responsible design alternatives, such as material choices and building orientation, together with other considerations based on program and aesthetics, in developing a design that is consistent with the Owner's program, schedule and budget for the Cost of Work. The Owner may obtain other environmentally responsible design services under Article 4.

This provision is another instance in which the theme of environmental responsibility pervades the 2007 edition of the AIA Documents.

The requirements of this provision are binding on the Architect but not on the Owner. The Architect is obliged to "consider environmentally responsible design alternatives," but the Owner is not obligated to select any such alternatives. Furthermore, although the Architect is obligated to "consider" these issues, it is not obligated to select or employ a more environmentally responsible alternative. Nothing in this provision requires even consideration of a superior environmental alternative if it has a negative impact on the Owner's program, schedule or budget.

This provision is included as one of the Architect's Basic Services. It is presumably limited to fundamental design issues, explicitly identifying "material choices and building orientation," but would presumably also include consideration of green roofs and other similar basic design issues. The last sentence of the provision refers to Article 4, of which Section 4.3.1.2 clarifies that more detailed environmental analysis, including "extensive environmentally responsible design alternatives, such as unique system designs, in-depth material research, energy modeling, or LEED® certification," are available at extra charge.

5.8   AIA B101 - §3.4.1 Construction Documents Level of Detail

Most of this paragraph is substantively equivalent to Sections 2.4.4.1 of B141-1997 and 2.4.1 of B151-1997. However, a new sentence has been added to the end, which states:

> The Owner and Architect acknowledge that in order to construct the Work the Contractor will provide additional information,

including Shop Drawings, Product Data, Samples and other similar submittals, which the Architect shall review in accordance with Section 3.6.4.

Although issues involving shop drawings and other submittals are dealt with in Section 3.6.4 of the B101-2007 and in all of the prior versions of the AIA Owner-Architect Agreements, this is the first time that they have been discussed in the section on Construction Documents.

There are probably two primary reasons for including the new sentence in the paragraph describing the Construction Documents. The first reason is to clarify that although the Construction Documents are supposed to set forth "in detail the . . . requirements for the construction," a further level of detail, to be provided by the Contractor, is necessary before construction can begin. The second reason is the trend in the construction industry toward architects detailing the Construction Documents less fully than in past practice. The new sentence clarifies and codifies current architectural practice.

5.9   AIA B101 - §3.4.2 Compliance with Laws

This paragraph relates to and supplements Section 3.1.5, discussed above. It states: "The Architect shall incorporate into the Construction Documents the design requirements of governmental authorities having jurisdiction over the Project." This provision is similar to paragraph 1.2.3.6 of the B141-1997, but it differs in one very important respect. The earlier version of this clause merely required the Architect to "respond in the design" to governmental requirements. This former language was awkward, and its meaning was never clear. The new provision clearly requires the Architect to comply with governmental requirements by incorporating these requirements into the design.

5.10   AIA B101 - §3.6.1.1 Administering the General Conditions

This paragraph preserves the same concept but changes the language found in paragraphs 2.6.1.1 and 2.6.1.3 of the B141-1997 and paragraphs 2.6.2 and 2.6.4 of the B151-1997. It states:

The Architect shall provide administration of the Contract between the Owner and the Contractor as set forth below and in AIA Document A201™-2007, General Conditions of the Contract for Construction. If the Owner and Contractor modify AIA Document A201-2007, those modifications shall not affect the Architect's services under this Agreement unless the Owner and the Architect amend this Agreement.

The prior edition of this paragraph required the Architect to approve any modifications to the A201 in writing before it would become effective with respect to the Architect. Many owners disliked and attempted to delete this provision because they did not want the architect to have approval rights over the terms in their contract with contractors. The solution in the B101-2007 is to delete all reference to architect approval rights and to instead require a modification to the Owner-Architect Agreement before a change to the A201 General Conditions effectively modifies the Architect's duties as set forth in B101.

It is advisable for both the Architect and the Owner to ensure that all provisions involving or affecting the Architect be consistent between the two documents.

5.11   AIA B101 - §3.6.1.2 Responsibility for Construction Means and Methods

This paragraph closely follows the language of Section 2.6.1.1 and 2.6.1.3 of the B141-1997 and Sections 2.6.2 and 2.6.4 of the B151-1997. The relevant portion reads:

> The Architect shall not have control over, charge of, or responsibility for the construction means, methods, techniques, sequences or procedures, or for safety precautions and programs in connection with the Work, nor shall the Architect be responsible for the Contractor's failure to perform the Work in accordance with the requirements of the Contract Documents.

However, there is a significant omission: the clause, "since these [construction means, methods, etc.] are solely the Contractor's rights and responsibilities under the Construction Documents," which was in the prior version of this paragraph is no longer included.

This omission changes the way that the paragraph can be characterized. As currently drafted, it could potentially be interpreted purely as an exculpatory provision, simply identifying certain duties and responsibilities as not belonging to the Architect, rather than as a division of duties between the design and construction teams.

5.12   AIA B101 - §3.6.2.1 Evaluations of the Work

This paragraph is a reworking of Sections 2.6.2.1 and 2.6.2.2 of the B141-1997. The basic concept has remained the same, but the wording has been changed to the following:

> The Architect shall visit the site at intervals appropriate to the stage of construction, or as otherwise required in Section 4.3.3, to become generally familiar with the progress and quality of the portion of the Work completed, and to determine, in general, if the Work observed is being performed in a manner indicating that the Work, when fully completed, will be in accordance with the Contract Documents. However, the Architect shall not be required to make exhaustive or continuous on-site inspections to check the quality or quantity of the Work. On the basis of the site visits, the Architect shall keep the Owner reasonably informed about the progress and quality of the portion of the Work completed, and report to the Owner (1) known deviations from the Contract Documents and from the most recent construction schedule submitted by the Contractor, and (2) defects and deficiencies observed in the Work.

The major change has been to delete the phrase, "to endeavor to guard the Owner against defects and deficiencies in the Work."

Although the Architect's purpose remains, in part, to try to detect or prevent construction defects and deviations, the promise to attempt to do so has been deleted. Many owners, as well as some courts and arbitrators, have interpreted the deleted clause to be more in the nature of a promise by the Architect to the Owner to protect the Owner against these construction problems. Although the clause only states that the Architect will "endeavor" to provide this protection, a frequently litigated issue has been whether the Architect has expended sufficient and appropriate effort to provide this protection. By deleting the clause, the AIA is apparently hoping to turn the paragraph into a more objective test: one which requires the Architect to advise the Owner of any problems actually observed, but which creates no obligations with regard to construction defects that are not detected. Consistent with this goal, the word "observed" has been added to the previously existing phrase, "if the Work is being performed in a manner indicating that the Work, when fully completed, will be in accordance with the Contract Documents." The addition of the word "observed" limits the Architect's determination to the Work actually visible for review.

5.13   AIA B101 - §3.6.2.5 Judge of Disputes

Prior versions of the AIA Owner-Architect Agreements have always designated the Architect as the initial dispute decider. For the first time, the B101 allows the Owner and Contractor to designate someone else to fill this role. This provision states:

> Unless the Owner and the Contractor designate another person to serve as an Initial Decision Maker, as that term is defined in AIA Document A201 – 2007, the Architect shall render initial decisions on Claims between the Owner and Contractor as provided in the Contract Documents.

The 2007 A201 General Conditions defines "Initial Decision Maker" in Section 1.1.8 as "the person identified in the Agreement to render initial decisions on Claims in accordance with Section 15.2 and certify termination of the Agreement under Section 14.2.2."

5.14   AIA B101 - §3.6.3.1 Certificates for Payment

This paragraph obligates the Architect to review and certify amounts due to the Contractor and contains the Architect's representations regarding the progress and quality of the construction, as well as caveats to those representations.   Only the second sentence has changed from paragraph 2.6.3.1 in the B141-1997 and paragraph 2.6.9.1 in the B151-1997. The new sentence reads:

> The Architect's certification for payment shall constitute a representation to the Owner, based on the Architect's evaluation of the Work as provided in Section 3.6.2 and on the data comprising the Contractor's Application for Payment, that, to the best of the Architect's knowledge, information and belief, the Work has progressed to the point indicated and that the quality of the Work is in accordance with the Contract Documents.

The substantive language has not changed, but the sequence of the clauses has changed, which changes the nature of the Architect's representation.

In the prior version of this provision, the Architect simply represented that the Work had progressed to the point indicated. There was no limitation of this representation to the Architect's knowledge, information or belief (although the four caveats in the next sentence constituted certain limitations). In the current version, however, the limitation to knowledge, information and belief precedes and modifies the representation regarding the progress of the Work, rendering it more of a representation regarding the Architect's state of mind then a pure factual representation.

This change reflects the reality that an Architect often is not in a position to know to a fine degree of certainty what percentage completion the Project has attained. Architectural site visits for the purpose of pay request certification involve general observation of Work progress but usually do not include a quantitative analysis of the percentage complete. For precise percentages, the Architect typically depends on the Contractor's Schedule of Values, not having access to any kind of quantity survey or analysis of materials and labor for the job.

5.15   AIA B101 - §3.6.4.1 & §3.6.4.2 Review of Submittals

For the first time, the AIA Documents link the Architect's time for reviewing shop drawings and other submittals to a submittal schedule prepared by the Contractor. Section 3.6.4.1 states:

> The Architect shall review the Contractor's submittal schedule and shall not unreasonably delay or withhold approval. The Architect's action in reviewing submittals shall be taken in accordance with the approved submittal schedule or, in the absence of an approved submittal schedule, with reasonable promptness while allowing sufficient time in the Architect's professional judgment to permit adequate review.

Section 3.6.4.2 echoes this concept, requiring the Architect to review shop drawings and other submittals "[i]n accordance with the Architect's approved submittal schedule."

5.16   AIA B101 - §5.2 Budget for the Project

This provision requires the Owner to establish and update or modify the budget for the construction work. The prior version of this paragraph, Section 1.2.2.2 of the B141-1997 and Section 4.2 of the B151-1997, forbid the Owner from significantly increasing or decreasing the budget or its key components without the Architect's approval. The B101-2007 recognizes that the issue of budget is within the discretion of the Owner over which the Architect should not have approval rights. The new language provides: "If the Owner significantly increases or decreases the Owner's budget for the Cost of the Work, the Owner shall notify the Architect." The budget change may require redesign, which may entitle the Architect to payment for Additional Services, but the Architect can no longer veto the budget change.

5.17   AIA B101 - §5.6 Owner's Consultants

This provision adds significant additional detail to the prior version of the provisions governing Owner's consultants, Section 1.2.2.4 of the B141-1997 and Section 4.6 of the B151-1997. The new provision reads:

> The Owner shall coordinate the services of its own consultants with those services provided by the Architect.   Upon the Architect's request, the Owner shall furnish copies of the scope of services in the contracts between the Owner and the Owner's consultants. The Owner shall furnish the services of consultants other than those designated in this Agreement, or authorize the Architect to furnish them as an Additional Service, when the Architect requests such services and demonstrates that they are reasonably required by the scope of the Project. The Owner shall require that its consultants maintain professional liability insurance as appropriate to the services provided.

Several concepts in this paragraph are new. It is the Owner who is responsible for coordinating the consultant's services with those of the Architect. The "scope of service" portion of the consultant's contract must be furnished to the Architect. The Architect must "demonstrate" the need for the Owner to hire the consultants. The Owner may authorize the Architect to hire the consultants directly. And the consultants are required to maintain the same kinds of insurance as the Architect.

Some of these provisions are likely to be controversial. It is unusual to require the Owner to coordinate professional services, and many owners may be unable to do so. It is also unusual for the Architect to be able to require particular insurance of the Owner's consultants, particularly since in many jurisdictions the economic loss rule would prevent the Architect from maintaining a direct claim against the consultants pertaining to typical design or construction defects.

5.18   AIA B101 - §5.10 Communications

This provision governs the Owner's communications with the Contractor and Architect's consultants. The predecessor provisions, Section 2.6.2.4 of the B141-1997 and Section 2.6.8 of the B151-1997, required the Owner to endeavor to communicate with the Contractor through the Architect. This requirement is retained and applied to the Architect's consultants as well. However, the new provision recognizes that there may be some direct communication between the Owner and either the Contractor or the Architect's consultants. The new language requires the Owner to "promptly notify the Architect of any direct communications that may affect the Architect's services."

5.19   AIA B101 - §5.11 Coordination of Contracts

This provision is entirely new. It requires the Owner to make consistent the description of the Architect's services in the Owner-Architect Agreement and the construction contract, stating:

> Before executing the Contract for Construction, the Owner shall coordinate the architect's duties and responsibilities set forth in the Contract for Construction with the Architect's services set forth in this Agreement. The Owner shall provide the Architect a copy of the executed agreement between the Owner and Contractor, including the General Conditions of the Contract for Construction.

This is a different approach to the issue in Section 3.6.1.1, which clarifies that the Architect is not bound to any provisions in the A201 General Conditions that are inconsistent with the Owner-Architect Agreement.

This provision contains two different requirements. The first requirement is that the Owner "coordinate" the provisions of the two contracts. Presumably this means not agreeing to provide any architectural services in the construction contract that are not set forth in the Owner-Architect Agreement. The other requirement is for the Owner to provide the Architect with a copy of the construction contract. This is presumably to allow the Architect to identify any such inconsistencies and to perform its construction administration functions more accurately.

5.20   AIA B101 - §6.1 Cost of the Work

This provision is a modification of similar predecessor provisions found
in Sections 1.3.1.1, 1.3.1.2 and 1.3.1.3 of the B141-1997 and Sections 5.1.1,
5.1.2 and 5.1.3 of the B151-1997. The new paragraph provides:

> For purposes of this Agreement, the Cost of the Work shall be the
> total cost to the Owner to construct all elements of the Project
> designed or specified by the Architect and shall include
> contractors' general conditions costs, overhead and profit. The
> Cost of the Work does not include the compensation of the
> Architect, the costs of the land, rights-of-way, financing,
> contingencies for changes in the Work or other costs that are the
> responsibility of the Owner."

There are three new concepts in this paragraph. The definition of the
Cost of the Work is limited to the purposes of this Agreement, presumably so
that it cannot be used against the Owner in a dispute with the Contractor
where the term is defined differently.   The provision clarifies that the
definition is to include General Conditions costs, overhead and profit.   It
further clarifies that contingencies are not to be included in the definition of
the Cost of the Work.

5.21   AIA B101 - §6.3 Estimates of the Costs of the Work

This provision defines the process for the Architect to estimate the Cost
of the Work and clarifies the previous provisions found at Section 2.1.7.3 of
the B141-1997 and Section 5.2.2 of the B151-1997. The more significant
change clarifies that the Architect's estimates are merely conceptual and that
more detailed estimating would be an Additional Service:

> The Architect's estimate of the Cost of the Work shall be based
> on current area, volume or similar conceptual estimating
> techniques.   If the Owner requests detailed cost estimating
> services, the Architect shall provide such services as an
> Additional Service under Article 4.

The other change permits the Architect to modify the Owner's program
for the Project if necessary to maintain budget. There is no requirement that
the Owner approve the Architect's modification to the program or scope,
although Section 6.6.4 requires the Owner to consult with the Architect

regarding such modifications. This is somewhat surprising because the Owner's program reflects the Owner's personal preferences and one would expect that the Architect would need the Owner's permission to modify it.

5.22   AIA B101 - §7.1 Copyright and Electronic Documents

This is a new provision without a predecessor in earlier versions of the AIA Owner-Architect Agreement. It consists of two separate topics and states:

> The Architect and the Owner warrant that in transmitting Instruments of Service, or any other information, the transmitting party is the copyright owner of such information or has permission from the copyright owner to transmit such information for its use on the Project. If the Owner and Architect intend to transmit Instruments of Service or any other information or documentation in digital form, they shall endeavor to establish necessary protocols governing such transmissions.

The first sentence is a warranty of the right to use any drawings or other documentation that one party transmits to the other. This applies not only to design and construction documents prepared by the design team but also to drawings, such as "as-builts" or preliminary sketches, or other information provided to the design team by the Owner. The second sentence requires the parties to agree on terms and conditions under which the Architect would provide its drawings or other documents in digital format. This is an important issue because the electronic nature of the medium may cause errors or other glitches to appear in the documentation that do not appear in the hard copy of the same documentation.

5.23   AIA B101 - §7.3 License to Use the Plans

This provision makes several changes to the predecessor paragraph found at Sections 1.3.2.2 and 1.3.2.3 of the B141-1997 and Section 1.6.2 of the B151-1997. The last sentence states: "If the Architect rightfully terminates this Agreement for cause as provided in Section 9.4, the license granted in this Section 7.3 shall terminate." The usual reason that an Architect would terminate the contract is for non-payment, and this sentence revokes the Owner's license to use the Drawings and Specifications in that case. This paragraph also makes the following minor changes and clarifications:

- The license granted to the Owner is for the "use" of the Drawings and Specifications, not merely their reproduction as in prior versions of this provision.
- Although the previous language stated that the license was "solely" for the purposes set forth in the paragraph, the meaning has been clarified by changing the limitation to the phrase, "solely and exclusively."
- For the first time, the Owner's permissible uses for the Drawings and Specifications include "altering and adding" to the Project.
- The breadth of the license is clarified to allow not only the Owner but also its "consultants and separate contractors" to reproduce the licensed documents, provided that the reproduction is only "for use in performing services or construction for the Project.

5.24 AIA B101 - §7.3.1 Owner's Use of Plans Without Architect

This paragraph has been almost completely rewritten from its predecessor provisions, Section 1.3.2.2 of the B141-1997 and Section 6.2 of the B151-1997. The new paragraph reads as follows:

> In the event the Owner uses the Instruments of Service without retaining the author of the Instruments of Service, the Owner releases the Architect and the Architect's consultants from all claims and causes of action arising from such uses. The Owner, to the extent permitted by law, further agrees to indemnify and hold harmless the Architect and its consultant(s) from all costs and expenses, including the cost of defense, related to claims and causes of action asserted by any third person or entity to the extent such cost and expenses arise from the Owner's use of the Instruments of Service under this Section 7.3.1. The terms of this Section 7.3.1 shall not apply if the Owner rightfully terminates this Agreement for cause under Section 9.4.

Note that this provision does not address the consequences of terminating the Architect in the middle of the Project or of hiring the Architect for very limited services only.

This provision provides both for a release and for indemnification. The indemnity is limited to claims by third parties against the Owner. One of the reasons for a release in addition to an indemnification is that some jurisdictions have anti-indemnity laws that would limit or forbid a party from contractually agreeing to indemnify another in some circumstances.[3]

5.25   AIA B101 - §8.1.1 Statute of Repose

The B101-2007 adopts a new approach to establishing a contractual statute of repose on claims arising out of the Owner-Architect Agreement. A statute of repose sets forth the maximum amount of time in which a claim must be brought, regardless of when the claim is discovered. Its predecessor provisions, Section 1.3.7.3 of the B141-1997 and Section 9.3 of the B151-1997, merely established that the applicable statute of limitations would begin to run no later than Substantial Completion for claims arising before then, and no later than Final Completion for claims arising between Substantial Completion and Final Completion. The local state statute would then determine the length of time after Substantial Completion or Final Completion for filing the claim. The new B101 provision does not establish when the statute of limitations will begin to run but, instead, contractually establishes a 10-year statute of repose commencing at Substantial Completion, stating:

> The Owner and Architect shall commence all claims and causes of action, whether in contract, tort or otherwise, against the other arising out of or relatied to this Agreement in accordance with the requirements of the method of binding dispute resolution selected in this Agreement within the period specified by applicable law, but in any case not more than 10 years after the date of Substantial Completion of the Work. The Owner and Architect waive all claims and causes of action not commenced in accordance with this Section 8.1.1.

The effect of this language is to establish contractually a 10-year period of repose beginning with Substantial Completion but without superseding any applicable state or other law that may set forth other restrictions, including a shorter repose period. Thus, claims between the Owner and Architect under B101 must both be timely as defined by the applicable jurisdiction's law and be filed within ten years of the date of Substantial Completion.

5.26   AIA B101 - §8.2.4 Choice of Binding Dispute Resolution

This paragraph contains the most highly publicized change in the B101-2007 from the prior versions of the Owner-Architect Agreement. The 1997 (and earlier) versions of B141 and B151, as well as every applicable AIA Document of the last several editions (except for the 2004 Design-Build Documents, which adopted the same approach as the new B101), specified arbitration as the binding dispute resolution method agreed to by the parties. In negotiating the contract, it was not uncommon for one party or the other to delete the arbitration clauses and all references to arbitration because the default binding dispute resolution forum was arbitration.

The new B101 employs a check-box approach to selecting a binding dispute resolution forum. There are three boxes available to check: the first provides for "Arbitration pursuant to Section 8.3 of this Agreement"; the second is for "Litigation in a court of competent jurisdiction";and the third is labeled "Other" and requires the parties to spell out the type of binding dispute resolution that they have agreed to employ.

The AIA appears to have structured this provision to establish litigation in court as the default binding dispute resolution method if no boxes are checked. The introductory language to the check-box states:

> If the Owner and Architect do not select a method of binding dispute resolution below, or do not subsequently agree in writing to a binding dispute resolution method other than litigation, the dispute will be resolved in a court of competent jurisdiction.

5.26.1   AIA B101 - §8.3.1.1 Timing of Arbitration

There is new language added to the B101 paragraph for the purpose of resolving issues regarding the timing of the filing of a demand for arbitration that had arisen under the predecessor versions of this provision, Section 1.3.5.3 of the B141-1997 and Section 7.2.2 of the B151-1997. In order to emphasize that mediation is a binding condition precedent to proceeding with an arbitration, the new provision now provides that a "demand for arbitration shall be made no earlier than concurrently with the filing of a request for mediation."

Another question that has been raised regarding arbitration commenced under AIA Documents was whether the filing of an arbitration demand tolled the statute of limitations. Although the filing of an arbitration demand logically should constitute the prosecution of a claim for statute of limitations purposes, the fact remained that arbitration is a private process and that many statutes of limitations contain language requiring a court filing to toll the limitations period.[4] A new sentence has been added to the end of paragraph 8.3.1.1 to clarify this issue:

> For statute of limitations purposes, receipt of a written demand for arbitration by the person or entity administering the arbitration shall constitute the institution of legal or equitable proceedings based on the claim, dispute or other matter in question.

The intent of the new sentence is to create a binding agreement between the parties establishing that the claim shall be deemed timely for statute of limitations purposes if the arbitration demand is filed timely. This follows the well-known principles that parties can agree in their contract to limit or otherwise modify an applicable statute of limitations.[5]

5.26.2   AIA B101 - §8.3.4.1 and 8.3.4.2 Consolidation of Arbitrations

These paragraphs represent a significant conceptual change from prior editions of the AIA Owner-Architect Agreement. It had previously been the philosophy of the AIA that arbitrations between the Owner and the Architect should not be consolidated with any other arbitrations involving different parties. Paragraph 8.3.4.1 of the B101-2007, however, now allows either the Owner or the Architect, without needing the consent of the other, to consolidate any arbitration between them with any other arbitration to which the consolidator is a party if three conditions are met:

> (1) the arbitration agreement governing the other arbitration permits consolidation; (2) the arbitrations to be consolidated substantially involve common issues of law or fact; and (3) the arbitrations employ materially similar procedural rules and methods for selecting arbitrator(s).

The provision does not offer any guidance as to what would constitute "common issues of law or fact," but a large body of case law involving consolidation of claims serves as precedent.[6] Paragraph 8.3.4.1 also does not provide any guidance regarding how similar the arbitrator selection procedures must be, and there is little to no precedent available on this point.

§ 8.3.4 CONSOLIDATION OR JOINDER

§ 8.3.4.1 Either party, at its sole discretion, may consolidate an arbitration conducted under this Agreement with any other arbitration to which it is a party provided that (1) the arbitration agreement governing the other arbitration permits consolidation; (2) the arbitrations to be consolidated substantially involve common questions of law or fact; and (3) the arbitrations employ materially similar procedural rules and methods for selecting arbitrator(s).

§ 8.3.4.2 Either party, at its sole discretion, may include by joinder persons or entities substantially involved in a common question of law or fact whose presence is required if complete relief is to be accorded in arbitration, provided that the party sought to be joined consents in writing to such joinder. Consent to arbitration involving an additional person or entity shall not constitute consent to arbitration of any claim, dispute or other matter in question not described in the written consent.

§ 8.3.4.3 The Owner and Architect grant to any person or entity made a party to an arbitration conducted under this Section 8.3, whether by joinder or consolidation, the same rights of joinder and consolidation as the Owner and Architect under this Agreement.

Paragraph 8.3.4.3 serves to flow down further joinder and consolidation rights to persons or entities that have themselves been made a party to an arbitration proceeding with the Owner or Architect as a result of joinder or consolidation. It applies to non-parties to the Owner-Architect Agreement who are participating in an arbitration that has been consolidated pursuant to paragraph 8.3.4.1 with the arbitration between the Owner and Architect under the B101-2007. Just as paragraph 8.3.4.1 allows the Owner or Architect to assume the role of Third-Party Plaintiff by consolidating the Owner/Architect arbitration with an arbitration against a downstream party, paragraph 8.3.4.3 allows the downstream party to assume the role of Fourth-Party Plaintiff by consolidating its arbitration against a party that is even further downstream. Thus, if the Owner is arbitrating a claim for design error against the Architect, paragraph 8.3.4.2 allows the Architect to add its consulting engineer as a party to the arbitration pursuant to an arbitration clause in the contract between the Architect and consulting engineer. Paragraph 8.3.4.3 would then permit the consulting engineer to fourth-party in a subconsulting engineer pursuant to an arbitration clause in the contract between them.

Although it may seem curious that paragraph 8.3.4.3 applies only to parties or entities who are not signatories to the B101 Owner-Architect Agreement, it is common for subcontracts, subconsulting agreements and other downstream contracts to incorporate by reference the terms and conditions of the upstream contract. As a result, the language of paragraph 8.3 may be incorporated by reference into a downstream contract. Furthermore, it operates to prevent the Owner or Architect from objecting to the efforts of the consulting engineer or other downstream party to consolidate a further downstream arbitration.

5.27 AIA B101 - §10.1 Choice of Law

This paragraph represents a conceptual change from the approach of the predecessor provisions, Section 1.3.7.1 of the B141-1997 and Section 9.1 of the B151-1997, both of which stated that the "principal place of business of the Architect" would provide the applicable law. The new approach in this paragraph is more realistic and was designed to comply with laws and court provisions that would void the previous incarnation of this provision.[7] The new provision defines the applicable law as that of the "place where the Project is located." However, to avoid running afoul of court decisions holding that the Federal Arbitration Act preempts any contrary state law,[8] the paragraph further provides "that if the parties have selected arbitration as the method of binding dispute resolution, the Federal Arbitration Act shall govern Section 8.3."

5.28 AIA B101 - §10.4 Certificates and Consents

This paragraph adds a new sentence to extend the principle in the prior version of this provision, Section 1.3.7.8 in the B141-1997, to consents as well as certificates. The prior edition allowed the Architect fourteen days of advance review of any certificate before having to sign it. The new paragraph extends the same principle to consents:

> If the Owner requests the Architect to execute consents reasonably required to facilitate assignment to a lender, the Architect shall execute all such consents that are consistent with

its Agreement, provided the proposed consent is submitted to the Architect for review at least 14 days prior to execution.

This reflects the concern that the language of lender's consent is often imprecise or overbroad, requiring negotiation and modification. However, to be consistent with the language in the prior sentence applicable to certificates, the final words of the new sentence should probably read: "at least 14 days prior to the requested dates of execution."

5.29   AIA B101 - §10.8 Confidential Information

This paragraph has been completely rewritten from its predecessor provision, Section 1.2.3.4 of the B141-1997. It now reads:

> If the Architect or Owner receives information specifically designated by the other party as "confidential" or "business proprietary", the receiving party shall keep such information strictly confidential and shall not disclose it to any other person except (1) its employees, (2) those who need to know the content of such information in order to perform services or construction solely and exclusively for the Project, or (3) to its consultants and contractors whose contracts include similar restrictions on the use of Confidential Information.

For the first time, this provision has been made mutual, rather than applying only to the Architect. It also now applies to "business proprietary" information, which is only confidential for commercial purposes. And the three numbered exceptions now allow the party maintaining confidentiality to disclose it as necessary to perform its services or other obligations for the Project.

The new paragraph also deleted established exceptions to the obligation to maintain confidentiality as set forth in Section 1.2.3.4 of the B141-1997: "unless withholding such information would violate the law, create the risk of significant harm to the public or prevent the Architect from establishing a claim or defense in an adjudicatory proceeding." The quoted circumstances are arguably legitimate and proper exceptions to confidentiality. It is unclear why they have been deleted.

5.30   AIA B101 - §11.9 License Fee Upon Termination for Convenience

This is a new concept in the AIA Owner-Architect Agreement. It provides for a fee to be paid by the Owner to the Architect to retain a license to use the Drawings and Specifications after terminating the Owner-Architect Agreement for convenience. This paragraph states:

> ### § 11.9 COMPENSATION FOR USE OF ARCHITECT'S INSTRUMENTS OF SERVICE
>
> If the Owner terminates the Architect for its convenience under Section 9.5, or the Architect terminates this Agreement under Section 9.3, the Owner shall pay a licensing fee as compensation for the Owner's continued use of the Architect's Instruments of Service solely for purposes of completing, using and maintaining the Project as follows:

No predecessor provision exists in the 1997 editions of B141 or B151.

This paragraph responds to the concern of architects who are known for their design skills. Often their fee structure is higher than that of other architectural firms less known for design. The higher-fee design architects are concerned that the Owner will obtain the benefits of their design and then terminate them for convenience, hiring a less expensive architecture firm to complete the Project.

5.31   AIA B101 - §11.10.3 Withholding Architect's Fee

This paragraph prohibits the Owner from withholding a portion of the Architect's fee to offset other losses or damages unless the Architect agrees or has been found to be liable for the sum withheld. As such, it clarifies its predecessor, Section 1.3.9.1 of the B141-1997. The new paragraph states:

> The Owner shall not withhold amounts from the Architect's compensation to impose a penalty or liquidated damages on the Architect, or to off set sums requested by or paid to contractors for the cost of changes in the Work unless the Architect agrees or has been found liable for the amounts in a binding dispute resolution proceeding.

5.32   AIA B101 - §13.2.2 Digital Data Protocol Exhibit

This paragraph refers to an Exhibit which is new with the B101-2007. The paragraph states that the new Exhibit, denominated AIA Document E201-2007 and entitled "Digital Data Protocol Exhibit," is incorporated by reference if filled out. Presumably, if left blank, it is not part of the parties' agreement. The details of the exhibit itself are beyond the scope of this chapter.

Acknowledgement: This chapter is based on an earlier and longer paper addressing a draft version of the AIA Document B101-2007 presented by Mr. Friedlander for the ABA Forum on the Construction Industry program entitled, "The 2007 AIA Documents: New Forms, New Issues, New Strategies," January 31, 2008, in New York, New York.

---

[1]   See *Miller v. DeWitt,* 59 Ill.App.2d 38, 208 N.E.2d 249 (4th Dist. 1965).

[2]   *Id.*

[3]   See e.g., Illinois: 740 ILCS 35/1 *et seq.;* New York: General Obligations Law §5-322.1; California: Civil Code §2782.

[4]   See *Murphy v. United States Fidelity & Guaranty Co.,* 120 Ill.App.3d 282, 458 N.E.2d 54, 58, 75 Ill.Dec. 886 (5th Dist. 1983) (holding that statute of limitations may be tolled as long as arbitration is demanded by one of the parties to the contract within the applicable statute of limitations time period); *Booth v. Fireman's Fund Insurance Co.,* 253 La. 521, 218 S.2d 580 (1968); *Schleif v. Hardware Dealer's Mutual Fire Insurance Co.,* 218 Tenn. 489, 404 S.W.2d 490 (1966); *DeLuca v. Motor Vehicle Accident Indemnification Corp.,* 17 N.Y.2d 76, 215 N.E.2d 482, 268 N.Y.S.2d 289 (1966); *Lemrick v. Grinnell Mutual Reinsurance Co.,* 263 N.W.2d 714 (Iowa 1978); *Pickering v. American Employers Insurance Co.,* 109 R.I. 143, 282 A.2d 584 (1971); *Franco v. Allstate Insurance Co.,* 505 S.W.2d 789 (Tex.1974); *North River Insurance Co. v. Kowaleski,* 275 Or. 531, 551 P.2d 1286 (1976); *Sahloff v. Western Casualty and Surety Co.,* 45 Wis.2d 60, 171 N.W.2d 914 (1969).

[5]   See e.g., *Braye v. Archer-Daniels-Midland Co.,* 276 Ill.App.3d 1066, 659 N.E.2d 430 (1995) citing *Village of Lake in the Hills v. Illinois Emcasco Insurance Co.,* 153 Ill.App.3d 815, 106 Ill.Dec. 881, 506 N.E.2d 681 (1987) (agreement by contract to modify the statute of limitations upheld).

[6]   See e.g., *In re Repetitive Stress Injury Litigation,* 11 F.3d 368 (C.A.2.N.Y., 1993); *Johnson v. Celotex Corp.,* 899 F.2d 1281 (C.A.2.N.Y., 1990); *Henderson v. National R.R. Passenger Corp.,* 118 F.R.D. 440 (N.D.Ill., 1987); *Bottazzi v.*

Petroleum Helicopters, Inc., 664 F.2d 49 (C.A.5.La., 1981); *Dupont v. Southern Pac. Co.*, 366 F.2d 193 (C.A.5.La., 1966).

[7] See *Labor Ready, Inc. v. Williams Staffing, LLC,* 149 F.Supp.2d 398, 405 (N.D.Ill. 2001); *Manion v. Roadway Package System, Inc.,* 938 F.Supp. 512, 515 (N.D.Ill. 1996). *International Surplus Lines Insurance Co. v. Pioneer Life Insurance Company of Illinois,* 209 Ill.App.3d 144, 568 N.E.2d 9, 154 Ill.Dec. 9 (1st Dist. 1990).

[8] See *Aste v. Metropolitan Life Ins. Co.*, 728 N.E.2d 629 (Ill.App. 2000); *Doctor's Associates, Inc. v. Casarotto*, 517 U.S. 681 (1996).

Chapter 6

Introducing the ConsensusDOCS

Brian M. Perlberg, J.D.

---

6. 1   Introduction

The construction industry is too often fragmented, adversarial, litigious, and inefficient. The contract documents which govern the performance of stakeholders in the design and construction process are part of the problem. Twenty-two leading construction associations, representing a diverse coalition of owners, contractors, sureties, and design professionals, joined together to develop a set of consensus standard contracts intended to have reasonable risk allocation for all parties.[1] The result is ConsensusDOCS™, which includes more than 82 contracts and forms that address all project delivery methods, including the first standard Integrated Project Delivery (IPD) contract.[2] Publication of ConsensusDOCS marks the first time that the entire construction industry was invited to join together to draft standard contracts.[3]

Contracts ultimately written by one organization are often perceived as being biased towards that membership's interests. The American Institute of Architects ("AIA") has historically played the role of "decider" of industry standard contracts. However, some perceive the AIA contract documents as biased towards architects. The memberships of the Associated General Contractors of America (AGC) and the American Subcontractor's Association (ASA) unanimously elected not to endorse the 2007 edition of AIA documents based upon the substantive concerns that were left unaddressed.[4]

Judging by the general state of affairs in construction contracts, the old ways don't best serve the industry. Fair risk allocation generally follows the principal that the party in the best position to control and mitigate risk should be allocated that risk. However, many view contracts as an opportunity to push risk away rather than manage it. Consequently, parties downstream in the contractual chain, who are often in the weakest position, bear an inordinate amount of the risk. The lack of consensus has led a fragmented industry to fragment in its use of contracts. Some markets report use of 54 different "standard" contracts. Moreover, even if a standard contract is used, it is often so modified that it loses the predictability that it was intended to provide.

ConsensusDOCS are intended to solve the Gordian Knot of perceived bias by giving all the stakeholders in the construction process an equal seat at the table. The "DOCS" in ConsensusDOCS stands for Designers, Owners, Contractors, Subcontractors, and Sureties. Upon reaching consensus, AGC and COAA merged their previous contract documents programs into ConsensusDOCS, thereby proactively providing cohesion and predictability in a fragmented industry.[5] Some argue that the ConsensusDOCS are solely a re-branding effort of the old AGC contract documents. That conclusion is the result of a misunderstanding of the process which resulted in the publication of the ConsensusDOCS. In reality, the participating organizations built consensus from the foundation of both the previous AGC and the COAA contracts. In addition to creating entirely new and innovative contract documents, every document, article, and section was put on the drafting table and subjected to an intensive three-year process that explored fundamental, as well as intricate, details to craft contractual best practices for today's industry and beyond.

The ConsensusDOCS stress collaboration and cooperation between the primary parties to control their destiny and resolve potential disputes before they become intractable. The owner is empowered to decide who should serve and be paid to be an "impartial" decision-maker or "arbitrator" in the mix from the inception of the contractual relationship. The architect may, or may not, be assigned this role.

6. 2   How ConsensusDOCS are Different

Written by experienced construction professionals and attorneys, the contracts provide solutions drawn from multiple segments of the construction process. The ConsensusDOCS also address cutting-edge issues, such as electronic communications and Building Information Modeling (BIM). In addition, ConsensusDOCS includes an important new agreement—the "Tri-Party Collaborative Agreement" (ConsensusDOCS 300)—which was the irst standard Integrated Project Delivery (IPD) document published. The Tri-

Party Collaborative Agreement brings together three parties—Owner, Design Professional, and Constructor—to execute the same contract and create a core team to act on behalf of the project. Agreements of this type have been used in Australia for some time, where they are known as "alliancing" or "relational contracting."[6] The document allows the project's core team, which may include key specialty contractors and consultants, to make consensus decisions based upon the best interests of the project. The Tri-Party Collaborative Agreement helps facilitate the use of BIM and incorporates LEAN construction techniques.

6. 3   Claims Mitigation & Mediation

With respect to dispute resolution, the ConsensusDOCS encourage the parties to communicate directly and resolve potential disputes before they become claims. The drafters of the ConsensusDOCS believe it is important that parties expend effort to establish positive relations. To further this end, the first provision of each agreement states that parties are to proceed on the basis of mutual trust, good faith, and fair dealing.[7] When issues arise, the parties must go through several, pre-defined steps, in the attempt to resolve the claims.[8] Parties initially meet and discuss issues at the project level. If not successful, the issues are raised to a senior management level. If the issues remain unresolved, then parties may utilize a Project Neutral or Dispute Review Board to issue non-binding findings to help resolve potential claims. The next step in this process is mediation, using the current Construction Industry Mediation Rules of the American Arbitration Association (AAA).[9]

6. 4   Binding Dispute Resolution

The drafters of the ConsensusDOCS believe that parties should make a conscious decision at the time the contract is signed whether to use arbitration or litigation, rather than have a "default" contract clause make that decision for them. Of course, parties can always mutually agree to arbitration when a claim arises, but it is more likely that the method chosen at contract signing will remain. As a result, the ConsensusDOCS have a "check the box" provision by which the parties select litigation or arbitration for claims elevated to binding dispute resolution.[10]

The venue for dispute resolution proceedings is established as the location of the project. If arbitration is selected, the AAA rules in effect at the time of the proceedings are used (as opposed to old rules in effect when the contract was signed). This allows parties to utilize revised and improved procedural rules.[11]

6. 5   Project Financing Information

ConsensusDOCS obligates the owner to provide evidence of project financing only, as opposed to general financial information, but the owner is obligated to do so both before the work commences, and at any time thereafter upon written request of the contractor.[12]   The AIA A201-2007 limits a contractor's rights to obtain financial information.   While the contractor may still gain access to the owner's financial information prior to commencement of the work, its ability to do so after the work commences is now much more restricted.[13]   Given today's difficult financial climate, the ConsensusDOCS approach appears to place design professionals and contractors in a better position of maintaining their own financial viability and avoid providing goods and services to an owner who is no longer in a position to pay for them. Additionally, ConsensusDOCS provides an example questionnaire, along with guidance to request needed information in a balanced and easy to use manner.[14]

6. 6   Document Ownership

AIA expressly, and ConsensusDOCS implicitly, recognize that the contractor does not usually have an ownership interest in the design drawings.   While AIA continues to vest very strong copyright ownership rights in design documents through employing its "Instrument of Service" terminology, ConsensusDOCS emphasizes the need of the owner to provide appropriate documents to the contractor to enable the contractor to proceed with its work.[15]   Also, owners often seek design professionals' copyright. ConsensusDOCS recognizes that the design professional should be granted a full indemnification, and receive fair compensation for any transfer of intellectual property rights.

6. 7   Contract Construction

Like AIA, ConsensusDOCS provide that the contract documents are complimentary and that the contractor is to perform the Work consistent with them and as reasonably inferable from them. ConsensusDOCS also provide a mechanism for the contractor to call to the owner's attention omissions or errors in figures, drawings, or specifications.[16]   ConsensusDOCS provides an order of precedence for interpreting contract documents, with change orders being accorded the highest precedence.[17]

6. 8   Additional Insured Status

Additional insured coverage was the last area, and one of the most difficult issues, for the ConsensusDOCS drafters. Owners tend to prefer Additional Insured protection as a "cost-free" mechanism to protect them from liability exposure that is generally not within their control. Specialty contractors passionately believe that Additional Insured is a mechanism which transfers the burden of providing insurance to those weakest in the contractual chain, and carries the consequence of higher insurance premiums that can result from instances they bore no responsibility in creating. Complicating a solution further is the burdensome litigation costs associated with assigning culpability among parties.

Consequently, the ConsensusDOCS contracts give the parties best practice options with regard to additional insured coverage, thereby creating a framework for the parties to determine how to best handle the issue on any given project. As one option, a contractor may decide not to require liability insurance over and above the insurance it has in place. If the contractor requires more insurance, it chooses from a menu that includes additional insured status for ongoing and completed operations that is limited to the contractor's negligence. Alternatively, an Owners and Contractors Protective Liability Insurance ("OCP") policy can be used for ongoing operations either alone or in combination with additional insured coverage for completed operations. It is also possible to use the OCP insurance in conjunction with Additional Insured protection for completed operations only. If there are additional costs for selected insurance coverage, said costs are to be paid by the contractor and ultimately the owner.[18]

6. 9   Mutual Waiver of Consequential Damages and Liquidated Damages

In the drafting process, contractors voiced concerns about exposure to consequential damages that could easily exceed the total contract price, and greatly exceed any anticipated profit. On the other hand, owners seek to ensure timely performance by making the contractor face the risk of having to compensate the owner in the event of unexcused delays, such as through the use of liquidated damages provisions or by having no waiver of consequential damages in the contract.

Balancing these considerations, the ConsensusDOCS owner/contractor agreements provide a limited waiver of consequential damages. The waiver is limited because owners are given an opportunity to delineate liquidated damages as well as items specifically excluded from the default waiver of consequential damages.[19] By precisely delineating the actual costs associated with unsatisfactory performance, the contract parties put everything on the table in negotiations upfront, before the work or disputes commence. This provides the financial incentives to protect against certain risk should they arise in a tailored manner.

6. 10   Termination for Convenience

Both the AIA and ConsensusDOCS forms allow the owner to terminate the contractor for convenience. In the event of such a termination, both sets of documents entitle the contractor to be paid for the work actually performed up to the time of the termination, and to be reimbursed for other costs incurred by such termination, including demobilization costs.[20] AIA expressly allows the contractor to recover "reasonable overhead and profit" on work not executed, but does not provide any guidelines for determining reasonableness.[21]

In contrast, ConsensusDOCS allow a separate premium to be awarded to the contractor in the event of a convenience termination. The amount of the premium is to be agreed upon between the parties at the time of contracting.[22] The AGC Guidebook[23] states that this premium better balances the owner's and the contractor's risks and interests. Care needs to be taken in arriving at, and articulating the basis for, the amount of the premium, so that it is tied to actual anticipated losses by the contractor, such as lost business opportunities. Otherwise, the premium may be construed as a penalty, in which case it might not be recoverable under applicable state contract law.[24]

6. 11   Retainage

ConsensusDOCS adopts an innovative approach that permits the owner to release retainage applicable to the work of early finishing trades and other subcontractors once their work has been accepted. Once the overall work of the project is 50% complete, the additional retainage is not withheld.[25] ConsensusDOCS believe that its approach allows for payment to flow in a more fair and equitable manner on the project. Another innovative provision of the ConsensusDOCS is the option given the owner to utilize a retention bond or other form of security interest in lieu of retainage.[26]

6. 12   Contractor Reporting of Problems with the Contract Documents

The contractor must report those errors it discovers, and the contractor is liable only to the extent it "knowingly fails" to report a recognized problem.[27] Unlike the new 2007 edition of the AIA A201, which places increased burdens, the ConsensusDOCS take a more consistent approach in both contractor and design professional liability exposures.

6. 13   Interim Change Directives

Both AIA and ConsensusDOCS allow the owner to issue an interim change directive, requiring the contractor to implement a change in the work until the parties reach a final agreement, in the form of a change order, regarding any impact to the contract sum or time for performance.[28] The AIA and ConsensusDOCS differ, however, on the procedures for resolving a dispute regarding the impact of the directed work on the contract sum.

AIA A201-2007 provides that the architect shall determine both the method for and the adjustment of the contract sum.[29] The "Initial Decision Maker" (IDM)—the person chosen by the parties to make initial decisions when disputes arise—is not part of the process at that point.[30] Instead, the architect's decisions are binding, subject to the parties' right to invoke the dispute resolution procedures set forth in Article 15, which would involve the IDM.[31] Consequently, if the architect rejects the contractor's anticipated costs, the contractor may be left having to fund costs of the directed change until a final resolution is reached, which could be long after the directed work was performed and, indeed, long after completion of the project.

While ConsensusDOCS similarly allow a final resolution to disputed adjustment in the contract sum, they differ from AIA in two significant respects. First, they require the owner and the contractor, as the parties most directly impacted by the resolution, to try to reach an accord themselves, rather than relegating that authority to the architect.[32] Second, they provide interim relief to the contractor where AIA does not. Specifically, in the event of a dispute regarding an adjustment to the contract sum based on the contractor's estimated costs of the directed work, ConsensusDOCS require the owner to at least pay 50% on the contractor's estimated costs of the directed work.[33] This will result in an immediate infusion of funds to the contractor to defray the cost of the directed work until a final resolution occurs. In this regard, the drafters of ConsensusDOCS believe that they struck a reasonable balance , allowing the contractor to maintain financial viability, while allowing the owner to retain legitimate claims in dispute.

6. 14   Electronic Communications

When evaluating the merits of documents proposed for use on a particular project, practitioners should ask, "Can the parties rely on information that is provided in electronic format or through Building Information Modeling (BIM)?" Under previous editions of standard contract documents, the answer is, "No," because in the absence of a protocol document, the hard copies solely govern.[34] This limitation includes basic electronic communications, such as fax transmissions and emails.

The ConsensusDOCS handle this differently. The ConsensusDOCS 200.2 Electronic Communications Protocol Addendum provides a comprehensive mechanism for parties to identify which technologies they want to utilize and who will be responsible for their adequacy.

6. 15   Building Information Modeling

The ConsensusDOCS 301 BIM Addendum is intended to navigate the legal issues using BIM. The BIM Addendum answers a host of legal and contractual questions that arise from the use of BIM, including:

> Does it alter the traditional allocation of responsibility and liability exposure among owners, designers, contractors, and suppliers? What are the risks of sharing digital models with other parties? Does the party managing the modeling process assume any additional liability exposure? What risks arise from potential interoperability of the various BIM software platforms in use? How should intellectual property rights be addressed? What risks arise for the party taking responsibility for establishing and maintaining the networked file-sharing site used as a depository for models? How might BIM alter the set of post-construction deliverables on a project, and what are the implications of the changes? And, perhaps most importantly, how can the project contracts enhance rather than limit the benefits to be gained through the use of BIM?[35]

The BIM Addendum provides for management of the BIM process through election of an Information Manager (IM). An existing project participant, such as an architect or contractor, could serve in this function, but just as easily an outside professional may be specified (Section 3.1). The Addendum also addresses compensation associated with BIM services (to be paid by the owner unless specified otherwise), as well as a detailed list of duties to be performed by the IM (Article 3). In addition, a BIM Execution Plan in Section 4.3 provides a detailed list of minimum elements that are required in the Plan. Ideally, the BIM Execution Plan will be completed at contract signing, but does provide the flexibility to be completed within 30 days of the execution. Significantly, the Addendum gives parties three options to determine their reliance on the model that range from full reliance for dimensional accuracy to using BIM for informational purposes only in Section 4.3.11.

6. 16   Materials Escalation/De-Escalation Amendment

The ConsensusDOCS 200.1 "Potentially Time and Price-Impacted Materials Amendment" is an amendment that provides an owner and contractor a baseline price and calculation method for potential adjustments to material prices. Although not commonly used, attention to this issue appears to be at an all-time high in light of dramatic price increases for materials such as steel, asphalt, and other materials which continue to experience volatile price swings. When material price fluctuations are a concern, the Amendment provides a sensible framework for owners and contractors to protect themselves against construction material price's volatility. Only commodities specifically identified in Schedule A potentially adjust up or down (Section 3.1), and parties may limit the amount of price adjustment (Section 3.3).

Using this document may avoid an owner receiving higher bids for anticipated price increases that may or may not occur. While the owner may receive credits if prices go down, an owner would need to be able to fund increased costs if materials do in fact rise. Moreover, price adjustments require documentation and do not include overhead and profit. Amendment A also addresses time extensions in the event of a project delay caused by material scarcity or delivery delay. The 200.1 may be used with ConsensusDOCS Agreements, and other standard agreements such as AIA and EJCDC contracts. The core substance of the 200.1 has been endorsed by EJCDC.[36]

6. 17   Conclusion

Putting the owner and contractor at the center of the contracting arena is critically important, and is one of the defining principles of the ConsensusDOCS. The ConsensusDOCS endeavor to revise and present contract terms and conditions in a more balanced approach.

---

[1]   See   http://www.consensusdocs.org/about_member-organizations.html.   The organizations are as follows: National Association of State Facilities Administrators (NASFA);   Construction   Users   Roundtable   (CURT);   Commercial   Owners Association of America (COAA); Associated General Contractors of America (AGC); Associated Specialty Contractors (ASC); Construction Industry Round Table (CIRT); American Subcontractors Association (ASA); Associated Builders and Contractors (ABC); Lean Construction Institute (LCI); Finishing Contractors Association (FCA); Mechanical Contractors Association of America (MCAA); National   Electrical   Contractors   Association   (NECA);   National   Insulation Association (NIA); National Roofing Contractors Association (NRCA); Painting and Decorating Contractors of America (PDCA); Plumbing Heating Cooling Contractors Association (PHCC); National Subcontractors Alliance (NSA); Sheet Metal and Air Conditioning Contractors' National Association (SMACNA); National Association of Surety Bond Producers (NASBP); The Surety & Fidelity Association of America (SFAA); Association of the Wall and Ceiling Industry (AWCI); and National Association of Electrical Distributors (NAED).   In addition, the Construction Management Association of America (CMAA) endorses the ConsensusDOCS 301 Building Information Modeling (BIM) Addendum, which was published on June 30, 2008.

[2]   www.consensusdocs.org/information.html

[3]   See Kevin Davis, The Role of Nonprofits in the Production of Boilerplate, 104 Mich. L. Rev. 5 (March 2006).

[4]   AGC's CEO Stephen E. Sandherr commented that, "the A201 does not reflect the collaboration that is necessary for a successful project [and] . . . does not fairly balance risk among all parties but instead significantly shifts risk to general contractors and other parties outside of the design profession," in an October 12, 2007, Press Release. AGC MEMBERS UNANIMOUSLY VOTE AGAINST A201 ENDORSEMENT. The ASA went further and commented that the AIA A201 and AIA A410 Subcontract "incorporate the worst industry practices" in a January 7, 2008, Press Release entitled "New FASA CD-ROMs Help Subs Navigate and Avoid the Perils of AIA's New A201 and A401."

[5]   In reality, there is actually one *less* set of standard construction contracts as a result of the consensus reached with the new ConsensusDOCS because two of the major producers of standard agreements, AGC and COAA, have folded their contract documents programs into the ConsensusDOCS. COAA and AGC discontinued publishing their individual contracts which have equivalent ConsensusDOCS contracts or forms. Moreover, some of the many other organizations which currently produce standard contracts may endorse ConsensusDOCS contracts without having to stop publishing their own individually produced contract documents.

[6]   See Wike, Mike. "Project Alliancing – Sharing Risks and Rewards Through a Collaborative   Agreements"   http://www.legalist.com/chicago2008/faculty.html   at Plenary 6-2.

[7] *E.g.,* ConsensusDOCS 200 § 2.1.

[8] *E.g.,* ConsensusDOCS200, § 12.2.

[9] *E.g.,* ConsensusDOCS 200, § 12.3.

[10] *E.g.,* ConsensusDOCS 200, §12.5.

[11] *E.g.,* ConsensusDOCS 200, § 12.5.

[12] *See* ConsensusDOCS 200, § 4.2.

[13] *See* AIA A201-2007, § 2.2.1.

[14] ConsensusDOCS 290 Owner Financial Questionnaire, and 290.1 Guidance to Owner Financial Questionnaire.

[15] Compare ConsensusDOCS 200, §2.3 to AIA A201-2007, § 1.5.

[16] *See* ConsensusDOCS 200, § 3.2.4.

[17] *See* ConsensusDOCS 200, § 14.2.5.

[18] *E.g.,* ConsensusDOCS 200, § 12.5.

[19] ConsensusDOCS 200, §§6.5, 6.6.

[20] *See* AIA A201-2007, §14.4; ConsensusDOCS 200, §11.5.3.

[21] *See* AIA A201-2007, §14.4.3.

[22] ConsensusDOCS 200, §11.4.2.3.

[23] www.consensusdocs.org/information.html

[24] Restatement (Second) of Contracts §356 (1981)

[25] ConsensusDOCS 200, §9.2.4.

[26] ConsensusDOCS 200, §9.2.4.3.

[27] *See* ConsensusDOCS 200, §3.32.

[28] AIA A201-2007, §7.3; ConsensusDOCS 200, §8.1.

[29] AIA A201-2007, §7.3.

[30] *See* AIA A201-2007, §15.2.

[31] AIA A201-2007, §§7.3.9, 15.2.

[32] ConsensusDOCS 200, §12.22.

[33] ConsensusDOCS 200, §8.22.

[34] ConsensusDOCS 200, §4.6.1.

[35] *See* Dwight A. Larson & Kate Golden, *Entering the Brave New World: An Introduction to Contracting for BIM*, 34 Wm. Mitchell L. Rev. 75 at 77.

[36] EJCDC endorses the AGC 200.1, which is no longer published. This document included the same core substance of the ConsensusDOCS 2001 as the ConsensusDOCS drafters deemed the content represented best practices.

Chapter 7

The ConsensusDOCS Owner-Architect Agreement

Jerome V. Bales, Esq.
Ricardo Aparicio, AIA, Esq.

7.1   The Role of the Architect/Engineer During Construction

Anyone reading ConsensusDOCS 200, *Standard Agreement and General Conditions Between Owner and Contractor* ("Owner-Contractor Agreement"), for the first time may be struck by the limited references to the Architect/Engineer throughout the document.   Indeed, one of the most remarkable differences between the approach of ConsensusDOCS and the AIA documents is the role played by the Architect/Engineer during the construction phase.   Generally, where the AIA interposes the Architect/Engineer in every critical step of the Owner-Contractor relationship, ConsensusDOCS opts for a direct relationship between the two parties to the Agreement, with the Architect/Engineer playing the limited role of consultant to the Owner or designer.

The definition of this role begins within ConsensusDOCS 240, *Standard Form of Agreement Between Owner and Architect/Engineer*, Paragraph 2.3, which states:

> Neither the Architect/Engineer nor any of its agents or employees shall act on behalf of or in the name of the Owner except as provided in this Agreement or unless authorized in writing by the Owner.

This clause is clearly intended to preclude the Architect/Engineer, among others, from acting as the Owner's representative or agent during the construction phase. In keeping with this approach, Subparagraph 3.1.4 goes on to require:

> Except as provided in this Agreement or unless otherwise directed by the Owner, the Architect/Engineer shall communicate with the Contractor and Subcontractors only through the Owner.

This does not mean that the Architect/Engineer ceases to play an important role as the Owner's consultant during the construction phase. Indeed, the services contemplated of the Architect/Engineer under Article 3 of ConsensusDOCS 240 include:

- assisting the Owner during the bidding and/or contract negotiation phase;
- receiving notifications from the Owner as to the commencement of construction;
- reviewing the Schedule of Values and Project Schedule;
- preparing design documents in connection with change orders, and responding to Contractor's requests for information;
- reviewing submittals;
- visiting the site at specific intervals, including Substantial and Final completion; and
- reviewing and certifying the Contractor's payment requests.

These services, however, are provided to and through the Owner, respecting the independent and distinct nature of the design services agreement and the contract for construction.

It is in keeping with this overall approach that ConsensusDOCS 200, Owner-Contractor Agreement, limits the references to the Architect/Engineer's role in the administration of the contract and the relationship of the Owner and Contractor. Where the Architect/Engineer is mentioned, it is done either to clarify that the Owner, for purposes of efficiencies, may direct the Contractor to provide certain documents concurrently to the Architect/Engineer, or to delineate the specific role the Architect/Engineer has been appointed to fulfill. For example, the schedule of values, construction schedule, shop drawings, samples, and product data are submitted to the Owner for approval and, only if directed, to the

Architect/Engineer.[1] If the Contractor has not been instructed to provide these submittals to the Architect/Engineer, then it is up to the Owner to transmit them to the Architect/Engineer or other consultants as the Owner may deem necessary for their review and comments.

Design professionals might be concerned that the Contractor is not required to provide shop drawings and submittals to them for review and appropriate action. Under the approach of the ConsensusDOCS, the Owner determines whether to involve the Architect/Engineer in the submittal process. With respect to payment applications, under ConsensusDOCS 200 and 240, the design professional still plays a key role. The Contractor submits them to both the Owner and Architect/Engineer, and the Owner is obligated to pay the amount certified by the Architect/Engineer within the prescribed period.[2]

Likewise, ConsensusDOCS 200 assures the Architect/Engineer's role in assisting the Owner in the determination of Final Completion of the Work under Subparagraph 9.8.1:

> Upon notification from the Contractor that the Work is complete and ready for final inspection and acceptance, the Owner with the assistance of its Architect/Engineer shall promptly conduct an inspection to determine if the Work has been completed and is acceptable under the Contract Documents.

Two noteworthy provisions of the Owner-Contractor Agreement recognize the continued importance of the design professional's role and responsibility for the Project. Subparagraph 3.16.2 of ConsensusDOCS 200 requires the Contractor to notify the Architect/Engineer directly if the Contractor discovers any concealed or unknown condition.

In addition, consistent with a parallel clause in the Owner-Architect Agreement,[3] ConsensusDOCS 200 states that the Contractor must facilitate the access of *"the Owner, Architect/Engineer and Others to Work in progress."*[4]

Although the Architect/Engineer does not act as the Owner's representative during construction under ConsensusDOCS 240 and 200, the documents do not prohibit such a role. Paragraph 4.7 of ConsensusDOCS 200 requires the Owner to name a representative, and the Owner could designate the Architect/Engineer to represent it with binding authority.

Finally, unlike the traditional AIA approach, under the ConsensusDOCS, the design professional does not have the right to reject Work or to interpret and decide matters concerning performance under, and requirements of, the Contract Documents.[5]

In contrast to the limitations on the Architect's role imposed by ConsensusDOCS, the AIA documents continue to accord the Architect a central and critical role during the construction process and in the Owner-Contractor relationship. Article 3 of AIA Document B101-2007, *Standard Form of Agreement Between Owner and Architect* ("AIA B101-2007"), outlines the Architect's scope of Basic Services during design and construction. Specifically, Section 3.6.1.1 states:

> The Architect shall provide administration of the Contract between the Owner and Contractor as set forth below and in AIA Document A201-2007, General Conditions of the Contract for Construction. If the Owner and Contractor modify AIA Document A201-2007, those modifications shall not affect the Architect's services under this Agreement unless the Owner and the Architect amend this Agreement.

This language is consistent with prior versions of the AIA documents providing that the Architect is the only party empowered to administer the construction contract between the Owner and the Contractor. The B101-2007 document also defines the scope of services, authority, and responsibility of the Architect during the construction phase by incorporating AIA A201-2007, *General Conditions of the Contract for Construction* ("General Conditions").[6]

Also, the AIA documents continue to require that communications between the Owner and Contractor be conducted through the Architect.[7] However, as to claims and disputes, the 2007 AIA documents have, for the first time, introduced the possibility of a third-party *"Initial Decision Maker"* ("IDM"), other than the Architect.[8] It is likely that the Architect will serve as the IDM on many projects, since the AIA documents provide that the Architect continues to be the "default" IDM if no one else is selected; the Basic Services offered by the Architect already include this role; and the Owner and Contractor are not likely to designate an IDM until the construction contract is subsequently executed, if then.

7.2   Site Safety

Subparagraph 3.2.8 of ConsensusDOCS 240 defines the construction phase services of the Architect/Engineer. As to job site safety, Subparagraph 3.2.8.4 provides that the Architect/Engineer *"shall not be responsible for the Contractor's safety precautions and programs."* This is consistent with AIA

Document B101-2007, which places the responsibility for job site safety on the Contractor.[9]

ConsensusDOCS 240 and ConsensusDOCS 245, *Standard Short Form Agreement Between Owner and Architect/Engineer* ("Short Form Agreement"),[10] include a disclaimer similar to that of AIA Document B 101 - 2007, but ConsensusDOCS 240 adds the following sentence:

> However, if the Architect/Engineer has actual knowledge of safety violations, the Architect/Engineer shall give prompt written notice to the Owner.[11]

Does this sentence, which also appeared in the previous AGC Document 240 (2000), *Standard Agreement Between Owner and Architect/Engineer,* [12] create liability exposure for the design professional? The answer varies from state to state.

7.3   Indemnity and Waiver of Consequential Damages

Paragraph 7.1 of ConsensusDOCS 240 provides for mutual indemnities between the Architect and Owner. Both provisions have been narrowly drafted to encompass only the indemnitor's negligent acts and omissions. In addition, the indemnitor is entitled to be reimbursed for any defense costs paid above its comparative liability.

In ConsensusDOCS 240, the Architect/Engineer's indemnification obligation extends to the Contractors, Subcontractors, and the Owner's other contractors and consultants.[13] Likewise, the Owner is also obligated to indemnify the Architect/Engineer, its subconsultants, and anyone for whose acts they may be liable.[14] These indemnities exclude property damage to the Work itself.[15] Unlike the Owner-Contractor Agreement,[16] ConsensusDOCS 240 does not contain a separate indemnity regarding hazardous materials or substances.

In addition to a fairly narrow indemnity clause, ConsensusDOCS 240 provides a further limitation on the parties' respective liabilities as to each other and their respective indemnities by including a so-called "limited" (though in practice quite broad) waiver of consequential damages. Under Paragraph 5.4, the Architect/Engineer and Owner mutually waive all claims for consequential damages arising out of or relating to the Agreement. This waiver includes all claims arising in contract, tort, strict liability, or otherwise and includes loss of use, profits, business, reputation, or financing. The clause, however, permits the parties to list specific items of damage that they wish to exclude from the mutual waiver.

The "limited" waiver of consequential damages in ConsensusDOCS does not apply to the category of general damages, but is written to speak specifically to the categories of damages that present the greatest uncertainty and risk. The provision is anything but "buried" in the document as some critics may contend; it is spelled out clearly.

ConsensusDOCS 240 allows the parties to delineate exceptions to the waiver. Thus, the parties are able to address the issue at the onset of the contracting process, instead of allowing a judge or arbitrator, far removed in time and place, to make the decision for them.

7.4 Ownership, Copyright, and License Issues

Few contract issues are more emotional to design professionals than the ownership of documents and the intellectual property rights accompanying them. This reaction is understandable since most of the work product and value of the design professional's contribution to the Project is memorialized in the drawings and specifications that it generates during the design and construction process. However, Owners and Contractors, by and large, have never fully embraced an approach that allows design professionals to jealously guard the Contract Documents to the potential detriment of the Project. Thus, it is not surprising that ConsensusDOCS and the AIA documents take different approaches to this issue.

7.4.1 Ownership of the Documents

ConsensusDOCS 240 and ConsensusDOCS 245, Short Form Agreement,[17] provide that upon making the contractually required payments to the Architect/Engineer, the Owner will receive ownership of the property rights, except copyrights, to the Contract Documents. Specifically, Paragraph 10.1 of ConsensusDOCS 240 states:

> The Owner shall receive ownership of the property rights, except for copyrights, of all documents, drawings, specifications, electronic data and information (hereinafter "Documents") prepared, provided or procured by the Architect/Engineer or by consultants retained by the Architect/Engineer and distributed to the Owner for this Project, upon the making of final payment to the Architect/Engineer or in the event of termination under Article 8, upon payment for all sums due to Architect/Engineer pursuant to Paragraphs 8.1 and 8.2.

To protect the design professional, this transfer of property rights is conditioned upon the Owner making final payment to the Architect/Engineer.

Under the AIA documents, the Architect retains all property rights, including copyrights, in the Instruments of Service.[18]

7.4.2   Copyright

In contrast to the AIA documents, ConsensusDOCS 240 provides that the copyright interest in the Documents may be transferred to the Owner for an agreed price. Subparagraph 10.1.1 provides:

> The Parties agree that Owner _____ shall/ ____ shall not (indicate one) obtain ownership of the copyright of all Documents. The Owner's acquisition of the copyright for all Documents shall be subject to the making of payments as required by Paragraph 10.1 and the payment of the fee reflecting the agreed value of the copyright set forth below:
>
> If the Parties have not made a selection to transfer copyright interests in the Documents, the copyright shall remain with the Architect/Engineer.

ConsensusDOCS 240 requires the parties to make a conscious decision about the ownership of the copyright by marking the box. If the parties fail to make that selection, the Agreement states that the Architect/Engineer will own the copyright interest.

ConsensusDOCS 245, Short Form Agreement, does not provide a check-the-box approach to ownership of the copyright. Instead, the Architect/Engineer retains its copyright in the Documents.[19] The Owner receives property rights to the Documents upon payment in full, either at completion of the project or at the time of termination.

7.4.3   Owner's License to Use the Documents

ConsensusDOCS and the AIA both grant a license to the Owner, its Contractor, and its consultants to use the Documents or Instruments of Service to construct the Project. Specifically, ConsensusDOCS 240 provides:

> Except as otherwise provided in this Agreement, the Architect/Engineer shall grant an appropriate license to use

design documents prepared by the Architect/Engineer to those retained by the Owner or the Owner's Contractor to perform construction services for the Project.[20]

This license is not tied to any performance obligations of the Owner, including payment to the Architect/Engineer for the Services rendered.[21]

Although AIA B101-2007 grants a broad license to the Owner (e.g., in using and maintaining the Project), it is conditioned upon the Owner's substantial performance of its obligations, including making prompt payments to the Architect.[22]

7.4.4   Rights of the Owner upon Termination of the Agreement

Not surprisingly, ConsensusDOCS 240 and 245 and AIA B101-2007 also take differing approaches to the Owner's right to use or reuse the Documents or Instruments of Service upon termination of the Agreement.

All three forms grant the Owner the right to terminate the Agreement for convenience and grant both parties the right to terminate for cause.[23] Paragraph 8.1 of ConsensusDOCS 240 is silent as to the Owner's payment obligation to the Architect/Engineer upon a termination for cause. Thus, the Owner's property rights in the Documents, including the right to use them to finish the Project, are apparently not affected by that termination. However, if the Owner terminates the Agreement for convenience, ConsensusDOCS 240 provides that the Owner may use the Documents to complete the Project provided it has made the required payments to the Architect/Engineer:

> In the event of a termination of this Agreement pursuant to Article 8, the Owner shall have the right to use, to reproduce, and to make derivative works of the Documents to complete the Project, regardless of whether there has been a transfer of copyright under Subparagraph 10.1.1, provided payment has been made pursuant to Paragraph 10.1.[24]

Paragraph 10.1 of 240 incorporates the payment obligations provided by Paragraphs 8.1 and 8.2. As stated above, under Paragraph 8.1, there is no specific obligation imposed on the Owner to make any payments to the Architect/Engineer in the event of termination for cause. If the Owner terminates for convenience pursuant to Paragraph 8.2, the Architect/Engineer is entitled to recover from the Owner, *". . . for all Services performed in accordance with this Agreement, and any proven loss, cost or expense in connection with the Services, including those resulting from the termination, and a premium as set forth in the schedule below [insert].*" Therefore, in a termination for convenience, the Owner must make these payments in order to be able to use the Documents to complete the Project.[25]

The AIA documents take a significantly different approach to the effect of termination. First, under Section 7.3, AIA B101-2007 provides for the automatic revocation of the Owner's license if the Architect terminates the Agreement for cause under Section 9.4. More importantly, however, Section 11.9, *Compensation for Use of Architect's Instruments of Service*, provides:

> If the Owner terminates the Architect for its convenience under Section 9.5, or the Architect terminates this Agreement under Section 9.3, the Owner shall pay a licensing fee as compensation for the Owner's continued use of the Architect's Instruments of Service solely for the purpose of completing, using and maintaining the Project as follows: [insert]

Thus, following a termination for convenience by the Owner or a termination for cause by the Architect as a result of the Owner's suspension of the Project, the Owner may complete the Project and use the Instruments of Service to maintain it by paying a specified licensing fee.[26] This provision facilitates the completion of the Project and addresses the complaints of owners that the Architect/Engineer should not be able to "hold the Project hostage" by refusing to permit the continued use of the Documents after termination of the Agreement.

The nature and timing of the termination will also affect liability and indemnity obligations. The Owner's right to use or reuse the Documents to complete the Project upon termination, whether for cause or convenience, is already a foregone conclusion under the ConsensusDOCS (provided, in the event of termination for convenience, that the Architect/Engineer has been paid for services performed through the date of termination), and there is no requirement for the Owner to indemnify the Architect/Engineer for that use. *Compare* the Owner's indemnity obligation toward the Architect/Engineer under Subparagraph 10.1.3 for <u>unauthorized</u> use of the Documents <u>after</u> completion of the Project.

In contrast, under AIA B101-2007, if the Owner pays the "*licensing fee*" but uses the Instruments of Service without retaining their author (except in the event of the Owner's "rightful" termination of the A/E for cause):

> . . . the Owner releases the Architect and Architect's consultant(s) from all claims and causes of action arising from such uses.[27]

In addition:

> The Owner, to the extent permitted by law, further agrees to indemnify and hold harmless the Architect and its consultants from all costs and expenses, including the cost of defense, related to claims and causes of action asserted by any third person or entity to the extent such costs and expenses arise from the Owner's use of the Instruments of Service under this Section 7.3.1. The terms of this Section 7.3.1 shall not apply if the Owner rightfully terminates this Agreement for cause under Section 9.4.[28]

ConsensusDOCS 245, Short Form Agreement, significantly varies from the approach of ConsensusDOCS 240 insofar as termination and reuse of documents are concerned. Under ConsensusDOCS 245 Paragraph 14, there is no distinction between termination for convenience or cause when it comes to the Owner's right to reuse the Documents. In either scenario, ConsensusDOCS 245 vests the Owner's right to reuse the Documents *"upon payment to Architect/Engineer for all Services performed."*[29] Also, under ConsensusDOCS 245, the Owner indemnifies and holds harmless the Architect/Engineer for the unauthorized reuse of the Documents, beginning apparently from the date of termination when the Project is still unfinished. In contrast, under ConsensusDOCS 240, that indemnity obligation only arises after completion of the Project.

Termination can have a significant impact on the Owner's ability to complete the Project and on the Architect's opportunity to be compensated for services performed. When using either the AIA documents or ConsensusDOCS, it is important for the parties to fully understand the implications of these complex provisions prior to the execution of the agreement and during its performance.

7.4.5   Rights of the Owner after Completion of the Project

Pursuant to Subparagraph 10.1.3 of ConsensusDOCS 240:

> After completion of the Project, the Owner may reuse, reproduce, or make derivative works from the Documents solely for the purpose of maintaining, renovating, remodeling or expanding the Project at the Worksite. The Owner's use of the Documents without the Architect/Engineer's involvement or on other projects is at the Owner's sole risk, except for the

Architect/Engineer's indemnification obligations pursuant to Paragraph 3.9, and the Owner shall indemnify and hold harmless the Architect/Engineer and its consultants, and the agents, officers, directors and employees of each of them, from and against any and all claims, damages, losses, costs and expenses, including reasonable attorneys' fees and costs, arising out of or resulting from any such prohibited use.

This provision contains two significant prongs. First, after completion of the Project, the Owner is only authorized to reuse the Documents for "*the purpose of maintaining, renovating or expanding the Project at the Worksite.*" If the Owner reuses the Documents without the Architect/Engineer's involvement, that use is at Owner's sole risk, except to the extent of the Architect/Engineer's indemnity obligations to the Owner. Second, the Owner must indemnify the Architect/Engineer if it reuses the Documents without the design professional's involvement.

7.4.6   Architect/Engineer's Use of the Documents

A somewhat less controversial issue is the Architect/Engineer's right to use the Documents or Instruments of Service. ConsensusDOCS 240 limits the Architect/Engineer's reuse of the Documents as follows:

> Where the Architect/Engineer has transferred its copyright interest in the Documents under Subparagraph 10.1.1, the Architect/Engineer may reuse Documents prepared pursuant to this Agreement in its practice, but only in their separate constituent parts and not as a whole.[30]

Thus, after payment for and transfer of the copyright, the Architect/Engineer may only use the Documents "*in their constituent parts.*"

In contrast, under AIA B101-2007, the Architect retains ownership of the Instruments of Service and the right to reuse them. By definition, the license granted to the Owner by the Architect to construct, use, maintain, alter, and add to the Project is nonexclusive.[31]

7.5   Dispute Resolution

Article 9 of ConsensusDOCS 240 outlines a three-step process for the resolution of a dispute:

1. Direct discussions between the parties.
2. "Dispute mitigation procedures" or mediation.
3. Binding dispute resolution through arbitration or litigation.

7.5.1   Step One - Direct Discussions

Under Paragraph 9.2, the first attempt to resolve the dispute is through direct discussions. Initially, the party representatives must *"endeavor to reach resolution through good faith direct discussions."* Those representatives must *"possess the necessary authority to resolve such matter"* and must *"record the date of first discussions."*

The concept of mandating direct discussions is not new to the AGC. The outdated AGC Document No. 240 (2000) required the parties to participate in direct discussions prior to nonbinding mediation.[32]

7.5.2   Step Two - Dispute Mitigation Procedures

The second step in resolving a dispute under ConsensusDOCS 240 is the use of dispute mitigation procedures, as defined in Paragraph 9.3, or mediation, as described in Paragraph 9.4. The parties may select a Project Neutral or a Dispute Review Board ("DRB") to issue nonbinding findings, but if they do not make that designation, they must submit to nonbinding mediation per Paragraph 9.4.

The findings of the Project Neutral or DRB may be introduced in a subsequent arbitration or litigation.[33] However, the agreement does not detail the procedures to be followed by the Project Neutral or DRB in rendering a decision. For example, there is no right to a hearing with the opportunity to present evidence and cross-examine witnesses, no prohibition against *ex-parte* communications, etc. Finally, the document does not indicate whether the Project Neutral or DRB members may be subpoenaed to testify in an arbitration or litigation to explain the findings.

If the parties do not designate a Project Neutral or DRB, they must proceed with nonbinding mediation. Paragraph 9.4 provides that the mediation will be governed by the current Construction Industry Mediation Rules of the American Arbitration Association or another set of mediation rules selected by the parties.

ConsensusDOCS 245, Short Form Agreement, Article 13, provides for mediation as the second step in the process of dispute resolution (after direct discussions), but does not include the option of using a Project Neutral or DRB.[34]

ConsensusDOCS 240 contemplates that the dispute mitigation procedure or mediation must be concluded before arbitration or litigation may be filed.

7.5.3   Step Three - Binding Dispute Resolution

The final step in the dispute resolution process prescribed by ConsensusDOCS 240 is binding arbitration or litigation as designated by the parties. The binding dispute resolution process begins when the dispute remains unresolved after completion of the dispute mitigation procedures (Project Neutral/DRB or nonbinding mediation). Paragraph 9.5 allows the parties to select arbitration or litigation.

ConsensusDOCS 240 outlines the following binding dispute resolution procedures:

- If arbitration is selected, it will proceed according to the current Construction Industry Arbitration Rules of the American Arbitration Association or another set of arbitration rules selected by the parties.
- The "*costs*" are borne by the non-prevailing party.
- Unless the parties agree otherwise, the venue of the arbitration or litigation will be the location of the project.
- All parties necessary to resolve a claim may be joined in the arbitration or litigation.[35]

ConsensusDOCS 240 also provides that the administration of any mediation or arbitration "*shall be as mutually agreed by the parties.*"[36] It is unclear what the drafters meant by this language, particularly if the parties designate AAA to administer the arbitration or mediation according to its procedures.

The "*non-prevailing party*" must pay the "*costs*" of the other party in the arbitration or litigation, but those terms are not defined.[37] A court would probably interpret the word "*costs*" to mean court costs, not attorneys' fees. ConsensusDOCS 245, Short Form Agreement, states that the prevailing party shall recover reasonable attorneys' fees, costs, and expenses.[38]

Subparagraph 9.5.2 of ConsensusDOCS 240 specifies that the venue of any arbitration or litigation will be the location of the project. The parties should verify that applicable state law permits the waiver of a litigation right such as venue.

The former AGC Document 240 (2000) compelled a party to commence an arbitration within the applicable statute of limitations,[39] but that provision was not carried forward to ConsensusDOCS 240. However,

ConsensusDOCS 245, Short Form Agreement, provides that the arbitration shall be commenced within a reasonable time, but not beyond the applicable statute of limitations.[40]

7.5.4   Joinder and Consolidation

ConsensusDOCS 240 encourages the joinder of other parties in the dispute resolution procedure (presumably all nonbinding and binding processes). Paragraph 9.6, "MULTI-PARTY PROCEEDINGS," mandates the joinder of *"all parties necessary to resolve a claim."* It also requires the parties to provide for that joinder or consolidation with appropriate terms in other contracts relating to the project, i.e., with consultants or subcontractors. AGC Document No. 240 (2000) contained the same clause.[41] Unlike AIA B101-2007,[42] ConsensusDOCS 240 does not define when a party is *"necessary to resolve a claim."*

ConsensusDOCS 245, Short Form Agreement, is silent on joinder and consolidation.[43]

7.5.5   Statute of Limitations/Repose

ConsensusDOCS 240 and 245 leave the statute of limitations and any statute of repose to the applicable state law. The 1997 AIA document defined when the statute of limitations commenced to run,[44] but that definition was eliminated from the 2007 version. Instead, AIA B101–2007 includes a ten-year statute of repose, which runs from the date of Substantial Completion of the Work.[45]

7.6   Standard of Care

7.6.1   Definition

AIA B101-2007 utilizes the following definition of the standard of care that the Architect must exercise:

> The Architect shall perform its services consistent with the professional skill and care ordinarily provided by architects practicing in the same or similar locality under the same or similar circumstances."[46]

ConsensusDOCS 245, Short Form Agreement,[47] includes a similar definition, as did the former AGC Document 240 (2000).[48]

ConsensusDOCS 240 does not define the standard of care. Instead, Paragraph 2.2 defines the relationship of the Owner and Architect/Engineer:

> The Architect/Engineer accepts the relationship of trust and confidence established by this Agreement and covenants with the Owner to cooperate and exercise the Architect/Engineer's skill and judgment in furthering the interests of the Owner. The Architect/Engineer represents that it possesses the requisite skill, expertise, and licensing to perform the required services. The Owner and Architect/Engineer agree to work together on the basis of mutual trust, good faith and fair dealing, and shall take actions reasonably necessary to enable each other to perform this Agreement in a timely, efficient and economical manner. The Owner and Architect/Engineer shall endeavor to promote harmony and cooperation among all Project participants.

The drafters of ConsensusDOCS determined that it would be better for design professionals to be held to the standard imposed on them by their own profession, rather than one defined by the Agreement.[49] Obviously, the legal remedy for violation of such a standard would be an action in negligence. However, Paragraph 10.9 of ConsensusDOCS 240 appears to eliminate all remedies in tort or negligence in favor of breach of contract remedies:

> RIGHTS AND REMEDIES: The Parties' rights, liabilities, responsibilities and remedies with respect to this Agreement, whether in contract, tort, negligence or otherwise, shall be exclusively those expressly set forth in this Agreement.

Paragraph 10.9 presents a problem, since the insurance provisions of ConsensusDOCS 240 contemplate coverage for "*negligent performance of professional services.*"[50] Further, the indemnity obligations set forth in Paragraph 7.1 are drafted so as to be restricted to a party's liability for negligent errors or omissions. It appears, therefore, that despite the problematic language of Paragraph 10.9, the drafters of ConsensusDOCS 240 intended that the design professional remain liable in tort or negligence.

7.6.2 "Trust and Confidence"

Paragraph 2.2 of ConsensusDOCS 240 bears on the standard of care. It provides as follows: *The Architect/Engineer accepts the relationship of trust and confidence established by this Agreement . . . ."* This language is absent from ConsensusDOCS 245, Short Form Agreement. The terms *"trust and confidence"* might imply a fiduciary relationship[51] and thus a heightened standard of care, which could be uninsurable under the typical Professional Liability policy.

7.6.3   Qualifications of Consultants

Paragraph 3.4 of ConsensusDOCS 240 states that the Architect/Engineer *"warrants and represents"* that the Architect/Engineer and its consultants are *"duly qualified, licensed, registered and authorized by law to perform the Services under this Agreement."* This warranty might not be insurable under the typical Professional Liability insurance policy.   There is no similar guarantee or representation in AIA B101-2007 or ConsensusDOCS 245, Short Form Agreement.

7.7   Insurance

ConsensusDOCS 240[52] and ConsensusDOCS 245, Short Form Agreement,[53] require the design professional to maintain insurance. The 1997 AIA documents did not require the architect to maintain any insurance. Now, AIA B101-2007[54] requires the design professional to maintain various insurance policies.

Specifically, under all of these form agreements, the design professional must maintain four types of coverage: Commercial General Liability ("CGL"), Automobile Liability, Workers' Compensation/Employers' Liability, and Professional Liability. ConsensusDOCS 240 has fill-in-the-blank forms for the applicable limits of coverage (e.g., for CGL insurance, the parties fill in the required limits for each occurrence, the general aggregate, products/completed operations aggregate, and personal and advertising coverage[55]). ConsensusDOCS 245, Short Form Agreement, includes an exhibit in which the parties must specify the details of the required insurance.[56]

ConsensusDOCS 240 requires the Architect/Engineer's consultants to maintain CGL, Automobile Liability, and Professional Liability coverages, with companies and limits that are satisfactory to the Owner. However, there is no requirement for the consultants to carry Workers' Compensation/Employers' Liability Insurance.[57] ConsensusDOCS 245, Short Form Agreement,[58] and AIA B101-2007[59] do not require the consultants to maintain insurance.

7.7.1 Professional Liability Insurance

Subparagraphs 7.2.4, 7.2.5, and 7.2.6 of ConsensusDOCS 240 provide the following terms with respect to Professional Liability coverage, none of which appear in AIA B101-2007:

- The insurance company and limits of the Architect/Engineer's and the consultants' policies must be satisfactory to the Owner.
- The required insurance must be maintained for the number of years agreed upon by the parties (following final payment to the Architect/Engineer).
- The deductible amount must not exceed the amount specified by the parties and must be paid by the Architect/Engineer.
- The design professional must furnish certificates of insurance and a copy of its Professional Liability policy.
- The Architect/Engineer cannot cancel or modify a policy without 30 days' prior notice to the Owner (except modifications caused by claims made against the policy).
- The Architect/Engineer and its Professional Liability insurance carrier must notify the Owner within 30 days of any claims made or loss expenses incurred against the Professional Liability policy.
- The Owner has the right to directly notify the Architect/Engineer's Professional Liability insurance carrier of a claim against the policy.
- The Architect/Engineer's and consultants' Professional Liability insurance must include prior acts coverage that is sufficient for all services performed for the Project.

Since Professional Liability insurance is written on a claims-made basis, the Owner will benefit from the approach of ConsensusDOCS 240, which requires the Architect to maintain the coverage for a specified number of years following final payment to the Architect.[60] The length of time selected by the parties should be reasonable, considering the applicable statute of limitations and the nature and size of the Project.

The design professional should be aware that it may be difficult to comply with notice requirements in ConsensusDOCS 240. Specifically, that document provides that the Architect/Engineer must notify the Owner within 30 days of "*any claims made or loss expenses incurred against the Professional Liability policy.*"[61] Professional liability policies normally have eroding limits, that is, the amount of coverage is reduced by the payment of claim expenses and defense costs. ConsensusDOCS literally requires the Architect/Engineer and the insurance carrier to notify the Owner each time the design professional or its carrier makes a payment to an attorney or expert in the defense of any claim, lawsuit, or arbitration. It is also important to note that the reporting requirement applies equally to claims unrelated to the project in question. Design professionals will want to consider modifying the Agreement to eliminate or modify this notice. Obviously, the Owner has an interest in knowing whether the limits have been eroded, but probably does not need to be told when each claim expense is paid.

7.7.2   CGL Coverage

ConsensusDOCS 200, Owner-Contractor Agreement, does not require the Contractor to maintain the Owner or Architect as an additional insured on its CGL policy.[62] By comparison, AIA A201-2007, General Conditions, requires the Contractor to include the Owner, the Architect, and the Architect's consultants as additional insureds on its CGL coverage during the Contractor's operations. AIA A201-2007 also requires the Owner as an additional insured during the Contractor's completed operations.[63]

ConsensusDOCS 240[64] and AIA B101-2007[65] do not call for the design professional to carry the Owner or Contractor as an additional insured on its CGL policy, but ConsensusDOCS 245, Short Form Agreement, includes that requirement.[66]

ConsensusDOCS 240 requires the Architect/Engineer to provide contractual liability insurance for the indemnity obligation set forth in Subparagraph 7.1.1.[67] However, this may be of limited value to the Owner since CGL policies typically exclude professional services, which are normally the basis of the Owner's claims against the design professional.

7.7.3   Property Insurance

The Owner must carry property insurance under ConsensusDOCS 240[68] and 245, Short Form Agreement.[69]

Subparagraph 7.3.1 of ConsensusDOCS 240 requires the Owner to name the Architect/Engineer and its consultants as additional insureds under its property insurance and provide certificates of insurance evidencing that coverage.

ConsensusDOCS 240 states that the Owner and Architect/Engineer waive subrogation rights against each other and the Contractor, Subcontractors, and Sub-subcontractors, to the extent of the property insurance, and that the Owner and Architect/Engineer must require similar waivers from their consultants for the project.[70] The Architect/Engineer's consultants are not named as beneficiaries of the waiver, but they are probably protected from subrogation because the Owner is required to list them as named additional insureds on the property insurance policies.

7.8   Design Services

7.8.1   Evolution of the Design

ConsensusDOCS 240,[71] ConsensusDOCS 245,[72] and AIA B101-2007[73] all describe the evolution of the design in terms of Schematic Design Documents, Design Development Documents, and Construction Documents. However, ConsensusDOCS 240 includes more protection for the Owner during the design process. First, the Architect/Engineer cannot proceed with the next design phase until receiving *written* approval from the Owner.[74] The same restriction appeared in the previous AGC Document 240 (2000).[75] ConsensusDOCS 245, Short Form Agreement,[76] and AIA B101-2007[77] mandate that the Architect obtain approval of the Owner at each stage of the design, but there is no requirement for that approval to be in writing.

Second, ConsensusDOCS 240,[78] similar to the former AGC Document 240 (2000),[79] requires the Architect/Engineer to "*identify in writing for the Owner's approval all material changes and deviations that have taken place*" from the prior version of the design. That is, the Architect/Engineer must show the material changes and deviations in the Schematic Design Documents as compared to the Preliminary Estimate of the Cost of Construction and Project Schedule.[80] Similarly, the Architect/Engineer must identify in writing all material changes and deviations in the Design Development Documents as compared to the Schematic Design Documents and the previous approved estimate of the Cost of Construction and Project Schedule.[81] Finally, the same requirement is included as to the Construction Documents.[82]

ConsensusDOCS 245, Short Form Agreement, also states that the design professional must identify these changes in the Documents, but the communications need not be in writing.[83]

AIA B101-2007 only requires the Architect to submit these various design documents to the Owner, advise the Owner of any adjustments to the Cost of the Work, and request the Owner's approval.[84] It does not require the designer to identify changes and deviations, verbally or in writing. Obviously, the goal of ConsensusDOCS is to avoid misunderstandings about the scope of the project and unauthorized changes. On some projects, the task of detailing all of the changes in each set of documents could be cumbersome. The failure to fully comply with this requirement could expose the design professional to a claim that certain changes were not authorized by the Owner or that the designer did not correctly understand the Owner's directions.

7.8.2   Construction Documents - Complete Design

Contractors and design professionals frequently debate whether disputed Work is reasonably inferable from the Construction Documents. ConsensusDOCS 240 requires these Documents to *"completely describe all work necessary to bid and construct the Project."*[85] This sentence is new to the AGC family of documents; it does not appear in the former AGC Document 240 (2000). Also, it is not contained in ConsensusDOCS 245, Short Form Agreement. The AGC explains: "This effectively addresses the dilemma which Contractors have faced in recent years of having to provide Work that the Architect/Engineer might argue was 'inferred' [*sic*] by the Construction Documents."[86] In reality, it is not practical for the Construction Documents to describe every square inch of the Work. However, the stipulation in the ConsensusDOCS that the designer must *"completely describe all work necessary to bid and construct the Project"* will undoubtedly aid the Contractor in a dispute over the quality of the Documents. ConsensusDOCS 200, Owner-Contractor Agreement, appears to be contradictory, requiring the Contractor to perform Work that is *"reasonably inferable"* from the Contract Documents.[87]

The requirement of a complete design might affect the designer's defense of betterment or added value with respect to an item that was omitted from the Documents. Some courts have denied the betterment defense where the designer agreed or represented that the design would be complete.[88]

7.8.3   Green Design

In its 2007 documents, the AIA requires the Architect to discuss with the Owner the feasibility of incorporating *"environmentally responsible"* design alternatives.[89]

By comparison, ConsensusDOCS 240 and ConsensusDOCS 245, Short Form Agreement, do not require the Architect/Engineer to consider sustainability issues.

7.8.4   Owner's Consultants

Under Subparagraph 3.2.6 of ConsensusDOCS 240, the Architect/Engineer must coordinate the services "*of all design consultants for the Project, including those retained by the Owner.*" The parties must designate those consultants or attach a separate exhibit listing the names and/or disciplines of the Owner's design consultants. This duty to coordinate also appears in ConsensusDOCS 245, Short Form Agreement,[90] and was contained in the prior AGC Document 240 (2000).[91] Under the wording of ConsensusDOCS, if the Owner's consultants do not properly perform, the Owner could claim that the design professional contributed to the problem by failing to properly coordinate the services of its consultants. Thus, the design professional should carefully consider the implications of this clause.

AIA B101-2007 states: "*The Architect shall coordinate its services* with *those services provided by the Owner and the Owner's consultants.*"[92] (Emphasis added.) Coordination of the Owner's consultants is considered an Additional Service of the Architect.[93] The AIA document requires the Owner to coordinate the services of its own consultants with those provided by the Architect.[94]

7.8.5   Redesign Obligation

Under ConsensusDOCS 240, the Architect/Engineer must "*promptly revise . . . without compensation*" those documents:

- "which have not been previously approved by the Owner and to which the Owner has reasonable objections."
- "identified by Contractor and accepted by the Owner as presenting constructability problems."
- "needing revisions to reflect clarifications and assumptions and allowances on which a guaranteed maximum price is based."[95]

These provisions mirror the former version of AGC Document 240 (2000).[96] There is no parallel provision in AIA B101-2007.

ConsensusDOCS 240 establishes a duty to revise the Documents without additional compensation, but none of the scenarios is tied to a violation of the standard of care. In addition, if the Contractor claims a constructability problem and the Owner accepts the Contractor's position, the Architect/Engineer must redesign the Documents without compensation. There is no requirement that the Contractor's position be reasonable or correct.

ConsensusDOCS 245, Short Form Agreement, takes a similar approach to constructability issues:

> Architect/Engineer must promptly revise without compensation those documents which have not been approved by the Owner and to which the Owner has reasonable objections or which present constructability [sic] problems.[97]

7.8.6   The Architect/Engineer's Consultants

ConsensusDOCS 240, like the previous AGC Document 240 (2000),[98] prevents the Architect/Engineer from entering into an agreement with a consultant that includes any limitation of liability, at least without the prior written approval of the Owner.[99]   ConsensusDOCS 245, Short Form Agreement, does not contain a similar clause.

Paragraph 3.5 of ConsensusDOCS 240 also provides that the Owner *"shall be considered the intended beneficiary of the performance"* of the consultant's services, which could support a direct claim by the Owner against a consultant.[100]   Conversely, the Agreement does not provide that the consultants are intended beneficiaries of the Agreement between the Owner and Architect/Engineer.

7.9   Conclusion

The approach of ConsensusDOCS 240 is significantly different from that of the AIA documents in many respects. Although many of the salient points have been outlined in this chapter, the nuances of each project might dictate a careful review of additional provisions. It is difficult to generalize about construction projects and their participants, so it is important for owners and design professionals to independently review any contract form in light of their specific needs and project issues.

Acknowledgement: *This chapter is based on a paper presented by the authors to the ABA Forum on the Construction Industry program "Winds of Change? The ConsensusDOCS," September, 11, 2008, Chicago, Illinois.*

---

[1]   ConsensusDOCS 200, § 3.14.1.

[2]   ConsensusDOCS 200, § 9.2.1, ConsensusDOCS 240, § 3.2.8.5.

[3]   ConsensusDOCS 240, § 3.1.3.

4   ConsensusDOCS 200,§ 3.20.

5   *Compare* AIA B101-2007, §§ 3.6.2.2 and 3.6.2.3.

6   § 3.6.1.1.

7   A201-2007 § 4.2.4, B101-2007 § 5.10.

8   A201-2007 § 15.2, B101-2007 § 3.6.2.5.

9   § 3.6.1.2.

10   § 6.3.2.

11   § 3.2.8.4.

12   § 3.2.8.4.

13   § 7.1.1.

14   § 7.1.2.

15   This exclusion makes more sense with respect to a contractor's indemnity obligation since it mirrors the CGL policy, which normally excludes liability for damage to the Work itself.

16   *See* ConsensusDOCS 200, § 3.13.6.

17   § 14.

18   *See, e.g.,* B101-2007 § 7.2.

19   § 14.

20   § 3.2.10.

21   Note, however, that similar license-granting language is conspicuously absent from ConsensusDOCS 245, Short Form Agreement.

22   This language is consistent with the 1997 version of the AIA Documents and, arguably, could result in the effective and immediate revocation of the license if the Owner fails to make any payment on a timely basis, even if the Agreement itself has not been terminated.

23   ConsensusDOCS 245 §§ 8.1 and 8.2; ConsensusDOCS 240,§ 12; AIA B101-2007 §§ 9.3, 9.4, and 9.5.

24   § 10.1.2.

25   Note that termination for cause by the Architect/Engineer, due to Owner's breach of the Contract, nonetheless expressly gives the Owner the right to *"use, reproduce, and to make derivative works of the Documents to complete the Project."*

[26] Although ConsensusDOCS 240 does not specifically provide for such a *"licensing fee"* upon termination for convenience by the Owner, Paragraph 8.2 provides for a termination *"premium"* to be agreed to by the parties at the time of contracting.

[27] § 7.3.1.

[28] *Id.*

[29] § 14.

[30] § 10.1.4.

[31] *See* Article 7.

[32] § 9.1.

[33] § 9.3.

[34] § 13.1.

[35] § 9.5.

[36] §§ 9.4 and 9.5.

[37] § 9.5.1.

[38] § 13.4.

[39] Exhibit E (Dispute Resolution Menu) to AGC Document 240 (2000).

[40] § 13.2.

[41] § 9.5.

[42] § 8.3.4.2.

[43] *See* Article 13.

[44] AIA Document B101-1997 § 9.3.

[45] § 8.1.1.

[46] § 2.2.

[47] § 1.

[48] § 2.1.

[49] AGC ConsensusDOCS Guidebook, p. 6, available at http://www.agc.org.

[50] § 7.2.4.

[51] *Roberson v. Paine Webber, Inc.,* 998 P.2d 193 (Okla. App 2000). ("A fiduciary relationship springs from an attitude of trust and confidence and is based on some

form of agreement, either expressed or implied, from which it can be said the minds have met to create a mutual obligation.")

[52] § 7.2.

[53] § 4.

[54] § 2.5.

[55] § 7.2.2.

[56] § 5, Exhibit C.

[57] §§ 7.2.3 and 7.2.5.

[58] § 4.

[59] § 2.5.

[60] § 7.2.4.

[61] § 7.2.4.

[62] *See* § 10.2.1.

[63] § 11.1.4.

[64] *See* § 7.2.2.2.

[65] *See* § 2.5.

[66] § 4.

[67] § 7.2.2.2.

[68] § 7.3.1.

[69] § 7.3.

[70] § 7.3.2.

[71] §§ 3.2.3, 3.2.4 and 3.2.5.

[72] §§ 6.2.4, 6.2.5 and 6.2.6.

[73] §§ 3.2, 3.3 and 3.4.

[74] § 3.1.2.

[75] § 3.1.2.

[76] §§ 6.2.4, 6.2.5 and 6.2.6.

[77] §§ 3.2.5, 3.2.7, 3.3.3, and 3.4.5.

[78] §§ 3.2.3, 3.2.4 and 3.2.5.

[79] §§ 3.2.3, 3.2.4 and 3.2.5.

[80] § 3.2.3.

[81] § 3.2.4.

[82] § 3.2.5.

[83] §§ 6.2.4, 6.2.5 and 6.2.6.

[84] §§ 3.2.7, 3.3.3 and 3.4.5.

[85] § 3.2.5.

[86] AGC ConsensusDOCS Guidebook, p. 7, available at http://www.agc.org.

[87] § 3.1.1.

[88] *Carter v. Wolf Creek Highway Water Dist.*, 635 P.2d 1036 (Or. App. 1981), and *Skidmore, Owings & Merrill v. Intrawest I L.P.*, 1997 WL 563159 (Wash. App.) (Unpublished Opinion), *rev. den'd, Skidmore, Owings & Merrill v. Intrawest I Ltd.*, 960 P.2d 939 (Wash. 1998).

[89] §§ 3.2.3 and 3.2.5.1.

[90] § 6.2.1.

[91] § 3.2.6.

[92] § 3.1.2.

[93] § 4.1.19.

[94] § 5.6.

[95] § 3.1.2.

[96] § 3.1.2.

[97] § 6.1.2.

[98] § 3.5.

[99] § 3.5.

[100] AGC Document 240 (2000) contained the same provision at § 3.5.

Chapter 8

The 2007 EJCDC Construction Contract Documents

Hugh N. Anderson, Esq.

8.1 Introduction: The Engineers Joint Contract Documents Committee

The Engineers Joint Contract Documents Committee (EJCDC) publishes standard contract documents that are used for design and construction of public and private infrastructure projects throughout the United States. In 2007, EJCDC issued a new version of its standard construction contract documents (the EJCDC C-Series). This chapter describes the EJCDC C-Series; presents the highlights of the 2007 revisions; and analyzes two construction contract provisions that are important to design professionals who use the EJCDC construction documents on their clients' projects.

The four EJCDC sponsoring organizations are the American Council of Engineering Companies (ACEC), the American Society of Civil Engineers (ASCE), the Associated General Contractors of America (AGC), and the National Society of Professional Engineers (NSPE). According to the Committee's Mission Statement, the three engineering societies formed EJCDC to "develop and endorse quality contract documents and encourage their use through education and promotion." The Associated General Contractors of America (AGC), a major trade organization representing U.S. construction contractors, actively contributed to drafting the EJCDC construction-related documents for over 20 years, and then in 2003 became a sponsoring EJCDC organization.

The EJCDC documents are drafted with the active participation of representatives of the four sponsoring organizations (engineers and contractors), together with   public owners; risk managers; professional liability insurers; surety and insurance experts; construction lawyers; various professional societies; and construction managers. The EJCDC documents are principally intended for use on public and private infrastructure projects designed by engineers, including water and wastewater treatment and conveyance facilities; utility work; solid waste handling and disposal facilities; highway and bridge projects; production, power, and processing facilities; site development work; environmental remediation projects; street, curb, and gutter work; tunneling and excavating projects; and similar applications.

8.1.1   The EJCDC Documents – Overview

The Construction Series is one of five principal EJCDC standard contract document series:

- Engineering (professional services) (E-Series)
- Construction (C-Series)
- Design-Build (D-Series)
- Procurement (major equipment purchase) (P-Series)
- Environmental Remediation (R-Series)

8.1.2   EJCDC's Mission

EJCDC's overall mission is to develop, publish, and maintain high-quality standard design and construction contract documents; to promote the use of the documents in the engineering profession and construction industry; and to provide guidance and information to users of the documents. EJCDC strives to identify, acknowledge, and fairly allocate risks, using a balanced approach that assigns a specific risk to the party best able to manage and control that risk. EJCDC's publications are intended to be objective and fair to all parties; to recognize and respect the separate interests, capabilities, and roles of those parties; and to contribute to the continual improvement of professional engineering services and construction contracting practices throughout the United States.

8.2   EJCDC – E-500 Standard Professional Service Contract

The Engineers Joint Contract Documents Committee (EJCDC) has issued the 2008 edition of its standard professional services contract, EJCDC

E-500, Agreement between Owner and Engineer for Professional Services. The new document replaces the 2002 edition of E-500 and is now available for purchase.

The 2008 edition of EJCDC E-500 maintains the solid base of terms and conditions found in prior editions of this flagship document, while making carefully considered changes that enhance clarity and reflect current design and construction-phase engineering practices. Highlights of the 2008 EJCDC E-500 are discussed below.

8.2.1 Safety

EJCDC has revised the Agreement to provide that the Owner must inform Engineer of specific safety requirements that Engineer must follow at the project site. In most cases, Engineer's compliance with Owner's and construction contractor's safety rules will be a basic included service. If a safety requirement is added after the effective date of the Agreement, and is more extensive than typically required, then compliance will be treated as an additional service.

8.2.2 Owner's Policies and Procedures

The new E-500 clarifies that to the extent that the Owner has policies or procedures that apply to the professional services to be rendered by Engineer (for example, required procedures for drafting and organizing specifications, or for reviewing contractor payment applications), such policies and procedures are to be provided to Engineer prior to entry into the Agreement. This will allow the parties to account in the pricing of Engineer's services for any costs associated with compliance with the policies and procedures. E-500 also notes that Engineer is required to comply with such policies and procedures only to the extent that doing so is not contrary to professional practice requirements.

8.2.3 Insurance

Because most design engineers do not provide insurance advice as part of their professional practices, the EJCDC documents provide that as between the Owner and Engineer, the Owner (presumably through its risk managers, attorneys, brokers, and other insurance advisers) must take responsibility for making insurance decisions, such as setting required policy limits—see EJCDC C-051, Engineer's Letter to Owner Requesting Instructions Concerning Bonds and Insurance. EJCDC has therefore added a provision to E-500 emphasizing that Engineer's services do not include providing insurance or bonding advice to Owner, or enforcing insurance-related requirements of the Owner's construction contract.   Also, the new edition lists the insurance coverages that Owner must require from the construction contractor (workers' compensation, commercial general liability, property damage, and motor vehicle damage), rather than merely cross-referencing the requirements set out in the EJCDC standard construction general conditions (EJCDC C-700).

8.2.4   Indemnification

Project owners typically require that engineers contractually indemnify them with respect to negligence that results in personal injury or damage to the property of others. It is less common for owners to provide the same indemnification to the engineer, often for public or corporate policy reasons, or based on the position that an owner's less active role in the design and construction reduces the call for such an indemnification. To be consistent with common practice, EJCDC has structured its indemnification provisions such that the Engineer's indemnification of Owner is a standard clause, and the Owner's indemnification of Engineer is an option that may be selected when appropriate for a particular project.

8.2.5   Definitions

The previous edition of E-500 incorporated many standard definitions from the EJCDC construction general conditions (EJCDC C-700) by reference. The 2008 edition contains the actual definitions, so the user does not need to refer to a second document to confirm a definition.

8.2.6   Certification against Corrupt and Collusive Practices

As part of an international initiative to improve procurement practices, the 2008 E-500 requires the Engineer to certify that it has not engaged in corrupt, fraudulent, collusive, or coercive practices with respect to obtaining the contract.   Other EJCDC documents contain similar requirements with respect to construction procurement.

8.2.7   Contested Invoices

The new document requires that if the Owner contests an invoice from the Engineer and withholds payment of all or a portion of the invoiced amount, then the Owner promptly must inform Engineer of the specific basis for doing so.

8.2.8 Review of Substitution Requests and Submittals

The Engineer's basic services are expanded to include the review of routine substitution and "or equal" requests made during the bidding process, if such requests are allowed by the instructions to bidders. The 2008 E-500 further provides that if it is necessary for the Engineer to conduct an excessive number of substitution or "or-equal" requests (whether submitted during the contractor selection process, or during the construction process), or review a shop drawing submittal more than three times, then the excess reviews will be treated as an additional engineering service.

8.2.9 Rejection of Defective Work

The previous edition of E-500 required the Engineer to identify defective work and recommend to the Owner that the Owner reject the defective work. Recognizing common construction practice, as described in current and past EJCDC standard general conditions, and the common expectation of the Owner that the Engineer is the party best positioned to identify and administer the rejection of defective work, the 2008 edition provides the Engineer with the authority to reject defective work directly, and further clarifies the standards under which work would be deemed defective.

8.2.10 Mediation

If a dispute between the Owner and the Engineer is mediated, the mediation process is expressly noted to be confidential, and must be conducted within 120 days.

8.2.11 Additional Services

The scope of services sections have been reorganized to clarify which services are basic, included responsibilities and which are additional services and thus entitled to compensation under the specific provisions for additional services. The modifications should allow for better pricing and budgeting for all parties.

8.2.12   Estimated Engineering Costs

Expanded discussion of the Owner's options when compensation for engineering services is estimated, not fixed, and costs approach the estimate prior to completion of services.

Beginning in 2009, EJCDC will also issue revised editions of its other professional services documents, including the standard master agreement (EJCDC E-505, Agreement between Owner and Engineer for Professional Services, Task Order Edition), the short form (EJCDC E-520), and various professional services subagreements, as well as a narrative guide to using the EJCDC Engineering Series documents.

8.3   Development and Content of the Construction Series

The EJCDC Construction Series (C-Series) is comprised (as of 2007) of twenty-one documents for use in establishing and administering the contractual relationships between a project owner and a construction contractor. The documents are premised on a traditional design-bid-build method of project delivery, with the design professional (Engineer) as an independent third party retained by the project owner. It is possible to revise the standard construction documents to reflect a negotiated procurement or other variations on the design-bid-build premise.

Legal and legislative developments are considered during the process of drafting and updating the documents. The C-Series documents are coordinated internally and among themselves in their use of terminology and allocation of responsibilities, and are also consistent with other EJCDC documents, including the owner-engineer agreements of the Engineering Series. The C-Series documents also serve an important administrative function by establishing practical, orderly, and standard procedures for bidding, contract formation, commencement of construction, progress payments, claims, completion of the project, and many other routine yet vital elements of the construction process.

The 21 Construction Series documents consist of the following:

- Narrative Guide, C-001

- Documents for initiating the selection and contracting processes:
    - C-050 (Bidding Procedures and Construction Contract Documents)
    - C-051 (Engineer's Letter To Owner Requesting Instructions Concerning Bonds And Insurance)

- C-052 (Owner's Instructions To Engineer Concerning Bonds And Insurance)

- Bidding-phase documents:
  - C-200 (Suggested Instructions To Bidders For Construction Contracts)
  - C-410 (Suggested Bid Form For Construction Contracts)
  - C-430 (Bid Bond – Penal Sum Form)
  - C-435 (Bid Bond – Damages Form)
  - C-510 (Notice of Award)

- Owner-Contractor Agreement Forms:
  - C-520 (Suggested Form of Agreement Between Owner and Contractor for Construction Contract (Stipulated Price))
  - C-525 (Suggested Form of Agreement Between Owner and Contractor for Construction Contract (Cost-Plus))

- Contract Commencement Documents:
  - C-550 (Notice to Proceed)
  - C-610 (Performance Bond)
  - C-615 (Payment Bond)

- Contract Terms and Conditions:
  - C-700 (Standard General Conditions of the Construction Contract)
  - C-800 (Guide to the Preparation of Supplementary Conditions)

- Contract Administration Forms:
  - C-620 (Contractor's Application for Payment)
  - C-625 (Certificate of Substantial Completion)
  - C-940 (Work Change Directive)
  - C-941 (Change Order)
  - C-942 (Field Order)

To obtain the most recent editions of these forms, guides, and other documents, please refer to EJCDC's webpage at www.ejcdc.org, or to one of the following websites of the sponsoring organizations:

- www.nspe.org
- www.agc.org

- www.acec.org
- www.asce.org

8.4   The 2007 Edition of the Construction Series

The 2007 EJCDC Construction series maintains the solid base of forms, terms, and conditions found in prior editions, while making carefully considered changes that enhance clarity and reflect current construction contracting practices. Highlights of the 2007 Construction series are the following:

- *Safety:* EJCDC's Standard General Conditions (EJCDC C-700) are revised to specify the responsibility of the Contractor to inform Owner and its Engineer of specific safety requirements that must be followed at the site, and the corresponding obligation of Owner and Engineer to comply with such requirements. Contractor is also required to comply with any applicable Owner safety programs. The new documents also expressly state that the site safety responsibilities that are contractually allocated to Contractor do not reduce the safety duties of subcontractors at the site. The subcontractor's duties must be determined by reference to the specific terms of the subcontract; EJCDC does not publish a standard subcontract.

- *Site Conditions:* The EJCDC approach to site conditions is explored in depth below.

- *Progress Payment Applications:* EJCDC's payment application form, EJCDC C-620, is for the first time provided in a spreadsheet format allowing for ease of use and accurate calculations of totals.

- *Insurance:* The insurance provisions of the Standard General Conditions (C-700) are updated to reflect changes in insurance terminology. Because most design engineers lack insurance expertise, the 2007 documents also confirm that as between the Owner and Engineer, the Owner (presumably through its risk managers, attorneys, brokers, and other insurance advisers) must take responsibility for making insurance decisions such as setting required policy limits—see EJCDC C-051, Engineer's Letter to Owner Requesting Instructions Concerning Bonds and Insurance.

- *Reporting Discrepancies in Design:* Contractor's duty is specified to be limited to reporting errors or conflicts in the specifications and drawings only if Contractor had actual knowledge of such discrepancies. 2007 Standard General Conditions (EJCDC C-700).

- *Bid Form:* The Suggested Bid Form (EJCDC C-410) has been made more user-friendly by eliminating the requirement that prices be stated in words—as of 2007 numeric figures are sufficient.

- *Certification against Corrupt and Collusive Practices:* At the request of The American Society of Civil Engineers (one of EJCDC's four sponsoring organizations), the 2007 Suggested Bid Form (EJCDC C-410) and Owner-Contractor Agreement Forms (EJCDC C-520, Stipulated Price; EJCDC C-525, Cost-Plus) require bidders and Contractors to certify that they have not engaged in corrupt, fraudulent, collusive, or coercive practices with respect to obtaining the contract.

- *Expanded Commentary:* EJCDC provides extensive commentary on use of the new documents in its Narrative Guide to the 2007 Construction Documents (EJCDC C-001). EJCDC has also expanded and revised the numerous notes to users that are interspersed throughout the text of various documents, including the Suggested Instructions to Bidders, Suggested Bid Form, Suggested Owner-Contractor Agreement Forms, and Guide to the Preparation of Supplementary Conditions (EJCDC C-800).

- *On-line Access to Supplementary Conditions:* EJCDC and its sponsoring organizations are providing free public access to the 2007 Guide to the Preparation of Supplementary Conditions (C-800) at their websites. From time to time, as the need arises, EJCDC will update this document to include more options for modifying the 2007 Standard General Conditions (EJCDC C-700).

8.5   Analysis of Two EJCDC Construction Contract Topics of Importance to Design Professionals

8.5.1. Site Conditions

Infrastructure projects are predominantly horizontal in nature. As a result, the intersection of the designed facilities with the ground below is typically of critical importance to the pricing and successful construction of the project. The risks and costs associated with encountering an unexpected subsurface condition may be allocated in a variety of ways.   The EJCDC General Conditions address the issues associated with underground construction in detail, using a risk allocation approach that is consistent with typical practices for engineered projects.   Other approaches are possible – there is no single simple answer to this challenging construction contract question.

The Site Conditions provisions are important to design professionals in two respects.   First, the design professional must understand the Owner's obligation to furnish certain information regarding the site, and to identify the technical information that the Contractor may rely on in establishing its price to perform the work, and in conducting construction. In most cases, the design professional will play a significant part in assisting the Owner in carrying out these obligations.   Second, the design professional must understand how to administer the site conditions clause if the contractor contends that it has encountered differing site conditions. A summary of the EJCDC approach may be helpful to an understanding of the complex provisions on this subject matter.

The 2007 Suggested Instructions to Bidders (EJCDC C-200), Suggested Bid Form (EJCDC C-410), and Suggested Owner-Contractor Agreement Forms (EJCDC C-520, Stipulated Price; EJCDC C-525, Cost-Plus) provide that contractors must take into consideration not only information furnished by the Owner but also their own actual knowledge of site conditions, and information commonly known about local conditions. The EJCDC position that owners should not typically require bidders to conduct their own subsurface testing is addressed in the Suggested Instructions.

8.5.2   Disclosing Site Information

The General Conditions and related documents (Suggested Instructions to Bidders, EJCDC C-200, and Guide to Preparation of Supplementary Conditions, EJCDC C-800) were revised in 2007 to state that the Owner will provide the Contractor with all known reports and drawings of site conditions, rather than merely providing reports and drawings relied on by the engineer in preparation of the design, which was the extent of the disclosure duty in previous editions of the documents.   The broader contractual disclosure commitment is intended to reflect prevailing caselaw holding owners responsible for full disclosure of information in their custody.   The revised disclosure provision also recognizes that the construction contractor may be interested in reviewing existing site information that was not important to the engineer in making design decisions.

The EJCDC documents contemplate that the Owner will inform prospective contractors of the identity of all reports known to the Owner of tests and explorations of subsurface conditions at or contiguous to the Site, and of all drawings known to the Owner of physical conditions related to existing surface or subsurface structures at the site (other than Underground Facilities discussed below). These known documents would include reports and drawings from the Owner's property files and facility records, as well as documents prepared or obtained by the Owner's Engineer during the planning and design of the current project. In paragraph 4.02.B of the General Conditions, the Contractor is entitled to rely on the accuracy of the "technical data" contractually identified by the Owner as being reliable, but not on non-technical data, interpretations, or opinions contained in the identified documents. In most cases, the Owner will delegate to the design professional the important task of identifying the reliable technical data through drafting of the bidding documents and supplementary conditions.

The EJCDC documents make clear that the Contractor may not assume that the documents that are furnished regarding site conditions are complete or sufficiently all-inclusive to provide the Contractor with all the information the Contractor needs for its construction purposes, particularly with respect to the particular means and methods and unique procedures of construction that the Contractor intends to use to do the Work. Any conclusion or interpretation that the Contractor draws from such documents is at its own risk.

The known documents are specifically indicated as "not Contract Documents" in order to overcome any possible claim that by implication such data was made available for reliance by the Contractor, when in fact it was made available in the interests of full, open disclosure, and to avoid any contention that relevant information had been withheld. Such documents will be made available on request under terms stated in the Instructions to Bidders. Another reason they are "not Contract Documents" is that they most likely will include outdated, unverified, and otherwise unreliable data. The Owner and Engineer most likely are not willing to assume responsibility for the accuracy of such data, nor are they willing to permit the Contractor to rely on it. Stating that such documents are specifically "not Contract Documents" will not, however, prejudice or defeat the Contractor's basic right to rely on expressly identified "technical data" contained in the documents.

The meaning and application of the term "technical data" undoubtedly will vary by project. Consequently, it is important for the design professional (Engineer) to assist the Owner in determining and establishing those portions of the reports of tests and explorations of subsurface conditions and those parts of the drawings of physical conditions that are "technical data" on which the Contractor will be entitled to rely. Examples of what might be considered "technical data" in such reports are: the boring method, plan, and logs; level of subsurface water; laboratory test methods and results; and similar factual data, all as of the dates made. As a general rule, all the factual information contained in <u>drawings</u> of physical conditions related to existing surface or subsurface structures (other than Underground Facilities) which are at the Site will usually qualify as "technical data" on which the Contractor should be entitled to rely. However, if reliance on such drawings is to be limited, the Owner should clearly identify in the Supplementary Conditions the information or data (such as comments or opinions) contained in or part of such drawings on which bidders, and after award the Contractor, may not rely. It should be understood that severely limiting the scope of information on which bidders and the Contractor may rely may require the bidders to assume additional risks which may in turn be reflected by higher bids.

Note that the General Conditions (paragraph 4.02) and the above discussion are based on the premise that some subsurface information exists. If no such data exists, the Instruction to Bidders and Supplementary Conditions should so note. See paragraph 4.02 of the supplementary conditions for suggested language.

8.5.3 Site Visits and Testing

During the bidding or negotiation phase, the Owner should have required prospective contractors to visit the site to become familiar with and satisfied as to the general, local, and site conditions that may affect cost, progress, performance, and furnishing of the Work. This should lead to an alert, heads-up, eyes-open, reasonable examination of the area and the conditions under which the Work is to be performed (see GC-4.03). It is expected that any special requirements for such examination will be set forth in the Instructions to Bidders (see article 4 of the Instructions and related Notes to User) or elsewhere in the Contract Documents if the contract is to be awarded on the basis of negotiation rather than after receipt of bids. The extent of such an examination will depend on the specifics of the job and the site as well as Owner's preference. EJCDC believes, however, that the requirements for any such pre-bid site examination should be realistic and clearly stated, and that detailed site and subsurface investigations should ordinarily not be required because of their cost, the constraints of time, insurance and liability concerns, and other practical considerations.

8.5.4 Administration of the Differing Site Conditions Clause

Paragraphs 4.03.A and 4.03.B of the General Conditions provide that when Contractor encounters an unanticipated subsurface or physical condition, Contractor is to notify Owner and Engineer if the revealed or discovered condition is of such a nature as to indicate that either (1) "technical data" on which reliance was permitted is inaccurate, (2) a change in the Contract Documents is required, (3) the condition differs materially from that shown or indicated in the Contract Documents, or (4) the actual condition is of an unusual nature and differs materially from conditions ordinarily encountered and generally recognized as inherent in Work of the character provided for in the Contract Documents. The Work in connection with the differing condition is then to stop and the Contractor may not further disturb such condition. The Engineer is to evaluate the situation and decide if a change in the Contract Documents is necessary to adapt to the actual conditions as discovered or revealed.

The third and fourth DSC triggers in EJCDC's clause are similar to the Type 1 and Type 2 differing site conditions recognized in federal statutes and in many states. The first and second triggers reflect the importance that EJCDC places on providing contractors with reliable technical data and on ensuring the integrity and soundness of the completed facility.

Under paragraph 4.03.C of the General Conditions, the rights of the Contractor and Owner to an adjustment in price or time because of the differing conditions are set out with the result that the Owner or Contractor is entitled to relief similar in most situations to that provided in the Federal Acquisition Regulations. The Contractor's entitlement to relief will be denied if the Contractor knew of the condition prior to formation of the contract, or if the condition should have been discovered during a reasonable pre-contract site visit, pursuant to specific terms to that effect.

The language of the Instructions to Bidders is closely coordinated with that of General Conditions. Also, in the Suggested Bid form language and the Owner-Contractor Agreements (see Article 8 of the Stipulated Price Agreement), Contractor is required to represent that such investigations, explorations, and studies with respect to subsurface and physical conditions at or contiguous to the Site have been made (in addition to those identified in the Contract Documents) to the extent necessary to enable the Contractor to do the Work at the Contract Price, within the Contract Times, and in accordance with the other terms and conditions of the Contract Documents.

Thus, a change in the General Conditions may well require change in these other documents.

8.5.5   Underground Facilities

The EJCDC General Conditions include a specific approach to underground facilities (existing utilities), as distinct from site conditions generally. Information regarding such utilities will often come from third parties, without verification by the Owner or Engineer during the design phase. The Contractor is given substantial responsibility for confirming the actual location of existing utilities and coordinating the work with the owners of such utilities, and presumably the Contractor includes the expected cost of those processes in the contract price. At the same time, the standard terms allocate to the Owner the risk that an underground facility either was not shown or indicated at all, or was not shown or indicated with reasonable accuracy. Contractor is entitled to a change in contract price and contract completion time to the extent necessitated by the inaccurate depiction of the underground facility.

Chapter 9

Contracting for Integrated Project Delivery: The AIA Documents

Suzanne H. Harness, Esq., AIA

9.1   Introduction

Over the last several years, observers of the construction industry have documented waste and inefficiency in the way buildings are designed, constructed, and maintained. Among other things, the industry has been slow to adopt new technologies. A 2004 National Institute of Standards and Technology study estimated that lack of interoperability among software programs cost the industry $15.8B annually. Fortunately, not all the news is bad. The United Kingdom's Office of Government Commerce (UKOGC) estimates that up to 30% may be saved in the cost of construction where integrated teams promote continuous improvement over a series of construction projects. UKOGC further estimates that single projects employing integrated supply teams can achieve savings of 2-10% in the cost of construction.

To encourage the U.S. construction industry to establish the kind of integrated teams that can increase efficiency and reduce waste, the American Institute of Architects (AIA) began taking steps in 2007 to introduce a new method for delivering design and construction projects: Integrated Project Delivery (IPD). Described more fully in *Integrated Project Delivery: A Guide* ("IPD Guide" or "the Guide"), this new method integrates people, systems, and practices from the very beginning of the project. Written jointly by the AIA's Documents Committee and AIA California Council, the IPD Guide sets forth several IPD principles and provides a roadmap, by project phase, for achieving those principles. The IPD Guide is free for download at www.aia.org/ipdg.

Building on the foundation of the IPD Guide, the AIA released in 2008 standard form contract documents for use on IPD projects. The documents take two different approaches. The first approach, called the transitional forms, or A295 family, provides an easy transition from traditional project delivery to IPD. The second approach, the Single Purpose Entity, fully implements IPD principles.

To address software interoperability concerns and to advance the sharing of digital information, the AIA launched in early 2007 two standard form contract documents: E201–2007™, Digital Data Protocol Exhibit; and C106™–2007, Digital Data Licensing Agreement. Those documents take the "fear factor" out of information sharing by allowing the project team to identify how, and in what file format, team members may transmit and use digital information across a project. To provide the project team the tools needed to manage the use of Building Information Modeling throughout the entire life of a project, the AIA published E202™–2008, Building Information Modeling Exhibit.

9.2   Integrated Project Delivery: A Guide

The AIA provided the IPD Guide in late 2007 not only to educate the industry about IPD but also, and primarily, to assist owners, designers, and builders in moving toward more integrated delivery models. Generally, the Guide identifies the characteristics of IPD and provides information about how to utilize IPD methods. It begins with introductory material that sets out and explains the principles of IPD and the issues that the project team must consider on an IPD project. The Guide then provides specific information about how to implement IPD, including descriptions of contractual arrangements. It culminates with a discussion of how to apply IPD principles to the project delivery models commonly used in the design and construction industry today.

As defined in the IPD Guide, IPD is a project delivery approach that integrates people, systems, business structures, and practices into a process that collaboratively harnesses the talents and insights of all participants to optimize project results, increase value to the owner, reduce waste, and maximize efficiency through all phases of design, fabrication, and construction. More fully described in the Guide, IPD principles include the following:

- Mutual respect and trust

- Mutual benefit and reward
- Collaborative innovation and decision-making
- Early involvement of key participants
- Early goal definition
- Intensified planning
- Open communication
- Appropriate technology
- Committed organization and leadership

IPD is not a rigid formula, but a process that project participants can follow in more than one way. IPD principles can be applied to a variety of contractual arrangements, and those contracts can include parties beyond the traditional trio of owner, architect, and contractor. Highly effective collaboration within the project team is a hallmark of IPD. Collaboration with the construction contractor commences early in design and continues throughout construction, thus distinguishing integrated projects from those delivered using traditional, linear processes where the contractor is selected at the completion of the design phase. IPD teams implement transparent processes, share information openly, and utilize full technological resources. When all IPD principles are employed, IPD contracts allow the project team to make decisions jointly and share risk and reward in an environment where assigning blame to others is counter-productive to individual success. In this all-for-one and one-for-all environment, project team members are motivated to solve problems quickly and collectively.

It's clear that IPD models require trust and mutual respect, attributes not always found on projects delivered traditionally. While some IPD principles may appear aspirational and out of reach, they provide the opportunity to design, build, and operate buildings as efficiently as possible, and thereby improve the productivity of the entire construction industry.

9.3   Exchanging Digital Data

The AIA was the first in the industry to advance the sharing of digital information when it launched E201–2007, Digital Data Protocol Exhibit, and C106–2007, Digital Data Licensing Agreement. These documents addressed a growing concern in the design and construction industry: transmitting data in a digital working environment and maintaining control over its future use. E201–2007 and C106–2007 address this concern by allowing contracting parties to share digital data in accordance with agreed-upon protocols for the transmission, format, and use of the data.

Architects, engineers, and other design professionals often rely upon Draconian disclaimer notices to ensure that drawings and other documents delivered in a digital format are not infringed upon or misused. To protect the sender's perceived risk of data degradation and downstream software incompatibility, as well as any unintended reliance on the accuracy of the information, these notices often disclaim any responsibility for errors or omissions in the data and forbid the receiving party's reliance on it. Instead, these notices require falling back to a printed paper record as the only true representation. These notices may serve to protect risk, but they also provide a significant barrier to the efficient design and construction of buildings in a digital age.

E201–2007 and C106–2007 take an entirely different approach that responds to the needs of both the party sending the data and the one receiving it. The party who receives the data should be not be saddled with concerns that the data may infringe a third party's copyright. For that reason, the transmitting party in both AIA digital data documents warrants that it is the copyright owner of the digital data, or has permission from the copyright owner to transmit the digital data for use on the project. Similarly, if the transmitting party is sending confidential information, the transmitting party warrants that it is authorized to do so. Because the receiving party needs to use the data to perform its work on the project, C106–2007 and E201–2007 do not forbid reliance on the data or disclaim responsibility for errors or omissions in the content; however, under certain circumstances parties may limit uses of the data by insertions in the Permitted Uses column of E201–2007, or in Article 3 of C106–2007.

The party sending data has two primary concerns: (1) the receiving party may, without permission, use the data on a different project than the one for which it was intended, and (2) the receiving party's alterations to the data, or unlicensed use of the data, may result in the sending party's involvement in a claim or dispute. To address those concerns, both AIA digital data documents specifically limit the receiving party's use, modification, and further transmission of the data to the design and construction of the project, in accordance with the terms of the project protocols in E201–2007 or the license conditions in C106–2007. Additionally, to the fullest extent permitted by law, the receiving party indemnifies and defends the transmitting party from and against all claims arising from or related to the receiving party's modification to, or unlicensed use of, the digital data.

Because these two documents require parties to identify the data transferred, to agree upon software formats and permitted uses, to warrant the right to transmit, and to indemnify for improper use, using C106 and E201 should eliminate most of the fear associated with information sharing and allow for more efficient use of digital data on the project.

9.3.1 AIA Document C106–2007, Digital Data Licensing Agreement

C106–2007 provides a licensing agreement for two parties who otherwise do not have a licensing agreement relating to the use and transmission of digital data on a design and construction project. AIA standard form agreements for design services and construction already include license provisions. These licenses, from consultant to architect and architect to owner, permit the owner to use the architect's and consultant's instruments of service, including the drawings and specifications, to construct the project. Under A201–2007 General Conditions of the Contract for Construction, the owner grants the further right to the contractor, subcontractor, sub-subcontractors, and material or equipment suppliers to use and reproduce the instruments of service provided to them solely and exclusively for execution of the work. Due to this existing chain of licenses, parties operating under unmodified AIA agreements do not need to execute C106–2007 and should consider using E201–2007, discussed below.

Design professionals may consider using C106–2007 under the following hypothetical circumstances: (1) a new building owner wishes to use the original architect's, or a consultant's, instruments of service to modify the building; or (2) a client-owner may wish its architect to distribute portions of the architect's instruments of service to a contractor or consultant for a use where architect will not be involved. As the circumstances in each case would be unique, the transmitting party may qualify the license granted in C106–2007 with respect to data format, transmission, and permitted uses. Where the design professional's intellectual property will be used without its involvement, the design professional may wish to add an indemnity to the license conditions in C106–2007 at Article 3.

Some or all of the transmitted digital data, such as the design professional's instruments of service, may be subject to copyright protection. C106–2007 allows the party transmitting the data to (1) grant the receiving party a limited non-exclusive license for the receiving party's use of digital data on a specific project, (2) set forth procedures for transmitting the data, and (3) place restrictions on the license granted. Additionally, C106–2007 allows the transmitting party to assess a licensing fee for the receiving party's use of the digital data.

9.3.2   AIA Document E201–2007, Digital Data Protocol Exhibit

When updating A201 General Conditions of the Contract for Construction for its release in 2007, the AIA recognized that the documents in the A201 family needed to address digital practice. The AIA quickly concluded, however, that adapting the text of each standard form agreement to suit digital processes was not realistic due to varying practices from project to project. In 2007, some projects used fully digital processes, many still used only paper, and most used a little of both. To respect the unique situation of each project, the AIA created a digital data protocol exhibit that contracting parties may incorporate into any agreement and modify to suit the specialized needs of the project. Because the exhibit is incorporated into the agreement, its terms are binding on the contracting parties. The exhibit may be used to standardize transmission methods and data formats across an entire project because it requires that each party incorporate the exhibit into all other agreements for design or construction for the project.

A Project Protocol Table in E201–2007 allows parties to determine the transmission method, data format, and permitted uses for a customizable list of the data to be transmitted throughout the design and construction phases. The Project Protocol Table contains a pre-printed list of digital data types in the first column, such as agendas, requests for information, and types of drawings. This list is merely a suggestion and should be modified to meet the needs of the project. The other column headings in the table identify essential categories of information: data format, transmission method, and permitted uses, as well as the identities of the transmitting and receiving parties.

To identify digital data, the parties should first consider identifying phases or activities in the project schedule when digital data may be exchanged. After listing the data, the parties may insert the required data format, transmitting party, required transmission method, receiving party, permitted uses, and any clarifying notes that are applicable to each data type. A portion of the Project Protocol Table, as it appears in E201–2007, is reproduced below.

ARTICLE 3 PROJECT PROTOCOL TABLE

§ 3.1 The parties agree to comply with the data formats, transmission methods and permitted uses set forth in the Project Protocol Table below when transmitting or using Digital Data on the Project.

(Complete the Project Protocol Table by entering information in the spaces below. Adapt the table to the needs of the Project by adding, deleting or modifying the listed Digital Data as necessary. Use Section 3.2 Project Protocol Table Definitions to define abbreviations placed, and to record notes indicated, in the Project Protocol Table.)

Digital Data	Data Format	Transmitting Party	Transmission Method	Receiving Party	Permitted Uses	Notes *(Enter #)*
3.1.1 Project Agreements and Modifications						
3.1.2 Project communications						
General communications						
Meeting notices					1	
Agendas						
Minutes						
Requests for information						
Other:						

Unintended uses of the data may be controlled by insertions in the Permitted Uses column of the table. In that column, the receiving party's usage rights in a listed data item may be restricted. To avoid confusion and misunderstandings, parties should discuss those restrictions prior to executing their agreements. Because entries in the table could conflict with provisions in the underlying agreement into which E201–2007 is incorporated, the exhibit specifically states that it takes priority over the agreement.

The Project Protocol Table Definitions section serves as a legend or key to define any terms or abbreviations used in the Project Protocol Table. It also provides a location to place explanatory notes that correspond to numbered entries in the Notes column of the table. Abbreviations pre-printed in the Project Protocol Table Definitions section are also merely suggestions and should to be modified to meet the needs of the project. A portion of the Project Protocol Table Definitions is reproduced below.

§3.2 PROJECT PROTOCOL TABLE DEFINITIONS
(Below are suggested abbreviations and definitions. Delete, modify or add as necessary.)

Data Format:
(Provide required data format, including software version.)
W   .doc, Microsoft® Word 2002

Transmitting Party:
O   Owner
A   Architect
C   Contractor

Transmission Method:
EM   Via e-mail
EMA   As an attachment to an e-mail transmission
CD   Delivered via Compact Disk
PS   Posted to Project Web site
FTP   FTP transfer to receiving FTP server

As explained briefly above, AIA agreements, including those outside of the A201 family, such as those in the 2004 Design-Build family, provide a chain of licenses that protect a design professional's intellectual property rights and, simultaneously, allow for using the designer's intellectual property to design and construct the project. Because these licenses already exist in AIA agreements, E201–2007 does not itself provide a license. Therefore, a party transmitting digital data under E201–2007 does not convey to the recipient any rights in the data itself (including the right to use, modify or further transmit the data), or in the software used to generate it. If those rights exist, they are found in the license provisions in the agreement into which the exhibit is incorporated, or in a separate license agreement such as C106–2007, Digital Data Licensing Agreement, discussed above.

9.4   Building Information Modeling

In late 2008, the AIA introduced E202–2008, Building Information Modeling Protocol Exhibit, to provide the contractual structure needed to manage the use of three-dimensional digital models. Like E201–2007, E202–2008 is not a stand-alone agreement, but is an exhibit to attach to any agreement for design services or construction on a project where the project team will use Building Information Modeling (BIM). To ensure consistency of BIM protocols and procedures across the project, parties executing E202 agree to incorporate it into any other agreement for services or construction on the project.

The AIA defines a Building Information Model (the Model) as a digital representation of the physical and functional characteristics of the project. BIM is defined as the process and technology used to create the Model. As a technology and process, BIM usage is not limited to any particular project delivery method. For that reason, the E202–2008 BIM exhibit may be incorporated into agreements used with any project delivery method.

E202's Article 1 provides general provisions and common definitions. Article 2 covers the protocols for file formats and standards, model management responsibilities, model ownership, conflict resolution, storage, viewing, and archiving. Article 3 establishes five progressively detailed levels of Model development and the authorized uses associated with each level of development. A Model Element Table at Section 4.3 divides a Model into component elements, using the Construction Specifications Institute's Uniformat™ system. Using the table, parties may assign Model element authorship by project phase, and specify the level of development that each Model element must achieve at the completion of each project phase. A portion of the Model Element Table is reproduced below:

§ 4.3 Model Element Table
Identify (1) the LOD required for each Model Element at the end of each phase, and (2) the Model Element Author (MEA) responsible for developing the Model Element to the LOD identified.

Insert abbreviations for each MEA identified in the table below, such as "A – Architect," or "C – Contractor."

NOTE: LODs must be adapted for the unique characteristics of each Project.

Model Elements Utilizing CSI UniFormat™				LOD	MEA	LOD	MEA	LOD	MEA	LOD	MEA	LOD	MEA	LOD	MEA	Note Number (See 4.4)
A SUBSTRUCTURE	A10 Foundations	A1010	Standard Foundations													
		A1020	Special Foundations													
		A1030	Slab on Grade													
	A20 Basement Construction	A2010	Basement Excavation													
		A2020	Basement Walls													
B SHELL	B10 Superstructure	B1010	Floor Construction													
		B1020	Roof Construction													
	B20 Exterior Enclosure	B2010	Exterior Walls													
		B2020	Exterior Windows													
		B2030	Exterior Doors													
	B30 Roofing	B3010	Roof Coverings													
		B3020	Roof Openings													
C INTERIORS	C10 Interior Construction	C1010	Partitions													
		C1020	Interior Doors													
		C1030	Fittings													
	C20 Stairs	C2010	Stair Construction													
		C2020	Stair Finishes													
	C30 Interior Finishes	C3010	Wall Finishes													
		C3020	Floor Finishes													
		C3030	Ceiling Finishes													

Section 4.1.1 of E202 states that Model content is intended to be shared with subsequent Model element authors and Model users throughout the course of the Project. Contractors at any tier and their suppliers are legitimately interested in knowing the extent to which they can rely on the content of Model elements to do their work. Design professionals are equally interested in knowing that a contractor will not rely inappropriately on Model element content and use it for an unintended purpose. To address those equally important concerns, E202 states at Section 4.1.2 that subsequent users may rely on the accuracy and completeness of a Model element only to the level of development required at the end of each phase, as that level of development is stated in the Model Element Table. E202–2008 further states at Section 4.1.3 that use of, or reliance on, a Model element that is inconsistent with the required level of development established in the Model Element Table will be at the user's own risk. Following the principle established in E201–2007, Section 4.1.3 of E202 requires that subsequent users indemnify and defend Model element authors against claims arising from the subsequent user's modification to, or unauthorized use of, the Model element content.

E202–2008 does not grant a usage license or any ownership right in the Model content or in the software used to generate the content. Rights to use, modify, or further transmit the Model must be provided in the agreement to which the exhibit is attached. E202 restricts those rights to the design and construction of the specific project that is identified in E202, unless further rights are granted in a separate license, such as C106–2007, Digital Data Licensing Agreement.

Among other things, E202–2008 answers the following questions:

- By project phase, who is responsible for each element of the Model and to what level of development?
- What are authorized uses of the Model elements?
- To what extent can users rely on the Model element?
- Who will manage the Model?
- Who owns the Model?

Because E202–2008 answers those questions, owners, design professionals, and contractors alike should find that it takes the uncertainty out of Model usage and creates an environment that encourages Model authors to share their Models with downstream users, including other designers, contractors, schedulers, cost estimators, and fabricators.

9.5   AIA Integrated Project Delivery Agreements

Although not essential for achieving IPD principals, BIM serves as a catalyst for IPD. BIM is a software product, not a project delivery method, but IPD processes work hand-in-hand with BIM and leverage the software's capabilities. BIM gives the project team the ability to build the project virtually before the first shovel of dirt is moved at the site by incorporating into the Model not only the architect's design information, but also the contractor's shop drawings and other means and methods of construction. Through this synergy, design professionals benefit from contractors' expertise, conflicts between building systems are discovered and avoided prior to construction, construction may proceed more efficiently, and construction claims due to errors and omissions may be reduced. Plainly, the most efficient and effective use of BIM demands that architects, engineers, and contractors collaborate during the pre-construction phase of the project. BIM opens the door to increased collaboration and the achievement of IPD goals. For that reason, the AIA's IPD agreements, released in 2008, all require the use of BIM to the fullest extent possible.

The traditional design process follows three familiar phases: schematic design, design development, and construction documents. Because it posits a different approach to the preconstruction phases, IPD adjusts the traditional project phases to allow for more intensified planning at the beginning of design, and for incorporating the contractor's shop drawings prior to the start of construction. The IPD preconstruction phases are identified as follows: conceptualization, criteria design, detailed design, implementation documents, and buy-out. When providing standard form contracts for IPD, the AIA created two new families, both of which require the use of BIM and follow the IPD phase sequencing identified above. These two families, the A295 family and the Single Purpose Entity (SPE) family, are more fully described below.

9.5.1   A295 Family

The A295 family, also called the IPD transitional forms, consists of B195™–2008, Agreement Between Owner and Architect for Integrated Project Delivery, and A195™–2008, Agreement Between Owner and Contractor for Integrated Project Delivery, a guaranteed maximum price (GMP), both of which incorporate A295™–2008, General Conditions of the Contract for Integrated Project Delivery. The A295 family provides a smooth transition from traditional delivery methods because it is based on a commonly used delivery model whereby the general contractor provides pre-construction services, such as cost estimating and constructability reviews, working in tandem with the architect during the design phase. The A295 General Conditions document departs from tradition because it integrates the duties and activities of the owner, contractor, and architect and describes them sequentially for each of the IPD phases, from conceptualization through construction. Through its organization by IPD phase, not by party, the General Conditions document encourages a more collaborative working environment among the owner, architect, and contractor.

B195–2008, the owner-architect agreement, covers primarily only business terms, such as insurance requirements, additional services, use of instruments of service, and compensation. Initial information, upon which the owner, architect, and contractor may rely, and the architect's scope of services are fully set out in A295. The architect's services specifically include "usual and customary structural, mechanical and electrical engineering services."

Similarly, A195–2008, the owner-contractor agreement, provides the business terms between the parties. The contractor's duties during both the pre-construction phases and the construction phase are described in A295. Pre-construction duties include cost estimating, scheduling, obtaining information from subcontractors to inform design decisions, and providing recommendations on constructability, purchasing, and bidding. After the owner accepts the GMP, the contractor is required to perform the work in accordance with the GMP documents, which compare to the contract documents in a traditional project. Unlike other AIA GMP agreements that do not prescribe when the contractor must provide its GMP, A295 requires that the contractor provide its GMP proposal for the owner's acceptance at the conclusion of the detailed design phase.

Although the owner and contractor may agree to bring certain specialty trades onboard prior to execution of the GMP, in most cases GMP execution will trigger the contractor to commence the buy-out of subcontracts. Having the trades under contract permits the flow of shop drawings for the architect to review and for the architect or the contractor, as may be agreed, to incorporate into the implementation documents using BIM. At the conclusion of the implementation documents phase, the implementation documents are incorporated into the GMP documents and the contractor uses them to construct the project.

The contractor is required to ensure that the implementation documents include sufficient and unambiguous information for completing the work. Because the owner is compensating the contractor, in part, to ensure that the implementation documents are suitable for construction, the owner is not liable to the contractor for damages resulting from inconsistencies in the

GMP documents that the contractor discovers during the construction phase. The contractor is not, however, responsible for ensuring that the GMP documents comply with laws and codes.

Due to the potential active participation of contractors, subcontractors, and fabricators during the design phase, the A295 family fosters better-informed design decisions, and fewer contractor claims based on errors and omissions in construction documents than under traditional delivery models. Utilizing BIM, the parties have the opportunity to construct the building virtually and avoid the collisions between building systems that often arise under the traditional project delivery process. The contractor may also use BIM to order and fabricate materials with greater accuracy, resulting in less waste.

The A295 family provides a contractual model for achieving many of the IPD goals, including the early involvement of key participants, intensified planning, open communication, and appropriate technology. The A295 family provides an easy transition to IPD because it does not significantly change the traditional risk allocation equations for the owner, architect, and contractor. It maintains the structure of two-party agreements that do not incorporate risk sharing provisions or opportunities to share rewards based on the establishment and achievement of mutual goals. As in any GMP agreement, the owner-contractor agreement may include a shared savings provision, but the architect does not participate in that savings. The A295 family requires that the owner, architect, and contractor work collaboratively from the beginning of the project, but does not require that they establish a project management team to make decisions jointly on behalf of the project. To fully implement all of the IPD goals established in the IPD Guide, the AIA introduced the Single Purpose Entity Family of IPD agreements, discussed below.

9.5.2 Single Purpose Entity Family

In contrast to the A295 family, the Single Purpose Entity family is not based on a traditional delivery model, but presents an entirely new way to deliver a project. To create a contract that would achieve the IPD goal of mutual benefit and reward to the maximum extent for all members of the project team, the AIA emulated the business model used for sophisticated product design and construction, such as automotive or aircraft manufacturing. In those arenas, one company designs and builds a product through a combination of its own forces and independent contractors. When key players are employed in the same company, their interests are the most closely aligned—all must pull together to achieve a common goal: the company's success. To achieve a similar alignment of interests, the AIA provided C195™–2008, Single Purpose Entity Agreement for Integrated Project Delivery.

Using C195, the owner, architect, construction manager, and perhaps other key project participants, each becomes a member of a single purpose entity (SPE), whose purpose is to provide the skills necessary to design and construct the project for a target cost that the SPE members mutually establish. The SPE is a limited liability company, a business entity readily recognizable and available in all jurisdictions, that provides the benefit of limited liability to its members. Except for decisions over which the owner wishes to retain control, and that are explicitly set forth in the SPE agreement at the time of its execution, the SPE's governance board makes all decisions unanimously.

The owner-member provides funding for the project under C196™–2008, Agreement Between Single Purpose Entity and Owner for Integrated Project Delivery. The architect, construction manager, and other non-owner members do not provide funding, but instead provide services to the SPE using C197™–2008, Agreement Between Single Purpose Entity and Non-Owner Member for Integrated Project Delivery. The owner, architect, and construction manager may invite other project participants to become SPE members. For example, where a project involves the design of a building and an adjacent park, perhaps the landscape architect would be a member of the SPE. For a project requiring substantial mechanical processing systems, perhaps the mechanical contractor would become a member.

The SPE itself does not perform professional services, but provides those services through contracts with its own members or with other licensed professionals. C197, the member services agreement, may be used to establish a contract between the SPE and any non-owner member providing services. C197 does not prescribe a fixed scope of services. Instead of a fixed scope, services are listed by project phase in an extensive services matrix that the members complete by assigning services to the member in the best position to complete the service. The SPE reimburses non-owner members for the costs, direct and indirect, that they incur in providing services. Non-owner members may earn profit two ways: (1) through the achievement of project goals (goal achievement compensation), and (2) by sharing savings realized at the completion of construction (incentive compensation). If one member earns profit, all members earn profit. For that reason, members are motivated to help each other achieve goals and monitor costs.

The SPE enters directly into contracts with non-member design consultants, specialty trade contractors, vendors, and material suppliers for services, labor, and materials to complete the design and construction of the project. The construction manager-member provides management expertise only and does not construct the building with its own forces, although the construction manager could construct the building under a separate contract with the SPE, if the other SPE members agreed it was in the best interest of the project. Under the terms of C195, the SPE is committed to managing costs and is required to enter into either a stipulated sum or guaranteed maximum price agreement with any construction contractor.

At the beginning of the project, the members form a project management team for the day-to-day management of the project's design and construction. Just as the SPE's governance board, the project management team must make all decisions unanimously. The project management team, which includes the owner, establishes goals for the project and the amount available to the non-owner SPE members as goal achievement compensation. The SPE pays the pre-established goal achievement compensation to all non-owner members, if, and only if, a goal is met. Failure to achieve a goal, regardless of fault, results in forfeiture of the goal achievement compensation established for that goal. The owner achieves a benefit when a goal is achieved. For that reason, the owner may not recover from members any previously paid goal achievement compensation, regardless of whether the project achieves other goals, including the achievement of the target cost.

The project management team prepares a target cost proposal for the owner's acceptance. If the members cannot unanimously agree on the amount of the target cost, the SPE dissolves. If the project continues, the members share, as incentive compensation, any savings achieved between the target cost and the actual cost of the project. Failure to design and construct the project for an amount less than the pre-established target cost, regardless of fault, results in forfeiture of any incentive compensation.

The members agree that maintaining the target cost is a primary goal and they must take the steps necessary to control costs; however, the members do not guarantee to the owner that the actual cost of the project will be less than the target cost. If the target cost is exceeded, the owner-member and the non-owner members share that burden in this way: non-owner members must continue to provide services without compensation, and the owner must continue to fund the SPE so that it can honor its commitments to non-member contractors and vendors. To protect the target cost, all members are required to monitor costs continuously, to make and distribute cost projections, and to develop recovery plans should it appear that the target cost may be exceeded. Absent the unanimous agreement of the members, the target cost may be adjusted for only two reasons: (1) a force majeure event, as defined in the SPE agreement, and (2) owner-initiated changes in the scope of the project.

Insurance plays an important role in the SPE agreement. Prior to the establishment of the target cost, the members are required to obtain commercial general liability, automobile liability, workers compensation/employers' liability, and if applicable, professional liability insurance. The SPE is required to retain an insurance advisor for the purpose of providing advice and assistance in establishing an insurance program controlled by the SPE (CCIP). After the target cost is established, the SPE is required to obtain, either through itself or its members, the insurance policies identified above in addition to builder's risk and other coverages that may be applicable to the project, such as for pollution liability. If a CCIP is established, members and non-members may be required to provide additional coverage, as the insurance advisor may recommend. Insurance costs, including deductibles, are an actual cost of the project.

Dispute resolution under the SPE is unique to the industry. Through a combination of limitations of liability, indemnities, and waivers of claims, the SPE aspires to protect its members from intramural claims, and to ensure that any claims that survive are covered by the insurance paid for as an actual cost of the project. Except in the case of a member's willful misconduct, (1) the members are not liable to the SPE, and to other members, for any amount in excess of the insurance required under the applicable agreements; and (2) the SPE holds harmless, indemnifies, and defends its members from and against all claims not covered by insurance. The members waive the right to pursue claims against each other, or against the SPE, except through the dispute resolution procedures of the SPE agreement. The members also agree to assign to the SPE, for resolution under the SPE dispute resolution procedures, all claims they may have against non-members providing work or services on the project. By agreeing to pursue all internal claims through the SPE, and to assign all other claims to the SPE, the members may resolve all member-initiated claims on the project out-of-court. All dispute resolution costs are actual costs of the project and, therefore, reduce the amount of incentive compensation available for members to share at the completion of the project. For that reason, members share a common disincentive to bring claims.

The SPE disputes procedures require members first to attempt to resolve disputes by consensus. If resolution is not achieved within 15 days, the dispute is transferred to the SPE's governance board for resolution. If the dispute is not resolved within 30 days, it proceeds to a dispute resolution committee for final resolution. The dispute resolution committee consists of the chief executive of each member and a neutral party, mutually agreed upon and identified in C195 SPE agreement. For up to 60 days, the neutral attempts to facilitate a resolution of the dispute. If those attempts fail, the neutral issues a decision that is binding on the members and enforceable in a court of competent jurisdiction. All members agree to resolve all claims and disputes that may arise after the SPE dissolves under the dispute resolution provisions of the SPE agreement.

This highly collaborative, all-for-one and one-for-all approach to project delivery offers a unique solution to the waste and inefficiency problems suffered in the design and construction industry. The AIA recognizes, however, that the SPE solution is likely not for everyone. The owner must be willing to assume the risk of cost over-runs, and to manage that risk through active participation in the design and construction process as a full member of the project management team. To motivate other members to achieve project performance goals, the owner must be willing to fund an amount sufficient to provide that motivation. Non-owner members must be prepared to provide their services at cost, with the conviction that through good performance, continuous risk monitoring, and the exercise of strict cost control, they can achieve profits in excess of those earned on a traditional project. The significantly decreased risk of claims and associated litigation should be attractive to all members and their insurers.

The SPE structure motivates its members to achieve a high level of performance. It requires all members to provide their expertise at the appropriate time, to share information, to collaborate, and to make unanimous decisions in the best interest of the project. It provides substantial incentives to excel and to solve problems collectively, rather than levying draconian penalties for failure. Through this combination of requirements and incentives, the SPE offers the potential to deliver a high quality project for the owner, and to achieve substantial monetary and intangible rewards for the other members.

Acknowledgement: This chapter was written and presented by the author as a paper by the same title at the Proceedings of the 48thAnnual Meeting of Invited Attorneys, on May 21, 2009, in St. Petersburg, Florida, and is reprinted with permission of Victor O. Schinnerer & Company, Inc.

Chapter 10

Building Information Modeling: A Framework for Collaboration

Howard W. Ashcraft, Esq.

10.1   Introduction

Building Information Modeling (BIM) technology has arrived and is being used by designers, contractors and suppliers to reduce their costs, increase quality, and in some instances, achieve designs that would be impossible without digital design and fabrication. Public[1] and private owners[2] in the United States are now requiring BIM and it has been widely adopted for complex projects.

Studies by Stanford University's Center for Integrated Facility Engineering report that BIM use has risen significantly and will continue to rise in the near future.[3] Between 2006 and 2007, the number of licensed seats of Autodesk's flagship BIM product, Revit, doubled from 100,000 to 200,000.[4] Moreover, McGraw-Hill estimated that that a tipping point was reached in spring 2008, with more teams using BIM than exploring it.[5] Pilot projects have now been completed where the entire structure was built using CNC[6] fabrication driven from the design model.[7] As the technical issues of standards[8] and interoperability are addressed, the software capabilities will develop further. This explosive growth has been supported by preliminary development of BIM standards[9] and of related issues, such as electronic data licensing and file transfer.[10] BIM is not tomorrow's vision; it is today's reality.

The legal and business structures for BIM, however, lag far behind. BIM's implications are just being realised and few solutions have been developed. Moreover, liability concerns have lead practitioners, and their lawyers, to contractually isolate the building information model – thus depriving the model of its greatest benefits.

BIM is more than a technology. Although it can be used without collaboration, such use only scratches the surface. Because the model (or models) is a central information resource, it leads naturally to intensive communication and interdependence. Building Information Models are platforms for collaboration.

But collaboration is not a construction industry hallmark. Rather, the industry, its practices, and its contract documents assume definite and distinct roles and liabilities. The insurance products used by the construction industry mirror these lines of responsibility and liability. However, collaborative processes, and BIM specifically, foster communication, joint decision making and interdependence that blur the distinctions between parties. Technology and business practices are in collision.

BIM also collides with traditional professional responsibility principles. Although virtually all professional licensing regulations require that designs be prepared by a person 'in responsible charge', much in a collaborative design is not supervised or directed by a single person or entity.

Change is required and change is coming.[11] This paper discusses attributes of BIM that conflict with traditional notions of responsibility and proposes alternative business and legal structures that support using BIM in a collaborative environment.

10.2   BIM: Definition and Characteristics

BIM broadly encompasses a series of technologies that are transforming design and construction. In essence, BIM uses information rich databases to characterise virtually all relevant aspects of a structure or system. It is qualitatively different from Computer Assisted Design and Drafting (CADD) because it is not just a depiction, it is a simulation of the facility.

The National Institute of Building Sciences (NIBS)[12] defines BIM as follows:

> A Building Information Model, or BIM, utilizes cutting edge digital technology to establish a computable representation of all the physical and functional characteristics of a facility and its related project/life-cycle information, and is intended to be a repository of information for the facility owner/operator to use and maintain throughout the life-cycle of a facility. [13]

Several aspects of this definition deserve discussion. Although the definition references a 'Building Information Model', in current practice the design is built from a set of interrelated models that can exchange information between their differing software platforms. It is this federated set of models that comprise the complete digital information about the facility and, for the purpose of this definition, are the Building Information Model.

The definition is also interesting for what it omits. It does not highlight three dimensional modeling, although this is one of the most visible and immediately understood aspects of BIM. This omission is explained in the phrase 'a computable representation of all the physical ... characteristics of a facility'. The computable representation is a simulation of all physical characteristic such that three dimensional views become just one logical manifestation of the model. In BIM, three dimensional design is an inherent feature, not an enhancement. Moreover, because it is 'computational,' the data can be extracted, analysed and manipulated with appropriate software.

Thirdly, the description 'all the physical and functional characteristics' expands BIM beyond earlier three dimensional design tools. In BIM, the building is not just a three dimensional picture. Instead, it is a digital simulation of the facility that can be viewed, tested, designed, constructed and deconstructed digitally. This promotes iterative design optimisation and the ability to 'rehearse' construction before ever moving labour, material, and equipment into the field.

The information maintained in a BIM also differs from the level and type of information maintained by traditional design tools. In traditional CAD, a wall or other elements is an assemblage of lines that, at most, define the geometric constraints of the wall. In BIM, the wall is an object[14] that contains a broad array of information in addition to physical dimensions. Rather than draw lines that describe dimensions of a design, designers organise intelligent objects into a design. Figure 1 is a screen shot from Revit Architecture 2008 showing element properties of a wall type (exterior: CMU insulated in this example) as well as values for the specific instance in the design.

Figure 1: Element Properties in Autodesk Revit

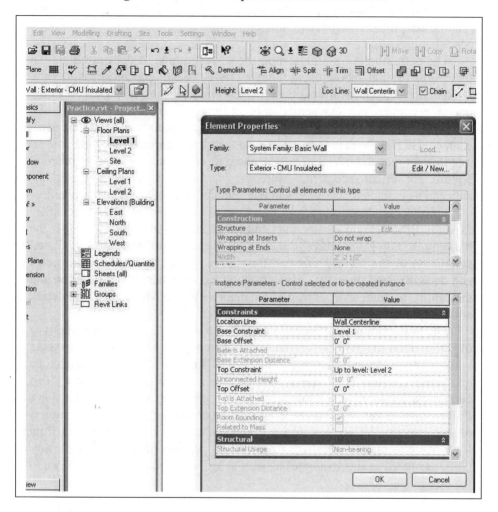

In addition to containing detailed information about the element, the building information model contains information about how the element relates to the design in general and to other objects. This parametric architecture allows the model to adjust to design changes without having to individually adjust every individual element. The CMU wall, in the example, 'knows' that it is supposed to extend from the foundation up to Level 1. If either of these parameters is changed, the height of the wall will automatically adjust to match. This increases design efficiency and reduces potential for errors.

Because the BIM is a 'computable representation' every manifestations of the model is automatically current. For example, sections or elevations are just different manifestations of the BIM information. If you make a change in plan view (and, therefore to the underlying BIM data), the elevation and section views that are built from the same BIM data will automatically reflect the changes. Without any further intervention, schedules, tables and other related data reflect the updated information. This also increases design efficiency and makes it virtually impossible for drawings to be internally inconsistent.

In addition, the model contains data concerning the object attributes that can be extracted as schedules, tables, bills of materials or other data that can be printed, evaluated, or sent to other programs for analysis. Again, because the information is based on the central model, and reflects the current design, the potential for error is reduced.

The definition continues by including, as information in the model, 'and its related life-cycle information'. This indicates that the model contains the functional information necessary to evaluate the operational facility and optimise its performance for efficiency, sustainability or other criteria.

Finally, the definition states that the model is to be a 'repository' of data for facility management. The model is meant to be a living document that owners can use to manage their facilities as well as build them. BIM's potential for facility management is perhaps its most important role, but it is a role that is just beginning to be explored.

10.3   How is BIM Being Used?

Single data entry; multiple use

Traditional construction practices require the same information to be used multiple times by multiple organisations. Identical information is entered into different programs that provide specific solutions, such as structural analysis, code compliance, material quantities or cost estimates. Every repetition is an opportunity for inconsistency and error. Moreover, even if information is digitally translated from one program to another, translation can alter or corrupt the data. And keeping track of different versions can be a nightmare, even with compatible programs. Drawing backgrounds are a recurring example of this problem.

The design consultants working alongside the architect need to upload and maintain the basic design backgrounds they receive from the architect.

These backgrounds, however, will change as the design develops and each party must take considerable care to ensure that they are working with the latest versions of the basic documents. The contractors and vendors must take the information provided by the designers, often in paper form, and enter it into their systems. As the design develops, changes in one party's documents must be transferred back to the others.

Errors begin to creep into the documents because updates are incompletely or incorrectly entered, and work can be wasted because parties are working from outdated information. Figure 2, on the following page, shows an example of structural design information in the Revit structural design model and in ETABS, a structural analysis program. By consolidating information into a unified data source, the likelihood of data entry, translation, or version errors is greatly decreased.

Design efficiency

Although the greatest efficiencies are obtained when BIM is used collaboratively, BIM design can aid a traditional design process. BIM software can reduce the cost of preparing 2D drawings in a conventional project, especially when designs are changing rapidly.[15] For example, in Revit®, any change in plan view automatically updates any section affected by the change. In Tekla Structures, changes in dimension or geometry automatically update details and related features. Moreover, using data rich elements instead of drawn objects accelerates the creation of contract drawings.

Figure 2: Structure design in Revit and ETABS

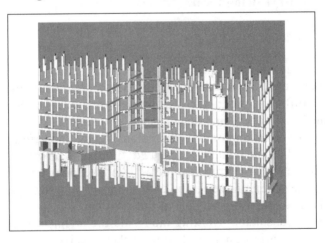

Consistent design bases

BIM modeling ensures that all parties working from the model share the same base. Under current practice, not all participants may be operating directly from the model. However, if the participants are using software that is compatible with the model, the base information can be moved, imported or exported from the model. Moreover, periodic imports into 3D visualisation software, such as NavisWorks's Jetstream®, quickly exposes inconsistencies.

3D modeling and conflict resolution

The BIM model can render the design in three dimensions and does not require separate software to explore the model visually. This allows better exploration of space, visualisation of light studies, and improved communication and understanding of design concepts within the team and with project stakeholders.

Conflict identification and resolution

On complex projects, conflict identification and resolution is an extraordinarily expensive and difficult task. In many instances, designers do not have the time or budget to fully explore and resolve conflict issues. In other instances, full coordination cannot be accomplished during the design phase because the contractor will later design key systems, such as HVAC or life safety equipment that is not reflected in the design drawings. Even in a complete design-bid-build project, construction details and layouts may require information regarding the actual equipment that will be installed.

This information deficit is typically addressed by warning the contractor that the design is 'diagrammatic' and that coordination will be required. Traditionally, the contractor coordinates physical drawings of different systems by overlaying them on light tables to determine if the various systems can actually be constructed in the allowed space. Alternatively, drawings for each discipline are merged and printed as color-coded composite drawings. Conflicts that are identified are brought to the designer's attention through the request for information process, where solutions can be developed and clarifications issued. But light table resolution is inherently a two dimensional process applied to a three dimensional problem. It is notoriously difficult and fraught with error. For these reasons, conflicts are a primary source of contractor claims.

BIM greatly reduces conflict issues by integrating all the key systems into the model. Design BIM systems can detect internal conflicts, and model viewing systems, such as NavisWorks®, can detect and highlight conflicts between the models and other information imported into the viewer. The solution can then be checked to ensure that it resolves the problem and to determine if it creates other, unintended, consequences.[16] In a complex project, the savings derived from coordination can completely offset the model's cost.

Figure 3: Clash detection in NavisWoorks Jetstream

Courtesy of University of California, San Francisco

Take-offs and estimating

The model contains information, or can link to information, necessary to generate bills of quantity, size and area estimates, productivity, materials cost, and related estimating information. It avoids processing material take-offs manually, thus reducing error and misunderstanding. Moreover, the linked cost information evolves in step with the design changes. The estimating advantages are so significant that some contractors will create models on 2D designed projects to use the model's estimating capabilities.

Shop and fabrication drawings

In some instances, the models can provide construction details and fabrication information. This reduces costs by reducing the detailing effort and increases fabrication accuracy. In addition, because conflicts are resolved through the model, there is greater confidence that prefabricated material will fit when delivered. This allows more construction work to be performed off-site in optimal factory conditions. Subcontractors in the steel and mechanical, electrical and plumbing trades, regularly use models to fabricate their products.

Visualization of alternative solutions and options

Because it is inherently a 3D process, models are excellent methods for evaluating alternative approaches. Moreover, the ability to evaluate how changes affect key attributes, such as energy use, enhances the model's usefulness as a thinking tool. However, the software interface can interfere with the creative process. In a study of one system, users noted that it was not 'sketch', and therefore impeded the initial creative process.[17] This may lead to using freeform design tools initially, with the results being loaded into the BIM system for refinement.[18]

Energy optimization

BIM systems, such as Autodesk's® Revit®, can provide information for energy analysis. They can be used to evaluate lighting design and options, and in conjunction with their material take-off capabilities, can generate the documentation necessary for LEED™ certification.[19]

Constructability reviews and 4D simulations

Using the model, the contractor can visualise the entire structure, gaining a greater understanding of the challenges involved in its construction. By integrating 4D capabilities, the contractor can also simulate the construction process, which significantly increases the contractor's ability to evaluate and optimise the construction sequence. The interaction between scheduling software and the model can also be used to evaluate the effect of construction delays and errors.

Reduced fabrication costs and errors

The ability to use information in the model to directly create fabrication drawings avoids a problematic and difficult step in the construction process. In a traditional work flow, the fabricators must review the plans and specifications, prepare fabrication drawings, compare them to other fabrication and design drawings, have them reviewed by the design team, and eventually release the drawings for fabrication. Errors can occur at any stage. By using the data in the model, dimensional errors, conflicts, and integration errors can be avoided or significantly reduced. In addition, the model can be updated with as-built information allowing accurate fabrication of custom components, such as building facades.

Facilities management

If the model is properly maintained during construction, it becomes a tool that can be used by the owner to manage and operate the structure or facility. Modifications and upgrades can be evaluated for cost effectiveness. Data contained in the model can be used for managing remodeling, additions and maintenance.

Functional simulations

The 3D and conflict checking mechanisms can be used to simulate and evaluate emergency response and evacuation. For example, NavisWorks® was used at the Letterman Digital Arts Center to ensure that fire response vehicles could navigate the parking structures.

BIM is the most powerful tool yet conceived for integrating design, construction and management of facilities. It allows designers to explore alternative concepts and iteratively optimise their designs. Contractors can use the model to rehearse construction, prepare cost data, coordinate drawings, and prepare shop and fabrication drawings. Owners can use the data to manage maintenance and facility renovation. And together, the parties can use BIM as a basis for collaboration.

10.4   Commercial Barriers to BIM

Despite BIM's advantages, its adoption faces significant barriers. Discussion of BIM generally focuses on the technology. Although this is a fascinating subject, the key question is how BIM alters current commercial models. Rather than view BIM as a technology, it should be analysed as a project delivery method, with new risks, rewards, and relationships. Unfortunately, new business models have not yet surfaced and early users are left attempting to integrate the new technologies into conventional practices.[20]

Immediate benefits do not accrue to the key adopter (the designer)

The benefits an owner accrues from BIM are easily seen. Using a flexible model allows design optimisation, fewer construction errors, fewer design coordination issues and, thus, fewer claims. The owner can also use the model for management and operation of the facility. Contractors also benefit through less coordination and engineering effort and reduced fabrication costs. Quality is increased, cost decreased and delivery times are shortened.

For designers, however, BIM's economic benefits are less apparent. Properly implemented, BIM design systems do increase efficiency by reducing duplicate and potentially inconsistent data entry. Multiple use of consistent data and the ability to quickly explore design alternatives also promotes efficiency and improved quality. But unless the designer shares in the economic benefits, the owner, not the designer, reaps the immediate benefits. Yet it is the designer, not the owner, who must adopt and invest in the new technology.

The asymmetrical rewards of BIM are a significant practical obstacle because design professionals are the linchpins of BIM. Design professionals must adopt the technology, install the software, train their employees and champion BIM's use. They need to restructure their workflows and reinvent the design process. If they do not share in the economic benefits, designers will have little incentive to adopt BIM processes. In fact, because BIM can increase the designer's potential liability, there is a significant disincentive to adopting BIM. This concern is echoed in comments from the American Institute of Architects (AIA) Technology Advisory Group, which stated in a recent monograph:

> We fear there will be a tendency, driven by valid concerns about liability and insurability, to prevent such use of the architect's design data. We believe this is the wrong answer and would jeopardise the future of architectural practice as we know it. If the architecture firm is not willing to deliver the potential value of the digital building model, the owner will seek delivery methods, probably contractor-led, that will deliver that value. The role of the architect will be diminished.
>
> We believe, rather, that the architecture firms' role and compensation should be enhanced by these technology developments. Obstacles to a free flow of data among the project participants should be overcome so that the architecture

firm can deliver the full value of its work to the client and be rewarded commensurately.[21]

Although designers should logically benefit from BIM, new business models have developed slowly. The Australian alliance model is promising because it allocates risks and rewards among all parties. In the United States, however, few projects are operating under new paradigms.

Absence of standard contract documents

The lack of standard contract documents also hinders the development of BIM. Standard contract documents perform four key functions. First, they validate a business model by providing a recommended framework for practice. As noted above, a consensus business model for BIM has not emerged. Secondly, standard documents establish a consensus allocation of risks and an integrated relationship between the risks assumed, compensation, dispute resolution and insurance. Bespoke agreements, unless crafted by seasoned practitioners, are often unbalanced and overlook key issues. Thirdly, standard contracts reduce the effort involved in documenting the roles and responsibilities on a project. Designers want to design structures, not structure contracts. Finally, drafting bespoke documents increases the transaction costs and thus reduces the profitability of every transaction. Unfortunately, the current standard contract documents are just beginning to address the use of BIM.

For example, regarding electronic information transfer, the AIA contract language in the owner-architect agreement states:

> 1.3.2.4 Prior to the Architect providing to the Owner any Instruments of Service in electronic form or the Owner providing to the Architect any electronic data for incorporation into the Instruments of Service, the Owner and the Architect shall by separate written agreement set forth the specific conditions governing the format of such Instruments of Service or electronic data, including any special limitations or licenses not otherwise provided in this Agreement.'[22]

In 2007, the AIA introduced the 'separate written agreements' envisaged by the 1997 documents: the Digital Data Licensing Agreement[23] and the Digital Data Protocol Exhibit.[24] These documents reflect a major shift from using transfer documents to insulate the creator from liability[25] to a more open and balanced approach. Essentially, the Licensing Agreement establishes the licenses and permitted uses of the documents. Under this document, the user is licensed to use and rely on the electronic document if used for the project and only indemnifies the creator from liability caused by unauthorised use. The Protocol Exhibit expands upon the Licensing Agreement by creating a Project Protocol Table that allows the parties to specify the data format, the transmission method and the permitted use of almost every common construction document. They AIA documents have recently been joined by ConsensusDOCS, which has published an Electronic Communications Protocol Addendum that differs in mechanics and emphasis, but shares the AIA documents' support for open communication protocols.[26]

Although these communication protocols are a distinct improvement, they do not attempt to address BIM's many legal implications. As of this date, the core contract documents, such as AIA document A-201-1997, General Conditions of the Contract for Construction, are silent regarding electronic documents, except to state that electronic documents provided by the architect are 'instruments of service,'[27] and do not discuss BIM at all. To fill this gap, both the AIA and ConsensusDOCS have published supplementary documents that are intended to amend the existing contract documents.

The ConsensusDOCS and the AIA BIM documents are quite different. Under the ConsensusDOCS Building Information Modeling Addendum, the owner appoints (and pays for) an Information Manager who is responsible for managing the model(s).[28] The project participants then meet to develop a BIM Execution Plan that will be executed by the parties. In addition, the document provides a liability waiver relating to use of the model information and provide licensing to use the intellectual property. The AIA Building Information Protocol, takes a very different approach.[29] It separates the process of using BIM from the substance of the models.

In the process portion of the document, the Protocol defines the process and responsibilities for model management, the model standard, model ownership, model archiving and conflict coordination. The most significant aspect of the document, however, is its handling of the model's substance. The Protocol defines five Levels of Detail (LOD 100 – LOD 500) for the modeled elements. Using a Model Element Table[30] (completed by the parties) it specifies who (Model Element Author) is responsible for developing the element and the Level of Development at each phase of design and construction. The individual elements are defined using the Uniformat[31] codes used for building specification, cost estimating and cost analysis. This allows the model information to directly relate to the cost estimating and specifications systems used by contractors.

10.5   Legal Concerns Inherent with BIM

The legal issues associated with BIM arise either from the technology itself or from the way the technology is used. BIM can be used solely to produce better quality design documents without any intent to share information or to use the more extensive functionality that BIM allows. Used in the former limited fashion, BIM is simply CAD on steroids. But BIM can also serve as a collaborative framework. Used in this way, BIM serves as a catalyst to change the relationships between the parties and eventually the fabric of their agreements. Collaboration through BIM is a profound change that creates great opportunities, but also creates new issues that need to be addressed and resolved.

Data translation / interoperability

As noted previously, there will rarely be a single BIM on a complex project. The architect may have its design model, the structural engineer its analysis model, the contractor its construction model, and the fabricator its shop drawing or fabrication model. In theory, these models will communicate seamlessly. But under current technology, this is an aspiration, not a reality.

In current practice, there are differences in capability between BIM software. Information must be translated or must fit into the standards for Industry Foundation Classes[32]. Translators may not transfer all information from one model to another. In addition, some translators can not 'round trip', that is move data from one platform to another, and then return it to the original platform after it has been modified or augmented. IFC classes do not exist for all data types and there can be data loss if the host application supports functionality not modeled in the IFC class. The net result is that differences can be created during the translation process that can cause model inconsistencies and errors.

Software is not perfect and residual flaws will remain, despite strenuous debugging efforts. Luckily, these bugs are most often annoying but not harmful. Sometimes, however, that is not the case. In *M A Mortenson Company Inc v Timberline Software Corporation*, a contractor's bid was $1,950,000 too low because of a software error.[33] In affirming the software vendor's motion for summary judgment, the Washington Supreme Court held that the software warranty contained in the instruction manual was incorporated into the purchase contract and that its limitation to the purchase price was valid and not unconscionable.[34] Thus, if errors in BIM software cause economic loss to the user, the injured party has no realistic remedy.

But the user's liability to other parties is not similarly limited, causing a liability gap if the errors cause deficiencies in plans or other deliverables.

Data misuse

Models can be created for a variety of uses. But a perfectly adequate model may cause difficulties if used for a different purpose than intended. Currency, adequacy and tolerances are three issues that need to be addressed when information in one model is used for another.

It seems obvious to state that a model needs to be up-to-date. However, a structural analysis model may not need to be absolutely synchronised with the architectural model to determine whether a structure is sound. But the structural fabrication model that can be derived from the structural model must be synchronised with the architectural model or dimensional conflicts will exist. Similarly, the detail required in a model depends upon its intended use. The end user of information must understand what information the offered model contains – and does not contain. Finally, even if the model is current and adequate, the tolerances required may differ between disciplines. The tolerances assumed for structural steel, for example, may differ from the tolerances assumed by a window wall manufacturer. If the tolerances are different, the window wall may not fit when the structural steel is attached. In addition, when performing conflict checking, the models may need to include space around modeled elements to accommodate tolerances or additional material, such as fireproofing.

Intellectual property

Many of the intellectual property issues are similar to those that existed before BIM. However, they are amplified by the amount of information contained in the BIM and its ease of transfer.

At the most fundamental level, who owns the information in the BIM? If the model is a collaborative work, then ownership may not be vested in a single party. If ownership issues are significant, they should be determined by contract. If information is confidential, then care must be taken to limit the distribution of information and have appropriate confidentiality agreements. Confidentiality issues can arise subtly when the embedded information is confidential, although the overall design is not inherently confidential. The upshot is that who owns the model, who owns information in the model, and who has access to the model should be considered when the BIM procedures are developed.

Loss of data

Building information models, like all digital data, are susceptible to data loss. If a party is hosting the information, it must take adequate steps to protect, and insure, against data loss or face possible liability for the ensuing losses.

Legal status of the model

Appendix A to the American Institute of Steel Construction's Manual of Practice states that the model is the contract document. Although this may be appropriate for steel fabricators and erectors, it is not yet appropriate in all contexts.

As noted previously, current practice uses a series of interlocking models to communicate the design and construction intent for a project. In many instances, the complete design is only visualised when imported into a viewing program, such as NavisWorks JetStream. Moreover, most models do not contain all of the construction details required for a project. Thus, the contract documents will include some 2D information that is added to the information in the model. Finally, many permitting agencies are not yet ready to review digital information and require traditional submissions. Then there is the pesky problem of how to stamp the model. In practice, these issues are currently resolved by using a printed submission as the contract document, even if the communication flow has been digital.

If the model is not the contract document, what is its legal status? There are several options being followed. The first is that it is a 'co-contract document' that is used between the parties, but is not submitted to permitting agencies. In this case, the contracts need to state how inconsistencies will be handled. Another option is to use the model as an 'inferential document'. Under this option, the model provides visualisation of the design intent inferable from the contract documents. Finally, the model can be used as an 'accommodation document' that can be used, but not relied upon, by the recipients. This last approach is similar to the CAD transfer liability waivers that designers use when providing CAD documents to contractors. But limiting reliance undermines the model's utility.

Standard of care

When CAD was introduced, it was viewed as a tool for very large companies and very large projects. Now it is the standard and within a few years BIM will be standard. This will change the standard of care with regard to design, especially in complex projects. Physical conflicts are an obvious example. If we can avoid virtually all conflicts by using a detailed model, we can expect the standard to say that we should. Resolving conflicts in the field or through post-design coordination drawings will not be acceptable.

Design delegation

Design delegation creates issues with licensing and responsible charge. BIM designs, especially when based on object technologies, can contain embedded information provided by manufacturers and subcontractors. In addition, some BIM software can react to changes in the model. Structural design software, for example, can change details in response to changes in the design. In neither of these cases will the architect or engineer of record have created the information or probably have checked the information before it is incorporated in the model.

A recent case decided in a different context highlights the licensing issue. In *Frankfort Digital Services v Kistler*, an individual used bankruptcy software to prepare his Chapter 7 bankruptcy. The software, which was not designed by a lawyer, was an 'expert system' that provided advice about filing options and 'knew the law' as respects various jurisdictions. A series of adversary proceedings were initiated against the software provider, and using California law, the Ninth Circuit held:

> Frankfort's system touted its offering of legal advice and projected an aura of expertise concerning bankruptcy petitions; and, in that context, it offered personalised – albeit automated – counsel. ... We find that because this was the conduct of a non-attorney, it constituted the unauthorized practice of law.[35]

Design and detailing software also 'knows' about the construction regulations, such as building codes. Moreover, they contain the specialised knowledge of engineering principles that is beyond the ken of laymen. From a legal perspective, there is little difference between Frankfort's bankruptcy software and advanced BIM tools.

There is a difference in use, however. In most instances, BIM design software is used by licensed professionals, rather than a lay individual, as in the *Frankfort* case. But this only raises a new issue.

In virtually all jurisdictions, the design professionals of record must be in 'responsible charge' of the design.[36] Responsible charge is generally achieved by either performing the work or having the work performed under the architect's or engineer's supervision.   But in this instance, work performed automatically by the software has clearly not been supervised by the architect or engineer of record.   Moreover, the software or embedded object is probably not prepared by an appropriately licensed professional. And design work provided by a subcontractor and embedded in the BIM may, or may not, have been prepared by a licensed professional.

Architecture and engineering practice will continue to evolve and use increasingly powerful design tools.   But as the above discussion demonstrates, the legal and regulatory structures have not adjusted to this change in practice.

Information ownership and preservation

A dynamic model creates challenging issues regarding ownership and preservation.   The model is immensely valuable, but can be fragile. Computer software is susceptible to power interruptions, viruses, and physical damage.   Although these dangers can be reduced by appropriate back-up strategies, there are risks involved with hosting data, and even small data losses can require significant effort to recover or replace.   If a failure occurs, what insurance, if any, will respond to the economic losses?   A design firm can purchase 'valuable papers' coverage that provides catastrophic loss protection, but this will not necessarily cover losses to other collaborative users.   Coverage under the designer's professional liability policy is problematic[37] and the designer's commercial general liability policy will not respond to purely economic losses.   The difficulty in characterising and insuring against this type of loss underscores the necessity of comprehensive risk allocation and waivers among all model users.

Data preservation can be challenging as well.   We have recently seen extraordinary judgments and sanctions levied against corporations that did not appropriately preserve relevant electronic evidence.   The duty to preserve evidence arises when litigation can be reasonably anticipated.[38]   On a construction project, however, claims are a normal aspect of project closeout, with only some claims proceeding to litigation.   Unfortunately, when they arise, claims that are eventually resolved by the parties look strikingly similar to claims that result in litigation.   After litigation commences, the likelihood of litigation will look 'reasonably anticipatable' in hindsight.

Even assuming that the design professional could recognise when information needed to be preserved, it is unclear how that should be accomplished.   An advantage of a dynamic model is that it can and does evolve.   This inherently involves replacing information with newer information and overwriting or discarding the obsolete data.   Although systems can track revisions, they may not be able to accurately roll back every change made to the system. Moreover, the model differs from traditional paper documents (or even electronic word processing files) in that there is no single paper representation of the model, and critical information is contained in the relationships between information. The model, and not its manifestations, needs to be preserved.

10.6   How BIM is Used: Risk Allocation

Our legal systems are essentially individualistic, focusing on individual rights and responsibilities. We expend great effort to determine where the responsibility of one party ends and the responsibility of another begins. Many of the most fiercely fought battles in construction law focus on the dividing line between entities.[39]   Privity of contract, the economic loss doctrine, means and methods, and third party reliance are all issues where drawing lines between parties is essential to determining responsibility and liability.   Insurance, because it tracks legal liability, is also focused on individual responsibilities.

In contrast, BIM is essentially collaborative. It is most effective when the key participants are jointly involved in developing and augmenting the central model. Although roles remain, the transitions between participants are less abrupt and less easily defined. Thus, there is a tension between the need to tightly define responsibilities and limit reliance on others and the need to promote collaboration and encourage reliance on information embedded in the model, regardless of how it was developed. BIM as a collaborative framework layers additional issues onto those inherent in the technology.

Risk allocation

Using BIM substantially alters the relationships between parties and blends their roles and responsibilities. Our legal framework, however, assumes a less collaborative environment with a clearer delineation of responsibility. As we move forward with BIM projects, risks will need to be allocated rationally, based on the benefits a party will be receiving from BIM, the ability of the party to control the risks, and the ability to absorb the risks through insurance or other means. Several key risk allocation issue are discussed below.

Standard of care

Design professional liability is almost always based on the standard of care. Tort liability is directly linked to the standard of care and contracts often reference it as the liability standard. Because roles are changing, clearly defined standards will not exist. A key question will be the extent to which the design professional can rely upon information provided by other participants and, to some extent, by the software itself. Clearly, the design professional's agreement should explicitly permit reliance without detailed checking of the software or others' contributions, but the ability to rely on another's work may be limited by professional registration statutes and ethics. This may lead to using risk transfer devices, such as limitations of liability or indemnity agreements, as methods to rebalance design professional liability.

Privity and third party reliance

The extent to which third parties may rely upon a designer's work is hotly contested across the U.S. Two defenses often interposed are: lack of privity and that the designer's services are not for plaintiff's benefit. The efficacy of these defenses varies widely between jurisdictions. However, using a collaborative model lessens the likelihood that the defences will be successful anywhere.

Restatement of Torts (Second) section 552 states the requirements for a negligent misrepresentation claim.

> (1)   One who, in the course of his business, profession or employment, or in any other transaction in which he has a pecuniary interest, supplies false information for the guidance of others in their business transactions, is subject to liability for pecuniary loss caused to them by their justifiable reliance upon the information, if he fails to exercise reasonable care or competence in obtaining or communicating the information.
> (2)   Except as stated in Subsection (3), the liability stated in Subsection (1) is limited to loss suffered:
>> (a)   by the person or one of a limited group of persons for whose benefit and guidance he intends to supply the information or knows that the recipient intends to supply it; and
>> (b)   through reliance upon it in a transaction that he intends the information to influence or knows that the

recipient so intends or in a substantially similar transaction.

(3)   The liability of one who is under a public duty to give the information extends to loss suffered by any of the class of persons for whose benefit the duty is created, in any of the transactions in which it is intended to protect them.

In a collaborative project, the designer is aware that other parties are relying on the model's accuracy. It is a short step from foreseeability to knowing that the model is intended to provide information for the contractors' and subcontractors' benefit. Liability under the Restatement only requires that there be intent to influence and reach a group or class of persons.[40] For this reason, contractors and subcontractors relying on the model are likely to be able to bring an action against the designer for damages caused by negligent errors.

Economic Loss Doctrine

The economic loss doctrine is another hotly contested defense in construction cases. Simply stated, the doctrine holds that purely economic losses cannot be recovered through a negligence cause of action.[41] As with the privity and third-party reliance defenses, the utility of the defense varies among jurisdictions and is dependent upon specific facts. Note, however, that the Restatement provision discussed above specifically addresses pecuniary losses. Where the parties intend to jointly rely on BIM information, it will be difficult to apply the economic loss damage.

Delegated and distributed design

These liability issues highlight concerns that arise from the distribution and delegation of design. Although design delegation issues can exist with or without collaborative use of BIM, they are clearly much more significant when more parties are involved and are involved more deeply.

In looking at this issue, it is useful to focus on three questions that highlight the change between traditional and BIM processes. They are: what is the design, who is the designer, and who is in 'responsible charge'?

What is the design?

The new design processes will be fluid and collaborative. Design elements, such as object properties, will be created by vendors or software manufacturers, not licensed design professionals. The design may be self-modifying, and to that extent, partially self-designed. The design deliverable may be a computer model or simulation, not paper drawings, and may be distributed between computer systems operated by different participants. The complete design may exist in a space defined by the internet, not plotting paper's narrow confines. The design will be flexible, but elusive.

Project design needs to be clearly expressed. Contractors need to know what they are bidding on. They need to be able to compare revised design elements to earlier versions to determine if there are changes in scope. Owners need to determine whether they have received a project that complies with the design. Inspectors must be able to compare physical construction to an objective design standard. Designers need assurance that their services are complete and, if problems later occur, that their designs can be compared against the constructed condition. Building officials and inspectors need a definite 'something' to review, not a moving target.

The design fluidity allowed by new technologies competes with the precision required for contract enforcement. Contract definitions of design should address two issues: first, the contracts between the parties should define the design deliverables in content, time, and type of electronic media used. Secondly, the contract documents should determine whether incorporated submittals, such as objects provided by vendors, are part of the designer's deliverables and which party takes responsibility for incorporation and coordination.

Once a design definition is adopted, it will be important for the parties, and particularly the designer, to adhere to the definition during project development.[42]

The design should be preserved in 'snapshots' at major design milestones. In some cases this may be accomplished by printing and saving these milestone documents. But in a multi-dimensional electronic design maintained in a diffused internet relationship, the total design package may not be encompassed by printed documents. It may be possible, however, to temporarily freeze this digital design world and save it, complete with linked documents and locations, on semi-permanent media, such as CD-ROMs. Revit®, for example, can preserve snapshots as 'Design Alternatives'.

The definition must consider the needs of inspectors and building officials to have a stable document to review or to compare against the actual construction.

Who is the designer?

Not only is the concept of 'the design' becoming less clear, the identity of the 'designer' is becoming equally vague. In the grand sense, we will always know the designer. The prime design professional will maintain responsibility for systems design, the overall layout of design elements, the flow through the structure, and 'artistic' building elements. Most disputes regarding design deficiencies, however, have little to do with these design elements.[43] Instead, they arise from deficiencies in details, inadequate coordination, deviations in submittals, excessive changes, and failure to meet budgetary or functional program requirements.

In a collaborative setting, the design details that create disputes may well be provided by subcontractors or vendors through submittals or object specifications. To this extent, those subcontractors and vendors become the 'designer'. The distribution and 'hiding' of the design process raises several significant questions:

- o How will the various designers' contributions be unwound to determine responsibility?
- o Will parties accessing the shared model be able to legally rely upon the contributions of others? Is privity an issue?
- o If the software can communicate between objects and cause them to adjust their properties, does the software become a 'designer' as well?
- o Do the standards committees that develop interoperability protocols and object specifications become project 'designers'?
- o What are the responsibilities of these secondary 'designer's?
- o To what extent can the design professional rely upon the products of these 'designers'?
- o If these 'designers' do have responsibility, do they have insurance for design risks? Do we need new insurance products better tailored to collaborative projects?

In the immediate future, owners and building officials will look to the architect and engineers of record as the project's designers. But, in a practical sense, these parties cannot check and be responsible for the work of the many 'designers' distributed throughout a collaborative design process. Just as tomorrow's designs will be distributed, so should design responsibility. In developing contract documents, careful thought should be given to integrating appropriate limitations of liability and waivers.

Who is in responsible charge?

The professional registration statutes generally require that a licensed professional be in 'responsible charge' of all work performed by a design firm. This work must either be performed or supervised by the responsible professional. The contract documents are sealed by the responsible professional to signify compliance with this requirement and acceptance of this responsibility. If design responsibility is distributed, however, is this even possible? How can a professional supervise design contributions by firms that are not under the professional's control? How can a design professional supervise changes to structural detailing that are performed by the software itself? In the short run, building officials are likely to accept sealed drawings without considering what portion of the content has been created under the responsible charge of the signing professional. But in the long run, the professional registration statutes must be modified to reflect the actual practices, and realities, of digital design.

Intellectual property

Given that the intelligent model is an inherently collaborative work, to what extent can anyone claim ownership of the intellectual property? In select instances, the designer's intellectual property rights have been used to preserve the integrity of the design itself. More commonly, the intellectual property rights are used to enforce payment obligations or to prevent reusing the design without compensation. Because the client will ordinarily have access to the model as it is being developed, care must be taken to ensure that the intellectual property rights are not lost because of the open and collaborative nature of model development.

The model may also contain confidential or trade secret information. For example, a model for a manufacturing plant may disclose what a company is planning to build and the processes it will use. If information is broadly circulated in a collaborative team, how will this information be protected legally and practically?

Spearin warranties

In 1918, the Supreme Court introduced the Spearin doctrine, which allocated liability for defects that occurred during the construction process.[44] The Spearin court found that 'the one who provides the plans and specification for a construction project warrants that those plans and specifications are free from defect.'[45] A contractor who adheres to the project's design specifications cannot be held liable for defects arising from the specifications, and can sue for financial costs accrued for fixing the defected condition.[46] Thus in the design-bid-build process, an implied warranty exists when the contractor is required to use a precise, detailed method in executing the contract.

The Spearin doctrine has had mixed results where the contractor has participated in preparing the design or the specifications. When contracts combine design and performance specifications, the courts have still allowed contractors to use an implied warranty theory if design specifications authored by someone else 'are defective to the degree that adherence to them results in an article that fails to satisfy a stated performance specification'.[47] However, in cases where the contractor could apprehend the potential for defect, the courts have found that the contractor assumed the risk of defect, and that no implied warranty exists.[48]

Where the contractor contributed pertinent information in designing a project, an implied warranty may not exist.[49] In *Austin v United States*, a contractor entered into a contract to design, manufacture, test and deliver an innovative, novel digital data recording system.[50] The contract already contained some detailed specifications as to the method of constructing the system, but the contractor determined that the contract would be impossible to perform using those specifications.[51] The contractor modified the design, but was still unable to successfully execute the contract.[52] The court denied the contractor the defence of impossibility, finding that because the contractor had integrated his own design into that of the original contract, he warranted his ability to successfully perform those substituted specifications.[53]

Although no cases currently exist that specifically discuss how Spearin warranties are affected by BIM collaboration, it seems clear from analogous cases that extensive contractor and subcontractor involvement may sharply curtail implied warranties.

Insurance

If BIM is used solely to prepare better contract documents, there are few insurance concerns. However, as a collaborative framework, it does create possible issues.

Many professional liability policies have exclusions for 'means and methods' and for joint venture liability. The 'means and methods' exclusions are designed to eliminate coverage for construction activities. In a collaborative setting, the designers may assist in developing sequences and construction procedures that at least skirt this exclusion. Sharing risk and reward, a hallmark of integrated project delivery, is also a joint venture characteristic and may lead insurers to deny or limit liability if joint venture liability is alleged.

Contractors also face insurance issues. Most standard commercial general liability policies exclude professional services and do not cover pure economic losses. As contractors become more deeply embedded in the design process, they must consider whether they should obtain contractor's professional liability coverage. And contractors must also recognise that their standard policies provide little protection from economic claims based on their negligent performance.

Hosting data can create additional insurance issues. Essentially, data loss more closely relates to valuable papers coverages than traditional construction policies. Moreover, if the parties are developing custom software for others' use, there are product risks involved that may not be covered by their usual policies.

The insurance industry is aware of these issues and may see a market in providing coverage for collaborative projects. But currently, the parties must work with their brokers to assure that the tasks they are undertaking on today's projects are adequately covered by their policies.

10.7   Technical Issues

Standards and interoperability

In its purest form, a BIM project would use a single data model for all purposes. Each participant would access the model, adding content that could be accessed immediately by all others. Exploration, analysis, and evaluation would take place within the model with information being exported as contract drawings, fabrication drawings, bills of materials, or other information. But there are several reasons why this goal is only partially realized.

Not every participant uses the same software and not all software is appropriate for all projects or tasks. Designing a software framework that can handle any conceivable project is a daunting task and can result in an overly complex program. In many instances, modeling software was developed to address issues affecting specific trades, such as piping, ductwork, or structural detailing. Not surprisingly, software developed for a specific purpose has advantages when used for that specific purpose. Thus, there are often multiple models existing on a single project that are optimised to a specific task. In a recent project in San Francisco, the subcontractor responsible for a complex structural steel sunscreen used the designer's 3D model to establish design intent and provide baseline data, but entered the information into a second model to generate shop and fabrication drawings. While the preference to use familiar software is understandable, using multiple models undermines the efficacy of the BIM process.

There are three current approaches to the multiple model problem. First, BIM models are becoming more powerful and capable of handling larger portions of the project. Additional software modules can be added to frameworks to customize the framework for specific uses.

Second, standards can be adopted to provide common definitions for the software emulating specific construction elements and systems. The IAI has developed, and is continuing to develop, standardized descriptions through the Industry Foundation Classes (IFC) and IFC/xml common model.[54] Many of the primary BIM software packages are IFC compatible. Under the IAI vision, information in any compatible program can be saved as an .ifc file and then opened and edited in another compatible program. Information is universal with specific tools being used to manipulate the common information.

The third approach, used by Autodesk's® Revit®, seeks to capitalise on the advantages of 'purpose built' modeling systems and lessen the difficulties caused by multiple models by using adjacent models constructed on a common framework that are separate, but closely linked. In addition to IFC compatibility, BIM software is often designed to interact with related software, such as structural or energy analysis programs. Although this approach is very effective if a common engine is used, it can be problematic when merging models built on engines from different software houses.

From the participants' viewpoint, the plurality of solutions makes it more difficult to develop a BIM project. Although all of the solutions may work, as long as participants are committed to different systems, integration will be challenging.

Archiving

Archiving also raises technical and practical issues. Although it is possible to save the model onto electronic media, this does not guarantee that the saved model will be usable. Properly prepared paper has an archival life of 100 years and, if carefully preserved, can last longer. We have limited experience with the long-term reliability of digital systems. We are aware that most magnetic media have limited lifespans. CDs and DVDs can last considerably longer, but that may be irrelevant. When the author began practicing law in 1979, word processing departments used eight-inch floppies and magcards. It would be hard to find any hardware that could read these formats, let alone run the software necessary to access and read the Displaywrite files. As succinctly stated by one commentator, '... the truth is that our digital storage media have a shorter lifespan than an old man with a good memory.'[55]

Technology obsolescence issues led The Rosetta Project to micro-etch analog information onto nickel disks rather than entrust the world's languages to the fickleness of digital technologies.[56] If data is archived on currently popular media, with currently popular software, it may be difficult or impossible to restore or view the data when needed. How long do we need to maintain models and how should this be accomplished?

10.8   Integrated Project Delivery: The Way Forward

BIM does not require a collaborative process. Designers can use the existing software to prepare traditional plans and specifications without providing the digital model to the contractor, its sub-contractors and suppliers, or even to the owner, itself. Contractors can create models for estimating, fabricating or construction simulation without ever sharing the information. However, doing so wastes the power of BIM as a collaborative framework and discards the cost and quality advantages of single entry, multiple use. This interrelationship between BIM and Integrated Project Delivery (IPD) was reflected in the AIA/AIACC Guide:

> A Note on Building Information Modeling
>
> It is understood that integrated project delivery and building information modeling (BIM) are different concepts – the first is a process and the second a tool. Certainly integrated projects are done without BIM and BIM is used in non-integrated processes. However, the full potential benefits of both IPD and BIM are achieved only when they are used together. Thus, the IPD phase descriptions included here assume the use of BIM.[57]

Moreover, an insular approach ignores current best practices favouring integrated project delivery with BIM at its core. To use BIM effectively, one must understand the trend to collaborative processes.

10.9   CURT White Papers – 2004 Report

The construction industry has long been plagued by fragmented and fractious project delivery processes. Competitive low bid procurement, guaranteed maximum price and similar contract structures have fostered an individualistic, zero-sum approach to construction. These processes, in conjunction with other influences, have resulted in declining productivity. The Construction Users Roundtable (CURT) has concluded that wholesale industry change is necessary to achieve successful projects.[58]

In response to these productivity concerns, CURT issued a 2004 report implementing a CURT policy favoring IPD methodologies.[59] The report proposed four elements of a new policy framework.

1. **Owner Leadership**: Owners, as the integrating influence in the building process, must engage in and demand that collaborative teams openly share information and use appropriate technology. CURT should establish policy and procedures to implement change in the AEC industry and encourage other building owner organisations to join the effort.

2. **Integrated Project Structure**: The building process cannot be optimised without full collaboration among all members of the design/build/own project. CURT and other owner organisations should establish policies that support such collaboration.

3. **Open Information Sharing**: Project collaboration must be characterised by open, timely, and reliable information sharing. CURT should advocate the establishment of procedures and protocols to achieve this end.

4. **Virtual Building Models**: Effectively designed and deployed information technology will support full collaboration and information sharing and will lead to more effective design/build/manage process. CURT should endorse establishing technology-based lifecycles that optimise the creation, interaction, and transport of digital information throughout the building process.

10.10 Second CURT Report

CURT's vision of an integrated project built around virtual building information models was sharpened in a later report on implementing the optimized building process.

Technology/BIM

Desire for re-use of project information beyond the building design created by architects and engineers will drive market adoption of building information models. Standards will be established for how building information models are developed with regard to content and modeling methods to produce information supporting downstream BIM automation services that are aligned with the owner's business objectives. Ultimately, for BIM to succeed, owners must acknowledge that all risk comes from them and ultimately returns to them.

Owners must set the tone for the project by requiring their design and construction teams to use the latest technologies. Including these requirements in requests for proposals is one simple step that owners can start using. Further, the owner should use the technology as well.

Owners should support industry initiatives to create standards where they are needed. Owners should also increase their awareness of the technology tools their consultants and contractors are using on their projects. Owners must recognise that the choice of technology solutions will affect their projects, not just during the development phase, but also after the project is completed and operating.[60]

Information Sharing

An essential element woven throughout the vision of transformation to an optimized model is the ability for all parties to communicate freely. Current practices of silence for fear of liability must be eliminated and a new process where decisions are made at the highest and most appropriate level of competency must be established to leverage team knowledge. ... This issue most certainly is the greatest obstacle to transformation and the realization of the optimized project. Owners must demand this openness and transparency from the team entity of which they are a part.[61]

CURT's message is quite clear. Projects should be capitalised on the competencies of all project participants and should promote open communication using the best technologies available. Building information models should be at the core of the process. But CURT does not explain how this radical transformation should occur, nor how to resolve the boundary problem.

10.11   Industry responses

In June 2007, the American Institute of Architects California Counsel issued 'Integrated Project Delivery: A Working Definition'.[62] This document sets forth the fundamental assumptions and framework for a fully integrated project. Summarized in the graphic below,[63] it defines a highly collaborative process where all key participants are involved throughout the project lifecycle and contribute on a 'best person' and 'best for project' basis.

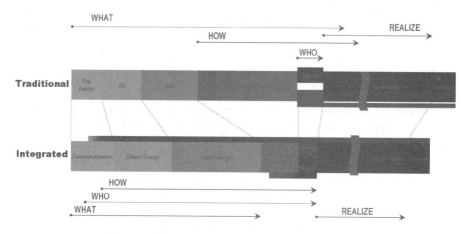

These concepts were further elaborated in the joint AIA/AIACC Integrated Project Delivery: A Guide,[64] and have now been embodied in form integrated project agreements using Single Purpose Entity[65] and a Owner-Architect[66]/Owner-Contractor[67] approaches.

The Associated General Contractors and others have recently released their ConsensusDocs Series 300 integrated project delivery agreement which is based on the earlier Lean Construction Institute agreement.[68]   It is a collaborative, multi-party agreement (owner/contractor/architect).

10.12   Contractual frameworks

Many of the legal issues related to collaboration are caused by duties and obligations that transcend boundaries.   When assessing contractual frameworks, it is useful to compare how they address (or ignore) boundary issues.

Status quo

BIM will be used regardless of business models. As stated to the author by a partner in a major international architectural firm: 'We are using it. We will use it. Owners should just demand it.' BIM can overcome the liability concerns and in the hands of experienced users, reduces risk even if responsibility increases. If BIM reduces drawing errors and miscommunications between the parties, the frequency and severity of loss will be lessened even if the pool of potential relying parties is expanded.[69] However, little is done to address boundaries, because they are simply ignored.

Design/build

Design/build solves the boundary problem by increasing the boundary's perimeter until it absorbs the key participants. Thus, information sharing and reliance issues are resolved by joining the provider to the relying party. For this strategy to be fully effective, the key participants must be identified and included in the design/build team. This is automatically accomplished if the designers are employed by the design/build firm. It is more challenging if the designers or key systems providers are subcontractors to the design/build firm. In this instance, the additional parties can become part of the 'virtual' design/build team if their liability is limited and their compensation, at least in part, is performance based.

Single Purpose Entities

Single Purpose Entities (SPE) also solve the boundary problem by bringing all parties within the boundary. The SPE is a limited liability enterprise (corporation, limited liability company, limited liability partnership, for example) created to design, construct and possibly own and operate a facility. The key participants sponsor the SPE and achieve gain by optimising the SPE's success. The SPE contracts with the sponsors for the services required to construct the facility, with the specifics of scope, responsibility and liability determined on a project specific basis. The parties within the boundary must release each other from most potential liabilities or agree that any 'in boundary' claims will be paid only by project insurance.

SPEs are common in off balance sheet asset financed projects (project finance). Under a classic project finance structure, non-recourse loans are used to design and construct a revenue generating asset that is owned by the SPE. The asset, and any guaranteed income streams, secure the loans. As might be expected, there are also numerous variations with limited recourse, limited sponsor guarantees and similar features. However, the fundamental economic principle of the SPE is that the sponsor's return is based on creating value in the SPE.

Unfortunately, SPEs burden the project with the additional costs of creating the SPE and managing its operations, precluding SPEs for smaller projects. Research on project finance shows that most projects exceed $100 million, and a significant percentage exceed $500 million.[70] Furthermore, because the created value may be locked into the SPE for some time, the structure may not meet the parties' liquidity requirements.

Interlocking risk allocation

Interlocking risk allocations leave boundaries in place, but lessen their importance. Under this approach, the key participants jointly negotiate specific limitations to their individual liabilities using releases, indemnifications and limitations of liability. The interlocking risk allocations lessen the liability fears that accompany free flow of information.

Interlocking risk allocation has three potential drawbacks. First, there is a risk that the provisions will be inadequately drafted or incomplete. Second, some jurisdictions have restrictions on liability limitations or indemnification that could undermine this approach. Finally, although the risk allocations lessen disincentives, they do not create any additional incentive to collaborate. To enhance their success, interlocking allocation should be balanced by performance incentives.

Relation based contracting (NEC3, Lean Construction)

The New Engineering Contract (NEC3) is a contract system currently published in the UK that is based on a collaborative management approach.[71]

The two principles on which the Engineering and Construction Contract (ECC) are based and which impact upon the objective of stimulating good management are:

- o foresight applied collaboratively mitigates problems and shrinks risk, and
- o clear division of function and responsibility helps accountability and motivates people to play their part.

A secondary but important theme is that people will be motivated to play their part in collaborative management if it is in their commercial and professional interest to do so. Reliance need not be placed upon exhortation, either within the contract or outside it.[72]

Lean Construction seeks to apply the Toyota management principles to the construction industry.[73] This includes recasting Toyota's just-in-time project delivery methodology into the concept of Last Planner, where project management becomes a workflow conversation from one precedent activity to the next. The Lean Construction approach has been applied in the Sutter Health system where it was distilled into Five Big Ideas.[74]

- o Collaborate; really collaborate, throughout design, planning, and execution;
- o Increase relatedness among all project participants;
- o Projects are networks of commitments;
- o Optimise the projects not the pieces; and
- o Tightly couple action with learning.

Relational contracting is based on early and deep collaboration between all members of the design and construction process. Although BIM is not required to accomplish these ends, it supports relational contracting at a fundamental level. However, neither of these approaches directly addresses the liabilities inherent with increased collaboration. They assume that more collaboration results in less risk, therefore less loss.

Alliancing

The alliance approach to contracting has been successfully used for oil exploration, the delivery of infrastructure, and at least one significant structure.[75] A recent definition of alliancing is:

> A project alliance is a commercial/legal framework between a department, agency or government-backed enterprise (GBE) as "owner-participant" and one or more private sector parties as "service provider" or "non-owner participants" (NOPs) for delivery of one or more capital works projects, characterised by:
> - o collective sharing of (nearly) all project risks;
> - o no fault, no blame and no dispute between the alliance participants (except in very limited cased of default);
> - o payment of NOPs for their services under a "3-limb" compensation model comprising:

- reimbursement of NOPs' project costs on 100% open book basis;

- a fee to cover corporate overheads and normal profit; and

- a gainshare/painshare regime where the rewards of outstanding performance and the pain or poor performance are shared equitably among all alliance participants;
  - o unanimous principle-based decision-making on all key project issues; and
  - o an integrated project team selected on the basis of best person for each position.[76]

Initially developed for risky projects,[77] alliancing has attributes that are attractive in a broader setting. Three alliancing features work particularly well with BIM.

First, in an Alliance, the parties agree that they will not sue each other, except for willful default. Sharing information can not lead to liability. The liability concerns that impede BIM adoption do not apply in an Alliance project.

Second, because a portion of compensation is tied to a successful outcome, there is an incentive to collaborate. In this context, BIM is an ideal platform for interactively sharing information, ideas and solutions.

During early project development, the parties develop a Target Cost Estimate that is used to calculate a Target Outturn Cost (TOC). The amount of each party's compensation depends on whether the Actual Outturn Cost (AOC) matches, exceeds or is less than the TOC. In all cases, the non-owner participants are guaranteed their direct project costs plus project specific overhead. Thus, if the AOC exceeds the TOC, the non-owner participants forfeit any profit or company overhead (painshare). If the AOC equals the TOC, the non-owner participants also receive their corporate overhead and 'usual' profit. If the AOC is less than the TOC, then the non-owner participants also receive a portion of the difference (gainshare).

Thus, there is a positive incentive for non-owner participants to assist each other. Contractors and vendors will want to participate in the design process to root out any source of error and suggest better, alternative methods of construction. Similarly, designers have an incentive to provide the model to contractors to allow accurate take-offs and construction simulations because they will increase project efficiency, as a whole. When compensation is tied to success, decisions are made on a 'best for project' basis. Similarly, if issues arise during project execution, it will be in everyone's best interest to seek the optimal solution for the project.

Finally, under a 'best person' philosophy, design can be delegated through the model, or by using interacting models, to the person, whether designer, subcontractor, fabricator or supplier, with the greatest knowledge and skill.

These attributes are tailor made for BIM. By limiting liability and tying compensation to firm success, alliancing makes boundaries irrelevant. BIM is also tailor made for alliancing. Because it is fundamentally collaborative, BIM provides a structure for 'best for project' decision making.

10.13   *Integrated Project Delivery*

Collaborative project approaches are beginning to appear in the United States under the general term 'Integrated Project Delivery.' Unlike Alliancing, which has generally been used for major civil and industrial infrastructure, IPD in the United States has been primarily used for complex vertical structures, such as hospitals. IPD is a radical departure from traditional prescriptive and adversarial contract approaches and offers the potential for increased project value and greater reward for all participants.

Most of the existing IPD projects have been performed using manuscript agreements.[78] Two of the primary publishers of standard agreements, the American Institute of Architects and ConsensusDOCS have also issued contracts for use in integrated projects although their approaches vary significantly. ConsensusDOCS has issued a multi-party agreement[79] that, depending upon the internal options chosen, can support a collaborative project. The American Institute of Architects has issued two very different contract sets. The most innovative uses a special purpose limited liability company that is owned by the project owner, architect and contractor.[80] The special purpose entity contracts with the architect and the contractor to design and construct the project subject to its direction with incentives and risks based on project performance. This approach is flexible, but complex and, depending upon where the project is located, can create corporate governance and licensing issues. The AIA's alternative approach[81] is more traditional. The contractor and architect separately contract with the owner under terms that encourage collaboration, but still adheres to traditional compensation models, risk allocation, and project management roles.

Although the custom and standard form IPD approaches vary significantly,[82] they all assume early involvement by key construction as well as design personnel. Moreover, they assume a high level of information exchange that is consistent with and supported by BIM. This leads recursively to BIM being best supported by collaborative project delivery methods that themselves are best executed using BIM.

10.14   Conclusion

BIM promises exponential improvements in construction quality and efficiency. But current business and contract models do not encourage its use and actively inhibit the collaboration at its core. To bring BIM into the mainstream, we need to recraft business models and contract relationships to reward 'best for project' decision making and to equitably allocate responsibility among all construction participants.

Acknowledgement: *This chapter was originally written as a paper delivered in London, U.K., at the Society of Construction Law in October 2008 and updated in June 2009. It is reprinted here with permission of the Society. Reprints are available from the Society of Construction Law at www.scl.org.uk.*

---

[1]   For example, the General Services Administration, the United States Army Corps of Engineers and the United States Coast Guard all have BIM requirements.

[2]   'Building Information Modeling,' McGraw-Hill SmartMarket Report (2008) reports increasing adoption of BIM throughout all sectors of the design and construction industry, albeit at different rates for different disciplines. In the author's personal practice, BIM has become standard practice in significant projects and commonplace in others.

[3]   Gilligan and Kunz, 'VDC Use in 2007: Significant Value, Dramatic Growth, and Apparent Business Opportunity' (Center for Integrated Facility Engineering, Report TR171, 2007).

[4]   Autodesk press releases in 2006 and 2007 reported 100,000 Revit seats sold through 8 June 2006 and over 200,000 seats sold through 4 May 2007.

[5]   'Interoperability in the Construction Industry' (McGraw Hill SmartMarket Report, 2007), page 11.

[6]   Computationally and Numerically Controlled. This is a manufacturing process where the fabrication of components is done by machines responding to computer directives, not human operation. Modern machining is often 'CNC' because of its accuracy and repeatability. It also allows creation of complex and curved shapes that would be very difficult to duplicate with manually controlled tools.

[7] An example is the Camera Obscura, Phase II at Mitchell Park designed by SHoP Architects. The structure was CNC manufactured from the design model and then 'installed' by the contractor. The 'installers' did not use plans, rather they had instructions, much as might be in a kit, explaining where parts went and how to connect them.

[8] The National Institute of Building Science, through the buildingSMARTalliance, is developing a National BIM Standard (the NBIMS Project, <www.buildingsdmartalliance.org/nbims>) and the buildingSMART International Alliance for Interoperability (<www.iai-international.org>) has long been working on standards for data exchange between modeling software. Moreover, there is growing demand for open-source data structures that support interoperability

[9] Most notably, the National BIM Standard, see note 8. Moreover, standard contractual addenda have been issued to support using BIM. See, for example, Consensus DOCS 301-2008 Building Information Modeling Addendum and AIA Document E202-2008, Building Information Modeling Protocol Exhibit.

[10] See, for example, the American Institute of Architects (AIA) standard documents C106-2007 Digital Data Licensing, E201-2007 Digital Data Protocol and the ConsensusDocs Document 200.2 Electronic Communications Protocol Addendum. For additional information and a comparison of the AIA and ConsensusDOCS approaches, see K. Hurtado and H. Ashcraft, 'Developing Meaningful Contract Terms for Electronic Communication on Construction Projects,' The Construction Lawyer, Vol. 29, Spring 2009.

[11] The Associated General Contractors is promoting the use of BIM and has published 'A Contractor's Guide to Building Information Modeling, Edition One', that is intended to show contractors 'how to get started' with BIM. The American Institute of Architects (AIA) Technology and Practice Committee has long supported the use of digital design tools and BIM. In April 2007, the AIA introduced its digital practice documents C106-2007 and E201-2007, see note 10.

[12] The NIBS is responsible for the National BIM Standard, see note 8.

[13] <www.buildingsmartalliance.org/nbims/about>

[14] The terminology varies between software platforms. However, there are at least three types of objects in any program. At the highest level are classes that abstractly represent a family of objects. Walls, for example, are an abstract family. These families or classes can be subclassed into specific object types, such as a masonry wall. Subclasses inherit the attributes of their family and add attributes appropriate to the subclass. Classes and subclasses are essentially descriptions, not the object, itself. Instances are the individual examples of a subclass in the design. This hierarchy makes it possible for designers to quickly create new component types by subclassing an existing component type, adding or modifying attributes, and then creating as many instances of the newly design component as desired.

[15] In discussion with myself, design firms with significant BIM experience have reported 50% reduction in time to produce drawings, compared with conventional 2D CAD drawings.

[16] NavisWorks® was used to model LucasFilm's Digital Arts Center; it identified several significant conflicts before construction commenced and was used to check field construction, again identifying mislocated elements and penetrations.

[17] L Khemlani, 'Autodesk Revit: Implementation in Practice (Arcwiz 2004).

[18] Supporting graphic creativity is already being addressed by the primary software houses, for example, Autodesk's Architectural Desktop® and Google's Sketch Up®.

[19] 'Building Information Modeling for Sustainable Design' (Autodesk® 2005).

[20] Design-build avoids the tension between collaboration and separateness by reducing the number of principal participants. Thus, many of the commercial and legal issues related to implementing BIM are obviated in the design-build project delivery system or its variants. However, design-build is not appropriate on all projects and is not permitted on others, such as some public agency projects. In any event, design-build does not address all of the issues relating to implementing BIM processes.

[21] 'Intelligent Building Models and Downstream Use' (Comments of the Technology in Architectural Practice Advisory Group submitted for the 2007 revisions to the AIA's documents B141 (Standard Form of Agreement Between Owner and Architect without a Predefined Scope of Architect's Services) and A201 (General Conditions of Contract for Construction), American Institute of Architects 2005).

[22] AIA document B141-1997, Standard Form of Agreement Between Owner and Architect without a Predefined Scope of Architect's Services, §1.3.2.4.

[23] AIA document C106-2007, Digital Data Licensing Agreement.

[24] AIA document E201-1997, Digital Data Protocol Exhibit.

[25] In contrast, the documents published by the Engineers Joint Contract Documents Committee (EJCDC) take a very conservative approach toward electronic information. They disallow any reliance on electronic information and place the risk of errors and discrepancies on the receiving party. This approach may be appropriate to the transfer of CAD files, but is totally inconsistent with a collaborative (BIM) approach. For example, EJCDC C-700, §3.06, states: '3.06 Electronic Data

> A. Unless otherwise stated in the Supplementary Conditions, the data furnished by Owner or Engineer to Contractor, or by Contractor to Owner or Engineer, that may be relied upon are limited to the printed copies (also known as hard copies). Files in electronic media format of text, data, graphics, or other types are furnished only for the convenience of the receiving party. Any conclusion or information obtained or derived from such electronic files will be at the user's

sole risk. If there is a discrepancy between the electronic files and the hard copies, the hard copies govern.

B. Because data stored in electronic media format can deteriorate or be modified inadvertently or otherwise without authorization of the data's creator, the party receiving electronic files agrees that it will perform acceptance tests or procedures within 60 days, after which the receiving party shall be deemed to have accepted the data thus transferred. Any errors detected within the 60-day acceptance period will be corrected by the transferring party.

C. When transferring documents in electronic media format, the transferring party makes no representations as to long term compatibility, usability, or readability of documents resulting from the use of software application packages, operating systems, or computer hardware differing from those used by the data's creator.'

[26] ConsensuDOCS 200.2 (2007). For a comparison of the ConsensuDOCS and AIA approaches, see H Ashcraft and K Hurtado, *Saving the Trees and Managing the Paper: Developing Meaningful Contract Terms for Construction Project Electronic Communications Protocols*, ABA Forum on the Construction Industry, Fall 2008.

[27] AIA document A201-1997, General Conditions of the Contract for Construction, §1.6.1.

[28] ConsensusDOCS 301 (2008).

[29] 'Building Information Modeling Protocol Exhibit,' AIA document E202 (2008). The E202 is available with Model Element Tables matching traditional AIA phase definitions, the newer Integrated Project Delivery phase definitions, or with blank phase definitions that can be defined by the user(s).

[30] The Model Element Table is based on the Model Progression Matrix developed by AIA California Council and can be downloaded at www.ipd-ca.net/Model%20Progression%20Spec%20V%2008-08-20.xls

[31] 'UNIFORMAT II Elemental Classification for Building Specifications, Cost Estimating and Cost Analysis' (National Institute of Standards and Technology, Department of Commerce, Doc NISTIR 6389).

[32] The Industry Foundation Classes specification is a neutral data format to describe, exchange and share information typically used within the building and facility management industry sector. The IFC specification is developed and maintained by buildingSMART International, bSI, (formally known as International Alliance for Interoperability, IAI). http://www.ifcwiki.org/index.php/Main_Page

[33] *M A Mortenson Company Inc v Timberline Software Corporation*, 140 Wn.2d 568; 998 P.2d 305 (2000).

[34] *M A Mortenson Company Inc v Timberline Software Corporation*, 140 Wn.2d 568, 584-588 (2000).

[35] *Frankfort Digital Services v Kistler* 477 F.3d 1117 (9th Cir 2007), at 1126.

[36] In California, for example, architects must be in 'responsible control' (Cal Bus & Prof, §5531.5) and engineers must be in 'responsible charge' (Cal Bus & Prof, §6703). These requirements reverberate through many other statutes and regulations.

[37] At least one insurer of design professionals is currently considering a 'technology rider' to expand professional liability coverage to include some information technology risks.

[38] See, *Zubulake v UBS*, 220 FRD 212 (SDNY 2003) ('Zubulake IV') and *Zubulake v UBS*, 229 FRD 422 (SDNY 2004) ('Zubulake V').

[39] Although there are many notable examples, it is interesting that one of the Supreme Court's earliest construction decisions, *US v Spearin*, 248 US 132 (1918) concerned where to place the boundary between the owner's responsibility and the responsibility of the contractor.

[40] See comment h to Subsection (2) of Restatement of Torts (Second), §552.

[41] Further exposition on the economic loss rule can be found in papers published in The Construction Lawyer, Vol 25, No 4 (2005) under the title 'Taking the Measure of the Economic Loss Rule'. See, also, Andrus, Gessford & Joce, 'The Economic Loss Doctrine in Construction Cases: Are the Odds for Design Professionals Better in Vegas?'(Journal of the American College of Construction Lawyers, Winter 2008), page 53.

[42] We have all experienced clients that will execute contract documents with detailed provisions governing change, notice, and dispute resolution and then ignore these provisions during contract performance. Or they will create entirely new mechanisms that deviate significantly from the systems provided in the contract. In this fashion, we must expect deviation from whatever prospective systems we and our clients develop. Technology may change, but people do not.

[43] In over 20 years of representing designers, the author has only once defended a designer sued because the design was 'ugly'.

[44] *United States v Spearin* (1918) 248 US 132.

[45] Golden, 25 Pub Cont LJ, at 48 note 2 (quoting Thomas L Patten, 'The Implied Warranty That Attaches to Government Furnished Design Specifications', 31 FED B J 291, 292 (1972)).

[46] *Hercules Inc v United States* (1994) 24 F.3d 188, 197.

[47] *RJ Crowley, Inc v United States*, 1990 US App Lexis 21618.

[48] *Blake Construction Co v United States* (1993) 987 F.2d 743, 746; *Austin*, 314 F.2d at 519; *TL James & Co v Traylor Bros* (2002) 294 F.3d 743, 751; *Martin K Eby*, 436 F. Supp 2d at 1310.

[49] *Austin Co*, 314 F.2d, page 520.

[50] *Austin Co*, note 49, page 519.

[51] *Austin Co*, note 49, page 519.

[52] *Austin Co*, note 49, page 519.

[53] *Austin Co*, note 49, page 520.

[54] Additional information concerning the IAI and IFC foundation classes can be found at <www.iai-international.org>

[55] M Wein being quoted by Norsam Technologies, the archival vendor for The Rosetta Project.

[56] www.rosettaproject.org/about-us/rosetta-disk/technolog

[57] 'Integrated Project Delivery: A Guide', explanatory note at page 20 (American Institute of Architects / American Institute of Architects California Council, 2008).

[58] 'Optimising the Construction Process: An Implementation Strategy', WP-1003, page 4, (The Construction Users Roundtable July 2006).

[59] 'Collaboration, Integrated Information and the Project Lifecycle in Building Design, Construction and Operation', WP-1202 (The Construction Users Roundtable August 2004).

[60] CURT Report 2004, note 59, page 14.

[61] CURT Report 2004, note 59.

[62] www.ipd-ca.net/images/Integrated%20Project%20Delivery%20Definition.pdf

[63] Reproduced with permission of the American Institute of Architects California Counsel.

[64] www.aia.org/ipdg

[65] Standard Form Single Purpose Entity Agreement for Integrated Project Delivery, AIA C195-2008

[66] Standard Form of Agreement Between Owner and Architect for Integrated Project Delivery, AIA B195-2008.

[67] Standard Form of Agreement Between Owner and Contractor for Integrated Project Delivery, AIA A195-2008.

[68] www.consensusdocs.org

[69] Risk management can take alternate routes. A person can choose to insulate him or herself from liability by contract, thus reducing the risk of being successfully sued. In the alternate, the person can embrace the risk, manage it, and avoid the failure that would give rise to the lawsuit. Although both are rational, they represent very different approaches to risk management.

[70] Benjamin C. Esty, 'Modern Project Finance' (Wiley 2004), Exhibit 2-9, page 38.

[71] NEC Engineering and Construction Contract (Thomas Telford) www.neccontract.com.

[72] 'Guidance Notes for the NEC Engineering and Construction Contract' (Thomas Telford).

[73] www.leanconstruction.org

[74] William A Lichtig, 'Ten key decisions to a successful construction project' (paper delivered at the American Bar Association, Forum on the Construction Fall Meet, September 2005).

[75] Australian National Museum.

[76] 'Project Alliancing Practitioner's Guide (Government of Victoria 2006), page 2.

[77] The Alliancing delivery system was developed for oil exploration in the North Sea. At the time of these projects, it was not clear that they could be accomplished and at what cost. Alliancing guaranteed recovery of costs and created incentives to collectively manage uncertainty and risk, thus eliminating the fear that causes participants to focus on their narrow self-interests.

[78] Sutter Health in California has undertaken a broad range of hospital and healthcare projects using its proprietary contract form. Variants of this form have been used for hospital and research laboratory projects in Missouri and Wisconsin. The author's practice has used an approach that was initially developed for Autodesk projects in California and Massachusetts that were closely modeled on IPD principles. This approach has also been used on hospital projects.

[79] 'Standard Form of Tri-Party Agreement for Collaborative Project Delivery', ConsensusDOCS 300 (2007).

[80] 'Standard Form Single Purpose Entity Agreement for Integrated Project Delivery' AIA Document C195 (2008). The Single Purpose Entity series also include the 'Standard Form of Agreement Between Single Purpose Entity and Owner for Integrated Project Delivery' AIA Document C196 (2008) and the 'Standard Form of Agreement Between Single Purpose Entity and Non-Owner Member for Integrated Project Delivery' AIA Document C197 (2008).

[81] 'Standard Form of Agreement between Owner and Contractor for Integrated Project Delivery' AIA Document A195 (2008); 'General Conditions of the Contract

for Integrated Project Delivery' AIA Document A295 (2008); and 'Standard Form of Agreement between Owner and Architect for Integrated Project Delivery' AIA Document B195 (2008).

[82] The key IPD elements are 1) early involvement of key participants; 2) designing to budget rather than designing to the programme; 3) joint project management; 4) economic risk and reward shared based on project outcome; and 5) waiver of claims to reduce internal conflict and defensiveness. These elements are not completely embraced in the current standard form agreements.

Chapter 11

Insuring IPD/BIM Risks

J. Kent Holland, Esq.

11.1   Introduction

The Integrated Project Delivery (IPD) method is an effort to bring the parties to the construction project together into a collaborative process – working together in a spirit of cooperation and trust for the mutual benefit of everyone – and particularly for the good of the project. This concept, which only a few years ago sounded too utopian to have any practical merit, seems to actually be catching on.

New contract forms by the American Institute of Architects (AIA) and Consensus DOCs have been created expressly for the IPD project. Meanwhile, Building Information Modeling (BIM), which has become the hottest topic of the day, is a powerful tool furthering collaboration.

BIM will lead to more IPD. Or IPD will lead to more BIM. But is all this new technology and collaboration realistically going to bring about the perfect project? Will most claims and litigation among contracting parties be avoided or eliminated? And if there are claims, will we be able to sort out who is responsible so that insurance coverage might cover the loss?

For risk managers and construction lawyers advising clients, it may be prudent to consider whether the next several years of navigating the bumps in the road to implementing IPD and BIM may result in greater risks instead of less – with some of those risks potentially resulting in uninsured losses. Because there will be such a strong connection or relationship between IPD and BIM, this paper addresses the insurability of the unique risks of IPD especially as impacted by BIM. For instance, one concern is that project owners are being oversold on the concept that IPD and BIM will provide answers to all their problems.   Another concern is that when problems inevitably arise, there will be no protection available under the traditional insurance programs maintained by the project participants. We focus here on a few of the increased risks that may result from the use of IPD and BIM to facilitate the design and construction of structures.

11.2.   What is Integrated Project Delivery?

A "working definition" of IPD has been developed by the AIA California Council as follows:

> Integrated Project Delivery (IPD) is a project delivery approach that integrates people, systems, business structures and practices into a process that collaboratively harnesses the talents and insights of all participants to reduce waste and optimize efficiency through all phases of design, fabrication and construction.   IPD principles can be applied to a variety of contractual arrangements and IPD teams will usually include members well beyond the basic triad of owner, architect, and contractor.   At a minimum, though, an Integrated Project includes tight collaboration between the owner, the architect, and the general contractor ultimately responsible for construction of the project, from early design through project handover.[1]

11.3   What is Building Information Modeling (BIM)?

A working definition of BIM, as published by the National Institute of Building Sciences, states that BIM "utilizes cutting edge digital technology to establish a computable representation of all the physical and functional characteristics of a facility and its related project/life cycle information, and is intended to be a repository for the facility owner/operator to use and maintain throughout the life cycle of a facility."[2]

BIM has also been described thus: "It goes beyond two-dimensional or three dimensional representations of a building design.   BIM perhaps is better imagined as a virtual simulation of the building's actual life cycle, including design, construction, usage, and maintenance."[3]

BIM is not a new project delivery system. Rather, it is a new tool to facilitate design and construction in any number of project delivery systems, including, among others, IPD, design-build, and design-bid-build.   To facilitate use of this new tool, the Facilities Information Council of the

National Institutes of Building Sciences[4] published a national BIM standard and the Associated General Contractors of America (AGC) has issued The Contractor's Guide to BIM.[5]

Although it is common to hear BIM referred to as though each project only involves one single BIM model, the reality most often is that, when BIM is used as a tool on a project, multiple models are in use. Each participant typically maintains its own separate model - the architect, civil engineer, structural engineer, contractor, subcontractors, and fabricators. Each of these project participants uses computer software of its own choosing for its model. Each participant uses its model for its own unique purposes.

Assuming that the individual models are compatible so as to permit them to communicate their data to a central model, it is possible that an integrated BIM model for a project may be maintained. We will address the practical and legal issues arising out of the use of the individual and integrated BIM models after addressing IPD and the interplay of BIM with IPD.

11.4   What is the Role of Building Information Modeling in IPD?

According to the AIA Guide, "BIM is a tool, not a project delivery method, but IPD process methods work hand in hand with BIM and leverage the tool's capabilities."[6] The AIA California Council goes so far as to say that BIM is an essential to efficient use of IPD.

> Although it is possible to achieve Integrated Project Delivery without Building Information Modeling, it is the opinion and recommendation of this study that Building Information Modeling is essential to efficiently achieve the collaboration required for Integrated Project Delivery.[7]

11.5.   What is Different about the Risks Inherent in IPD?

No single contractual means exists to create an IPD project. The AIA and Consensus DOCS, for example, take different approaches to establish an IPD project. For instance, the project may involve at least two essential contracts: A project alliance contract or a relational contract.

11.5.1   Project Alliance Contract

One type of agreement has been termed the "Project Alliance" agreement, because it includes all of the parties participating in the design and construction of the project. For instance, the alliance contract may include the architect, engineer, construction manager, major contractors, trades, and fabricators. The team members sign the contract stating their roles and how they will share in the total project performance risk, as well as the profit or loss. Depending upon the contract model used, the parties may agree to waive claims against each other (except for willful default).[8]

The AIA Integrated Project Delivery Guide explains the Project Alliance method of contracting as follows:

> The Project Alliance participants agree to waive liability among each other except for willful default. Willful default does not occur unless a party abandons the project. For all practical purposes, there are no liability concerns within the Project Alliance." However, the Project Alliance, and its participants, are still liable for damage inflicted on third parties.... Standard liability insurance will generally be sufficient to address third-party incidents, and the unified structure of a Project Alliance is well suited to Owner Controlled Insurance Plans (OCIP) or similar wrap-up policies. The insurances should, in all instances, be reviewed to identify potential coverage limitations, such as joint-venture exclusions, professional services exclusions, or limitations on coverage for construction level services (i.e. means and methods exclusions in professional liability policies.)[9]

With regard to dispute resolution in the context of Project Alliances, the AIA Guide suggests:

> Because liability is released within the Project Alliance, there are no dispute resolution mechanisms. Decisions made by and for the Project Alliance are by facilitated consensus. The parties have agreed to abide those decisions; as such there can be no further dispute to resolve.[10]

If issues are resolved entirely by consensus, without any formal dispute process, it may be impossible for an insured to demonstrate that it has legal responsibility to which the insurance policy is required to respond.

11.5.2 Relational Contract

At the other end of the spectrum is the "Relational Contract" signed by the project team members. As described by the AIA Integrated Project Delivery Guide,[11]

> Relational Contracts are similar to Project Alliance in that a virtual organization is created from individual entities. However, it differs in its approach to compensation, risk sharing and decision making. In a relational contract, the parties may agree to limit their liability to each other, but it is not completely waived. If errors are made, conventional insurance is expected to respond.

Under a Relational Contract, which creates the relationship between the parties designing and constructing the project, it is possible (depending upon the language between the team and the project owner) for a court to find joint and several liability arising out of the contract between the team and the project owner.[12] The agreement between the team and the project owner is the second primary contract between the project team and the project owner.

The AIA Guide states that under these contracts, parties are responsible for their own errors and omissions. Herein lays the distinctive difference between the two contracts: Liability among participants is *waived* in the Alliance Contract, while it is not in the Relational Contract. In reviewing various contracts, it is observed that project contingencies may be established to cover damages within a first dollar amount. For damages exceeding the contingencies, the contracts may require the relevant participant to accept responsibility for damages and losses resulting from its work. With regard to insurance coverage, the AIA Guide states:

> Conventional insurance products are used by the participants in relational contract projects. Each participant purchases its own insurance, which protects it against its own liability. But the policies should be carefully reviewed against the services each party will provide. If a contractor is providing incidental design or design-build services, Contractor's Professional Liability coverage should be obtained. If designers will be assisting with sequencing or other construction level services, the policies should be reviewed for exclusions that might limit coverage for means and methods or construction-related activities.[13]

11.5.3   Single Purpose Entity Contract

As another option, the owner may be one of the parties to the contract with the alliance team. Here, a contract model is used to bring all the parties to the project together into a Single Purpose Entity (SPE), which includes the owner along with the designers and contractors. As described by the AIA Integrated Project Delivery Guide:[14]

> A Single Purpose Entity (SPE) is a temporary, but formal, legal structure created to realize a specific project. The SPE can be a corporation, limited liability company, limited liability partnership, or other legal form. In an integrated SPE, key participants have an equity interest in the SPE based on their individual skill, creativity, experience, services, access to capital or financial contribution. Typically, equity owners are paid for any services they provide to the SPE. However, an additional element of compensation is tied to overall project success.

According to the AIA Guide, "Participant liability to the SPE and to other participants is theoretically unlimited, but in practice is often adjusted by contract. Typical risk management tools are limitations of liability, consequential damage waivers, waivers of liability, and waivers of subrogation."[15]

11.6   Collaboration Changes Responsibilities and Liabilities

Depending upon how the IPD is structured, and what contract documents are used, the emphasis on collaboration changes the individual responsibilities that each member of the team would typically have if the traditional project procurement and contracting methods were applied. Instead of carefully-delineated responsibility for each individual participant, the IPD seeks to establish a new culture of "no blame."

When things don't go as expected, and there are design errors, construction defects, time delays and cost overruns, liability may be assigned to the entire project team on some sort of shared basis, even if a particular participant had nothing to do with causing the problem. This approach to liability is in sharp contrast to the common allocation of liability along defined lines of responsibility for design issues or construction issues in a traditional project structure.

Just as IPD calls for collaboration and intersection of the designers, contractors, and trades in the design and construction of a project, so, too, does IPD allow for the blurring of the lines of liability. In effect, architects, engineers, contractors, trade contractors, and even fabricators work together in the planning of IPD projects, share design information, and incorporate shop drawing and fabrication details offered by contractors. The issue of who is legally liable for damages or financial losses is further complicated when the architects, civil engineers, structural engineers, general contractors, trade contractors and fabricators have contributed data into various BIM models that have become integrated into a single combined BIM model for the project. Because IPD does not create a "bright line" between design responsibility and construction means, methods and procedures responsibility, it also does not create a bright line between the parties for liability.

Due to the collaborative nature of BIM, it is likely to become synonymous with the use of IPD. BIM may, of course, also be used on projects using more traditional delivery systems such as design-build or design-bid-build.[16] Questions regarding the allocation of risk and insuring those risks may arise on any project using BIM, but those issues are magnified on the IPD project.

References in this report to the AIA Guide and IPD contract documents are not intended to slight the work of the ConsensusDOCS group of associations that represent owners, contractors, subcontractors and sureties. In September 2007, the ConsenusDOCS 300, a Standard Form of Tri-Party Agreement for Collaborative Project Delivery was published. In this contract, the project owner, designer and contractor join together in a collaborative effort to plan, design and construct the project. A management group of senior representatives from each party to the contract then directs the project. ConsensusDOCS 300 establishes shared responsibility and control and allocates risks and rewards along the lines discussed above for IPD projects. The issues and concerns discussed below regarding insurance apply to the IPD delivery system whether the contracts are based on ConsensusDOCS, AIA documents, or some other form of IPD contracts.

11.7   Shift in Responsibilities and Risks Resulting from IPD Affects Insurability of Risk

When the contractor and fabricators agree by contract to increase their risks by assuming liabilities arising out of design, how can this additional risk be managed – and can it be insured?[17]

On the other hand, when the architect, engineer or other design professional agree by contract to increase their risk by accepting responsibility and liability arising out of construction work, the means, methods and procedures, or the fabrication details, how will the designer manage and insure those risks?

Will insurance carriers writing general liability and professional liability coverages be able to effectively underwrite and insure these new contractually assumed responsibilities?

11.8.   BIM Affects the Roles, Responsibilities, and Risks of Project Participants

What are the key risk allocation issues that may be impacted by the use of BIM on a specific construction project?   According to some attorneys and commentators, the risks unique to BIM are minimal and more than offset by its many benefits.   For example, attorney Rick Lowe writes: "When all of these issues are analyzed, the perceived legal risks in using 3D modeling melt away and are outweighed by the obvious benefits of clash detection and greater project collaboration. It should only be a matter of time before insurers offer discounts to encourage clients to wear the clash-detection 'safety belts' of 3D modeling.   Ultimately, the question will morph into whether team leaders actually increase risks by *not* using 3D modeling, much like not using seat belts."[18]

While underwriters may agree that there are benefits of early conflict detection and resolution through 3D modeling, they are less likely to see how they can underwrite their single insured, who has a minor participation in the BIM model, and who may pick up full responsibility and liability for claims arising out of mistakes caused by use of or reliance on that model.   The challenge for the insurer is that this scenario resembles insuring someone "for all damages caused in whole or in part by their acts, errors or omissions."

The courts interpret language of this type to mean the responsible party is liable for all damages arising out of the acts of all parties involved in a transaction, so long as the assuming party was responsible *to any degree* for the resulting loss or damage.   The collaboration of contractors and subcontractors in the design has the potential to create uninsurable professional liability risks for themselves, as well as the design professionals, where BIM is used for design and construction of a project.   Similarly, the collaboration of the design professionals in the means, methods and procedures of construction has the potential to create uninsured general liability risks for the design professionals.   In fact, both professional liability and general liability risks may be difficult to insure in projects where BIM is utilized.

11.9   Risks as Viewed by a Professional Liability and Environment Insurance Broker

Many serious risk allocation and insurance concerns have been raised by the managing director of Aon Environmental Insurance Services Group, Rodney J. Taylor, in a white paper entitled: "Professional Liability Risks in BIM Applications: If BIM is Here to Stay, How Can We Insure Errors and Omissions?"[19]   Because of the major role he plays in one of the most significant insurance brokers for construction industry, we should consider carefully his view of the impact of BIM risks. Rather than paraphrase or edit his comments, I will quote him directly:

> Reliance on the information developed and maintained in a BIM system raises questions concerning the role of the architect in performing professional services associated with the construction process. With systems that are capable of generating beam sizes and concrete thickness from three-dimensional models, who is responsible for the specification of the final elements incorporated into a structure designed and built with BIM technology? Is the answer the same if the architect's data is supplemented by data from the contractors, vendors and the owner that result in the selection of different elements from those originally specified by the architect and/or the BIM system?
>
> Over-reliance on BIM technology presents a chance for heightened liability on the part of design professional if the information being input into a BIM system is incorrect or the software processes it incorrectly.[20]   Some architects and structural experts fear that this will result in catastrophic failures where no human judgment is applied after the fundamental construction components have been selected by computer programs based on the architect's design parameters. There is also fear that the new breed of architects that interface with the BIM systems may lack field experience and "street-sense". This could lead to construction using materials and systems that experienced personnel would intuitively understand to be unworkable.
>
> Legal issues will also arise in determining responsibility for design errors where greater collaboration among the construction team spreads decision-making for design elements beyond the traditional set of design professionals. Liability may

depend on what information is included in the database; who has the ability to add or change data and how much reliance contractors place on the output from the BIM system. With the lines of responsibility blurred, professional liability risks may spread from the traditional design professionals to include contractors, subcontractors and even building owners that alter the data in the BIM databases.

***

Another question that has been asked with respect to the use of BIM systems is whether they alter the standard of care applied to design professionals for their work in developing building concepts and specifications. It is important to understand that BIM does not promise "perfect" drawings. The work of the architects and engineers is still subject to errors that can result in change orders during construction or future structural problems. The owner still needs to set aside a contingency fund for construction coordination issues that arise during construction * * *.

In his White Paper, Mr. Taylor also makes several suggestions for design professionals that, if followed, may facilitate the availability of insurance to cover the risks arising out of BIM. If a design professional's current policy does not provide affirmative coverage for BIM, it should, at a minimum, not contain an exclusion expressly excluding claims arising out of BIM. An astute underwriter will want to inquire as to the following:

(1) Is the design professional obtaining risk allocation clauses in its contracts stating that the use of BIM is not intended to alter the normal standard of care applicable to the design professional's services?

(2) Who can input data into the BIM model and can that affect the data or the results of the data provided by the design professional?

(3) If the design professional's BIM content can be altered by future decisions of the Owner or contractors, is there a contractual indemnity provision to protect the design professional against liability resulting from those changes?

(4) Does the design professional's contract with its owner/client include a third-party beneficiary clause stating that use of the BIM model is not intended to create any contractual

relationship with third parties (e.g., contractors and suppliers) that may also be using the model?
(5) Does the design professional contract include a waiver of consequential (and even direct) damages resulting from flaws or failure of a BIM system for which it was not responsible?[21]

11.10   Additional Concerns with BIM that further Impact Insurability of IPD Projects

Attorneys Benton T. Wheatley and Travis Brown, writing for the Construction Lawyer[22], suggest that "If BIM is to succeed, construction professionals and their lawyers must resolve the following issues:

a.   Definition of professional services and the design process, and whether the standard of care will change;
b.   Is a BIM design a product, or an instrument of service;
c.   Ownership and control of the digital information;
d.   Record-keeping and archives;
e.   Conformity of completed construction to the model;
f.   Relationships of the various parties with concurrent design and construction authority;
g.   Risk that goes with any investment by the stakeholders;
h.   Payment for the creative efforts, control of information, and assumed or assigned risks;
i.   Whether the use of BIM changes the calculus of "per square foot" rules, in all of their varieties;
j.   What constitutes a failure to perform in accordance with the industry standard of care relative to BIM; and
k.   Whether a contractor/subcontractor's interactive participation in the design process sets them up for sanction with professional boards, or coverage questions with their own insurance?

In addition to the issues identified above, several others issues will be of concern to Commercial General Liability and Professional Liability insurance underwriters due to the practical impact of the risks undertaken by their insured design professionals and contractors. These issues include the following:

11.10.1 Who Constitutes the Risk being Underwritten?

Will construction managers and contractors become so involved in the design of structures that the professional liability carriers for the architect and engineers should base their underwriting not only on the reputation and experience of their insured As and Es, but also on the abilities and experience of other parties who are contributing to the designs?

11.10.2 Unreasonable Owner Expectations – Perfection instead of Standard of Care

Does the project owner have reasonable expectations with respect to the outcome of the design/construction process? Are the expectations of the owner being properly managed by the design professionals so that the owners do not expect the use of BIM will make designs "perfect"? Are change orders still likely to be necessary? Are cost overruns eliminated? Will the project be on a fast-track or other accelerated completion process?

Recent articles by individuals such as Paul Seletsky, Director of Digital Design, Skidmore Owings and Merrill, LLP, may cause insurance underwriters to become understandably nervous about what they are insuring in taking on the risks of the IPD/BIM project.[23] He suggests that the expectations of an owner of a building designed and constructed using BIM can be compared with the expectations of the buyer of a car who "unequivocally expect[s] that flawless engineering will be an integral part of every new car—from design through delivery."

Seletsky explains that the owner anticipates this expectation will be met through digital simulation tools and asks, "Should we not then expect the same from our architects and our buildings? Indeed, we should expect them to live up to the same high standards, employ the same advanced technologies, utilize the same simulation and analysis methodologies, and incorporate the same tacit and explicit knowledge into publicly-accepted, digitized, procedural methodologies as would be expected from any other profession."[24]

If "flawless engineering" is truly what project owners will come to expect as a result of using BIM, insurance underwriters will want to consider whether such expectations are patently unreasonable and make it impossible to insure projects where BIM is utilized. Construction risk management suggests the best starting point is the selection of a good client. A client that expects perfection because BIM is utilized on his project is, by definition, not a good client. This owner is also not a good risk for the insurance carrier that is underwriting participants in the BIM-assisted design team.

11.10.3   Designer Responsibility for Contractor's Means and Methods

Will the designer take on responsibility for the contractor's means, methods and procedures of construction by virtue of having worked hand-in-hand with the contractor in preparing and approving the BIM system that has incorporated such means, methods and procedures, fabrication plans and details into the basic design contained in the model?

11.10.4   Contractor's Loss of Spearin Doctrine Creates New Risk for Design Professional

Loss of the Spearin Doctrine defense for the contractor would likely affect the design professional and its insurer. Does the design professional assume greater responsibility and create additional liability for the contractor if the contractor cannot recover from the project owner under the Spearin Doctrine for implied warranty of the specifications? Could the contractor sue the design professional to recover its losses for defective designs? The answer to this question would depend upon the jurisdiction and whether a contractual relationship exists between the contractor and design professional, as would be the case in an IPD project.

Loss of the Spearin Doctrine defense will also be of concern to the insurer and surety for the contractor. Because the contractor may be participating in the development and entering of data that goes into the BIM models, they may lose their legal remedy for asserting reliance to their detriment on the owner's specifications.

11.10.5   Least Skilled Participant Creates Risks Shared by All

The performance of BIM may be adversely impacted by the lowest common denominator among the parties participating in it. Questions that need to be considered by all participants include: (1) Does each participant have the knowledge necessary to use the model? (2) Do they have computer hardware and software, plus Internet band-width capable of communicating vast amounts of data necessary for the model? (3) Do the parties have technicians on staff capable of working with BIM to input and manage data? And (4) is each party willing to play by the rules and comply with the contract requirements to share their data with the others?

11.10.6   Contractor Professional Liability for BIM Content Excluded in CGL Policy

Contractors providing design details for the integrated BIM model may be subjecting themselves to professional liability exposure that is typically excluded by their commercial general liability policy. To the extent, however, that a contractor has purchased a professional liability policy, the carrier may have justifiable concerns that by providing professional services that go into a BIM model, the contractor's liability exposure increases exponentially. Potential liability could include a catastrophic project failure that might be imposed on a joint and several basis due to lack of any clear delineation in responsibility between the participants in the design and construction processes.

This list of issues for CGL and professional liability carries is just a conversation starter and could be greatly expanded. Suffice it to say that many reasons exist for insurance carriers to refrain from jumping on the BIM bandwagon – They need time to evaluate the merits of the potential benefits versus the potential risks of using BIM and resolve some of the contract issues discussed here.

11.11   Recognizing the IPD-BIM Impact on Insurance Coverage Availability for Owners, Design Professionals, and Contractors

Based on the available information and experience of underwriters with BIM to date, the insurance industry will need several more years before the issues have sufficiently evolved so that insurance carriers can conclude whether BIM is a net positive when underwriting accounts. BIM is not the first time the insurance industry has had to address the impacts of a new set of relationships. With design-build projects, insurance carriers initially took a cautious approach, sometimes excluding coverage under the Professional Liability Policy if their insured was participating in a design-build project. Eventually, experience demonstrated that design-build was a safe risk and the exclusions were removed from the policies. It may be necessary to go through a similar learning curve where BIM – and especially BIM combined with IPD – is involved.

When BIM is used in conjunction with IPD, the AIA Guide acknowledges that insurance coverage under traditional insurance policies may be compromised or lost.

Using BIM and other tools to construct a building virtually in advance of actual construction substantially diminishes the risk of design errors and omissions. If the participants adopt "no suit" clauses, the risk of incurring internal first-party claims for economic loss can be eliminated through these waivers. However, where participants do not waive first party claims but assume non-traditional liability, traditional insurance products may not be available in today's insurance market. Insurance for third-party claims for personal injury and property damage may also not be available. It is now incumbent upon the insurance industry to develop and offer alternative insurance products that align with the project goals and the specific risk allocation terms established among the IPD project participants.[25]

Current professional liability policies that are standard in the marketplace for design professionals, however, are generally silent on the issue of BIM. Express language addressing BIM is neither in the insuring agreement sections of the policies nor in the exclusions sections of the policies. Since BIM is much like any other tool, such as CADD, which a design firm may utilize in providing its services, it can be argued that there is nothing so unique about BIM that would require it to be separately addressed in the policy. The professional services are covered regardless of what tools or means the design professional may use to deliver those services.

A key exclusion to be considered in the professional liability policy, however, is the contractual liability exclusion. That exclusion typically states that, if an Insured assumes the liability of others under a contract, that liability will be excluded from coverage except to the extent that the Insured would have been liable at common law even in the absence of the contract.

11.12 Conclusion

The discussion is just beginning about how IPD (particularly as combined with BIM) will impact the insurability of project risks.

With regard to insuring risks arising out of BIM as a tool for providing design professional services, it appears that existing language of professional liability policies does not specifically address service through BIM as a risk to be treated differently or to be excluded. Professional liability of an Insured for its negligent acts, errors and omissions are covered, regardless of whether the services have been delivered via the use of BIM.

It is too early to tell whether carriers will consider with favor or disfavor the use of BIM. Until contract documents more specifically address the roles and responsibilities for those using BIM, and more plainly establish reasonable expectations of project owners that are calling for the use of BIM, it is doubtful that insurance carriers will consider the use of BIM by their insureds as something to be rewarded by reduced premiums.

With regard to insuring risks arising out of IPD, the numerous exclusions and gaps in coverage in the typical professional liability policies and general liability policies will need to be addressed before project participants can feel comfortable that they are not accepting uninsured risks when embarking upon these projects.

Acknowledgement: This chapter is based on a paper entitled, "Insurability of Risks in the Marriage of IPD and BIM," presented by Mr. Holland to the ABA Forum on the Construction Industry program, "Coverages, Disputes and Tactics for Survival: Critical Insurance and Litigation Issues and Insights," January 15, 2009, in Bonita Springs, Florida.

---

[1]   A Working Definition: Integrated Project Delivery, AIA California Council (May 15, 2007), p. 1.

[2]   http://www.facilityinformationcouncil.org/bim/pdfs/NBIMSv1_p1.pdf.

[3]   Benton T. Wheatley and Travis W. Brown, *An Introduction to Building Information Modeling*, The Construction Lawyer, Fall, 2007, at 33.

[4]   The BIM Standard of the National Institutes of Building Sciences can be downloaded at www.facilityinformationcouncil.org/bim/pdfs/NBIMSv1_p1.pdf.

http://iweb.agc.org/iweb/Purchase/CatalogSearchResults.aspx?Option=1&ProductTypeText=All&ProductTypeValue=All&Title=2926E

[5]   http://iweb.agc.org/iweb/Purchase/CatalogSearchResults.aspx?Option=1&ProductTypeText=All&ProductTypeValue=All&Title=2926E

[6]   Integrated Project Delivery: A Guide, AIA National/AIA California Counsel (2007 Version 1), section 4.1.4.

[7]   A Working Definition: Integrated Project Delivery, AIA California Council (May 15, 2007), p. 1.

[8]   This is most typical of the "Project Alliance" contract model. See section 6.1.1, Integrated Project Delivery" A Guide, AIA National/AIA California Counsel (2007 Version 1).

[9]   Integrated Project Delivery: A Guide, AIA National/AIA California Counsel (2007 Version 1), section 6.5.3.1.2.

[10]   Integrated Project Delivery: A Guide, AIA National/AIA California Counsel (2007 Version 1), section 6.5.3.1.3.

[11]   Integrated Project Delivery: A Guide, AIA National/AIA California Counsel (2007 Version 1), section 6.1.3.

[12] Suzanne Harness, managing director and counsel for AIA, has been quoted as explaining "We are not publishing a multiparty agreements ... which is a major distinction between the AIA forms and the ConsensusDOCS 300 forms." Finance & Business: Job Collaboration Raises Many Issues (May 28, 2008).

[13] *Id.* at 6.5.3.3.3.

[14] Integrated Project Delivery: A Guide, AIA National/AIA California Counsel (2007 Version 1), section 6.1.2.

[15] Integrated Project Delivery: A Guide, AIA National/AIA California Counsel (2007 Version 1), section 6.5.3.2.3.

[16] Calling design-build a "traditional" delivery method is perhaps ironic in that it was only a few short years ago that it was the exciting "new" thing that upset the traditions of the day. But with the passage of time, the significant percentage of large projects using the design-build method, and the general acceptance of design-build by the public and private sectors, it has moved into the status of being "traditional."

[17] The contractual liability exclusion of the commercial general liability (CGL) policy, as well as the contractual liability exclusion of the professional liability, deny coverage for claims arising out of risks assumed by contract for which the firm would not have had at common law – except in the case of the GCL policy for tort actions arising out of bodily injury or property damage.

[18] Richard H. Lowe, Constructor Magazine, January/February 2007 (McGraw-Hill Co.).

[19] Rodney J. Taylor, J.D, P.E., CPCU, CLU, ARM – Director , *Professional Liability Risks in BIM Applications*, AON Risk Services, unpublished white paper (December 14, 2007), pages 7-9.

[20] Gary Prather, *Building Information Modeling: The Wave of the Future?*, INSIGHT, September 18, 2007.

[21] See Taylor, *Professional Liability Risks in BIM Applications*, supra, pages 8-10 for additional risk management suggestions from the insurance professional's perspective.

[22] Benton T. Wheatley and Travis W. Brown, *An Introduction to Building Information Modeling*, The Construction Lawyer, Fall 2007, p. 33.

[23] *Digital Design and the Age of Building Simulation*, Quarterly Review, (Zetlin & DeChiara, Vol. 11, No. 4, 2006, p. 6).

[24] *Id.* at 6.

[25] Integrated Project Delivery: A Guide, AIA National/AIA California Counsel (2007 Version 1), section 4.4.3.

Chapter 12

Public Private Partnerships:
A Primer for Design Professionals

Simon J. Santiago, Esq.
Heather L. DeBlanc, Esq.

12.1   Introduction

Public agencies in the United States are facing a potential crisis because there is insufficient public funding to maintain or improve the nation's aging public infrastructure. In a 2009 assessment, the American Society of Civil Engineers gave the condition of the nation's infrastructure an overall grade of "D" and estimated that $2.2 trillion would be needed over a five-year period to bring the nation's infrastructure to a good condition.[1]   The National Governor's Association – a bipartisan organization comprised of the governors from the individual states – reported that $222 billion (in 2005 dollars) was needed annually simply to maintain the current highway and transit system, but that only $177 billion annually was available.[2]   These assessments, however, have failed to stop a decade's long decline in the decreasing amounts of public funding available for infrastructure projects.[3]

Given the deteriorating infrastructure and public funding shortage, public agencies are increasingly considering the use of public-private partnerships (P3s) to help finance and develop infrastructure projects. Data suggest that private investment could significantly help address the funding needs. A February 2008 quarterly report from McKinsey & Company estimated that private investment funds raised $105 billion for infrastructure projects from 2006 to mid-2007.[4]   Several managing directors from global investment firms have opined that equity capital available globally for infrastructure may reach in excess of $500 billion, after leveraging.[5]

This chapter will explore the basic characteristics of P3s, their potential benefits, and some of the unique project risks that are encountered and must be addressed. Also, this chapter will discuss some of the key points for maintaining and managing risks in the context of P3s, especially those related to design and project management.

12.2   P3s Defined, and Preliminary Considerations

12.2.1   Defining P3s

The term public-private partnership can be used to describe a wide array of arrangements between the public and private sector, from design-build to long-term leases of existing infrastructure assets. Indeed, various organizations and agencies define P3s broadly. For example, the National Council for Public Private Partnerships ("NCPPP"), an organization that advocates and facilitates the formation of P3s at the federal, state and local levels, defines P3s as follows:

> A Public-Private Partnership is a contractual agreement between a public agency (federal, state or local) and a private sector entity. Through this agreement, the skills and assets of each sector (public and private) are shared in delivering a service or facility for the use of the general public. In addition to the sharing of resources, each party shares in the risks and rewards potential in the delivery of the service and/or facility.[6]

Similarly, the United States Department of Transportation (USDOT) in a 2004 report to Congress offered the following definition of P3s:

> A public-private partnership is a contractual agreement formed between public and private sector partners, which allows more private sector participation than is traditional. The agreements usually involve a government agency contracting with a private company to renovate, construct, operate, maintain, and/or manage a facility or system. While the public sector usually retains ownership in the facility or system, the private party will be given additional decision rights in determining how the project or task will be completed.[7]

Since access to private investment is one of the key advantages of using a P3, some consider true P3s as only those involving some degree of private sector financing of the project.[8]   In fact, subsequent to its 2004 report to Congress, USDOT provided a more focused definition of P3s that describes the private sector assuming a greater financial role and greater risk in the project.[9]   Sectors where P3s have been used include transportation, water/wastewater, urban development, utilities, and schools.[10]

12.2.2   Types of P3s

There are various types of project delivery methods that may utilize the P3 framework, each with varying degrees of risk to the public and private sectors. The delivery method appropriate for a particular project will vary depending on the needs of the public, the nature of the project, and the amount of risk that a private partner would be willing to accept for such project.

While there are many project delivery approaches, P3s can be grouped into two main categories: a development project and an existing asset lease project.   A development project (sometimes referred to as a greenfield project) involves the development of new or added capital improvements. Typically, there is no user fee (i.e. tolls) on the facility at the time that the development project is undertaken. Rather, the user fee is an added element of the development project and applies after the facility is put into service. For example, the SH-130 Segments 5&6 project in Texas is a development project to construct a new 40-mile tolled highway between San Antonio and Austin. The Capital Beltway HOT Lanes project in the Washington, DC area is a development project to add four high occupancy toll ("HOT") lanes on existing portions of I-495.

An existing asset lease project (sometimes referred to as a brownfield project) involves an existing, revenue-generating public facility that is leased to the private sector to operate and maintain on a long-term basis, sometimes with a responsibility to perform upfront capital improvements. Generally, the public sector uses existing asset lease projects as a way to extract value from existing infrastructure and raise funds for infrastructure or other uses. For example, the City of Chicago entered into a 99-year lease with the private sector to operate and maintain the Chicago Skyway, a 7.8 mile toll road connecting the Dan Ryan Expressway on the Chicago's south side with the Indiana Toll Road. In return, the City of Chicago received an upfront payment of $1.8 billion from the private concessionaire. The City of Chicago has also agreed to lease Midway Airport to a private concessionaire to operate and maintain the airport for a 99-year term. In exchange for the right to the airport's revenues from landing, terminal, parking, concessions and other fees, the private sector has agreed to pay the City $2.52 billion.[11]

12.2.3   Creating the Legislative Framework

P3s involve greater participation from the private sector than traditional project delivery methods, so public agencies require greater flexibility to use P3s to develop and maintain infrastructure. As mentioned above, P3s come in many shapes and sizes, and P3 legislation must allow the public agency to structure and develop approaches to procurements and contracting to address the specific characteristics and needs of a P3 project. Legislation should advance the objectives of taking advantage of the innovation and resources of the private sector to solve the individual project goals and challenges. At the same time, P3 legislation must preserve and promote the public agency's obligation and duty to protect the public's interest. This includes ensuring that the procurement process is fair and consistent, with a level of transparency that properly balances the public's right to be informed with protecting the private sector's competitive interests.

The scope of the authority that the public sector has to enter into P3s is a threshold issue P3 legislation should address. Specifically, public agencies must decide which types of infrastructure projects are eligible for P3s. This decision, in large part, rests on whether alternative procurement methods are needed because the existing procurement methods are not fully addressing the public's infrastructure needs. Often, the prime candidates for P3s are those types of projects that have dedicated revenue streams and are in need of private investment.

The traditional process for procuring infrastructure projects often precludes or unduly restricts the use of P3s. Typically, public agencies approach the development of a project sequentially, relying on separate entities to perform and complete each activity before proceeding to the next. This approach requires separate procurements, with design-related services based on qualifications and construction and maintenance services based on low bid. This process, however, is not well-suited for P3s, especially given that one of the inherent characteristics of P3s is the broadened scope of services furnished by the private sector partner. Therefore, P3 legislation should enable the public agency to procure services through a wide array of methods and chose the methodology that best fits the specific needs and objectives of a project.

One of the key benefits of P3s is the ability to access private capital. Since private investment allows public agencies to proceed with critical projects that otherwise would remain in the initial planning stages, P3 legislation should promote policies that maximize the use of all lawful sources of funding. In addition, to permit effective use of private capital, legislation should allow P3 projects to be funded by any mix of public funding and private capital.

12.3   Potential Benefits and Concerns of P3s

The public sector enjoys a number of potential benefits when using P3s. When a single entity performs most of the functions associated with planning, developing, designing, constructing, operating and maintaining a project, these activities can be coordinated and often performed concurrently, rather than sequentially, resulting in immediate time savings. For example, separate procurements for design and construction services are unnecessary with P3s. Also, construction activities can start before the project is fully designed because both design and construction are performed by a single entity.

Further, P3s may reduce the total project costs. As the private sector takes on more responsibilities associated with the project, significant risks can be shifted to or shared with the private sector because the private sector has more control over the project activities to manage and mitigate risks. As such, cost and schedule overruns can be borne primarily by the private sector. The private sector must also factor in lilfe-cycle costs when designing and constructing the project because P3s often extends the private sector's role beyond construction completion to operation and maintenance. In other words, the private sector can make decisions during the design and construction phase that will reduce its operations and maintenance costs in the long run.[12]

P3s are perhaps most beneficial because they can reduce or eliminate the public funding that would otherwise be required for a project. Because many P3s involve private sector financing, public agencies can: (1) allocate funds to other infrastructure projects or budgetary needs; (2) reduce the upfront costs of borrowing that may be needed to satisfy funding gaps; and (3) avoid legislative or administrative restrictions that regulate the amount of permissible outstanding public debt.[13]

There exist, however, concerns and criticisms with respect to P3s. One concern is that the user fees charged by a P3 project would be significantly higher than, and would not correlate with, the costs of operating and maintaining the facility, even taking into account a reasonable return on investment. Instead, the user fees may be dictated by market conditions, which may pose unfair burdens on the public.[14] Also, when the public sector relinquishes the right to the revenue stream of a facility for an extended period of time in exchange for a large upfront payment, the public risks giving up more over the long term to realize a short-term gain. Because there are many unforeseen circumstances and unquantifiable factors, a concern exists that there are no accurate or reliable ways to assess the value of future revenues from a facility with the market value of the facility. For example, in 1999, the Government of Ontario received a $3.1 billion upfront payment for the long-term lease of Highway 407 ETR in Toronto, Canada. Subsequently, commercial and residential development in the surrounding areas significantly exceeded the government's estimate. A valuation performed in 2002 estimated the new value of the facility to be $6.2 billion, inclusive of added improvements, parking lots, and increased tolls.[15]

In addition to the financial and market-related concerns, some have expressed reservations as to whether P3s advance the public's interest in improving and maintaining the nation's infrastructure. In 2007, the Chairmen of the House Committee on Transportation and Infrastructure and the Subcommittee on Highways and Transit released a letter and position paper outlining their concerns that P3s pose the risk of undermining the integrity of the transportation network:

> We are also very concerned about the impact that PPPs will have on our national transportation network, which is the mobility backbone that supports our economy. Our Federal-aid highway system was developed on the basis of a federal-state partnership. The need for an efficient, integrated national transportation network is even more compelling in today's global economy than when we began the work in the [sic] 1956. Shortsighted and unbalanced PPPs that mortgage our nation's surface transportation infrastructure for generations to come may favor parochial and private interests to the detriment of an improved 21st Century national transportation system.[16]

Indeed, there have been some recent legislative and political setbacks due to the public's misgivings over P3s. The Texas legislature imposed a partial, two-year moratorium on toll roads, the governors in Pennsylvania and New Jersey have been unable to garner political and legislative support to lease their states' turnpikes to the private sector.[17] Therefore, while P3s can be valuable tools to deliver infrastructure projects, they must be used in the proper context and with the adequate measures and controls to protect the public's interests.

12.4   Guiding Principles and Practices of Risk Management

One of the guiding principles that a public sector partner follows for a particular P3 project is to allocate and manage risk in the manner that is expected to produce the best overall value to the taxpayers. Similarly, the private sector partner assesses risks by, among other things, examining the financial "upside" of a P3 project and the expected return on investment. With these principles in mind, risks are assessed, allocated and managed by both the private and public sector based on common practices, including the following:

- Assessing, evaluating and understanding the particular material risks that the project presents.
- Reducing the likelihood and magnitude of the risk through pre-development efforts, data gathering and generation, and due diligence.
- Allocating the risk to the party in the best position to manage and mitigate it.
- Where the parties are fairly equally situated to manage and mitigate the risk (or have fairly equal inability to manage and mitigate the risk), providing for risk sharing, so that both parties have incentive to work together to solve the problem.
- Understanding how the financial markets perceive particular risks and whether they accept or reject them.
- Comparing the estimated cost to the public owner of retaining risk with the estimated contingency the private sector will reserve if the private sector bears the risk.

12.5   Procurement Risks

As an initial matter, one of the key risks that must be addressed early on is the risk that the P3 project will not have the institutional and public support to proceed with the award of the contract. As mentioned previously, there have been political and public policy concerns with respect to P3s in the United States. Because P3 procurements require substantial time and effort, the private sector will be more willing to compete for and participate in a P3 project if there is greater certainty that the procurement process is transparent and that the project has the necessary governmental approval and public support.

To mitigate the risk that a P3 procurement will be altered or cancelled, the public sector should determine the expected benefits and costs of using the P3 project delivery method as opposed to other project delivery methods.[18] This often involves conducting a "value for money" analysis or public sector comparator, which is used to evaluate whether a P3 is the best procurement option for the public.[19] This type of upfront analysis is helpful to counter allegations that the public sector is not being a responsible steward of public funds and infrastructure.

Further, the public sector partner should obtain input and buy in from all affected public stakeholders prior to commencing the procurement. It is preferable to resolve concerns related to the project, such as environmental, user fees, location, design, and financing, prior to initiating the procurement process. Often, this will require a coordinated effort among several governmental entities to ensure that the proposed infrastructure project meets and addresses the needs of all stakeholders. However, some public owners require approval by a non-procuring agency (such as a county or municipality affected by the project) as a condition to awarding a P3 project to a proposer.[20] Also, some require legislative approval or public input on the terms of a P3 agreement may impose commercial risks that are unacceptable to the private sector.[21] Public owners must be mindful not to impose undue uncertainties and risks once a P3 project is selected and the procurement is allowed to proceed. Otherwise, the private sector will be hesitant to participate in the process, thereby reducing competition.

12.6   Financial Risks

In its purest form, P3s require the private sector partner to develop infrastructure using private capital, with the private sector recouping its costs through user fees generated by the infrastructure asset or other dedicated revenue stream for a specified duration. Indeed, one of the primary reasons for the growing interest and use of P3s is the ability to access private financing and to shift the financial burden from general public funding to private capital and project revenues.

In cases where the private sector partner finances all or a significant portion of the costs of the P3 project in exchange for the right to the revenues generated by the infrastructure asset, the private sector partner assumes the risks with respect to the financial viability of the project for the duration of the P3 contract. In the design and construction period, it assumes the macroeconomic risks related to the availability and costs of labor and materials. During the operating period, the private sector partner also assumes the macroeconomic risks affecting the revenue stream. For example, in a P3 highway toll concession project, the private sector partner bears the risk of travel demand and other economic factors influencing use of the project, such as fuel costs.

There are, however, P3 arrangements where the public sector partner may retain the financial risks with respect to the ability of the P3 project to generate revenue. For example, under an "availability payment" regime, the private sector partner is compensated based on the "availability" of the infrastructure asset for the public's use and meeting certain performance requirements and standards set forth in the P3 contract. So long as the private sector partner complies with its contractual obligations, it receives the availability payment (typically a fixed periodic payment), regardless of the actual use of the infrastructure asset. In other words, payment is not dependent on how much revenue or user fees are collected from the asset.

There is also a "financial risk" to the public sector that P3 projects (in particular those involving a long-term lease of an infrastructure asset) may result in excessive profiteering by the private sector. One concern is that the user fees charged by a P3 project would be significantly higher than and would not correlate with the costs of operating and maintaining the facility, even taking into account a reasonable return on investment. Instead, the user fees may be dictated by market conditions, which may pose unfair burdens on the public.[22] Further, because there are many unforeseen circumstances and unquantifiable factors, a concern exists that there are no accurate or reliable ways to assess the value of future revenues from a facility with the market value of the facility. For example, in 1999, the Government of Ontario received a $3.1 billion upfront payment for the long-term lease of Highway 407 ETR in Toronto, Canada. Subsequently, commercial and residential development in the surrounding areas significantly exceeded the government's estimate. A valuation performed in 2002 estimated the new value of the facility to be $6.2 billion, inclusive of added improvements, parking lots, and increased tolls.[23]

To address these concerns, contractual provisions often require the private sector to share with the public sector revenues generated by the asset once a certain rate of return is achieved. Notably, several existing P3 laws expressly allow or require the use of these "revenue sharing" provisions in P3 agreements.[24] Also, restrictions are often imposed (contractually and/or legislatively) addressing how and when user fees can be adjusted on a P3 project.

12.7   Performance Risks - Allocation of Responsibilities

A general rule of risk allocation is that with the greater assumption of project responsibilities, the project risks assumed by a party should increase. Conversely, with the lesser assumption of project responsibilities, the project risks assumed by a party should decrease. Because P3s involve greater participation by the private sector in project development, a P3 arrangement results in the private sector's ability to absorb greater risks with respect to design, construction, operation and maintenance. In particular, greater risks are able to be transferred to the private sector because P3 contracts generally are "performance based" and give more control to the private sector partner than traditional contracting methods.

Under a design-bid-build arrangement, the public owner is responsible for the accuracy of the plans, assumptions in the design, and front line acceptance during construction. After construction is completed, the owner is responsible for operating and maintaining the project. Except for any post-completion warranties or latent defects, the contractor's responsibilities typically end at final acceptance and the owner must deal with deficiencies in the construction work for the remaining useful life of the project. Further, the owner is responsible for making engineering decisions with respect to the interpretation of the design and specification requirements and the sufficiency of construction materials and workmanship to meet the intended use.

In contrast, under a typical P3 concession arrangement, the private sector partner is responsible for developing the plans, making the assumptions in the design, and front line acceptance during construction. After construction is completed, the private sector partner also is responsible for operating and maintaining the project and must bear the consequences of the quality of the project (potential loss of revenue or increased maintenance costs) until the end of the contract term.

12.8   Risk Management Issues During Performance

Once the parties' respective roles are defined and the risks are allocated, the P3 project must be structured and implemented to reflect and preserve these roles and risk allocations. Some key methods for maintaining and managing the parties' pre-determined responsibilities and risk allocation under a P3 arrangement is the use of performance specifications as opposed to prescriptive specifications, and the implementation of the appropriate level of design reviews and inspections.

Generally, prescriptive specifications are those specifications that require the end product to be of a specific material, component, type, dimension, or weight, or to use a certain equipment, process, procedure or method for producing the end product. Performance specifications detail the performance or operational characteristics that the end product must meet, providing flexibility to achieve the required characteristic. The decision regarding if and to what extent to use performance specifications on a particular project should depend in large part on who bears the responsibility and risk for the performance of the end product. Because the private sector partner on a P3 project typically is the party responsible for operating and maintaining the project and has the financial risk of the project's nonperformance, the public sector partner should use performance specifications to define its objectives when appropriate. Performance specifications give the private sector partner the ability to innovate and pursue alternative design solutions to meet the project's objectives and needs, while holding the private sector partner accountable if the solutions do not meet these objectives and needs.

In contrast, when prescriptive specifications are used, the public sector partner may be liable if the P3 project is built in accordance with the prescriptive specifications yet the project does not perform in accordance with the stated requirements. Under this scenario, the use of prescriptive specifications may have the undesired effect of transferring back to the public sector partner the risk of the project's failure to meet the stated requirements.

Similarly, under a P3 arrangement, the design review and inspection program implemented by the public sector partner should take into account the expanded role and responsibilities of the private sector partner. Under design-bid-build, the public owner is actively engaged in the design process and front line inspection and testing, having the primary responsibility for the design and ensuring that the project meets the plans and specifications. As more design and construction responsibility and risks are shifted to the private sector partner under a P3, the public sector partner's role should shift to a more general design review for conformance with the project's requirements and confirming that the public sector partner's quality program is being adequately implemented. The imposition of owner preferences into the design or inspection process through excessive design reviews, dictating the project's design or overzealous inspections will likely negate the benefits of allocating design and construction responsibilities to the private sector partner, leading to project delays and claims.

Although public owners have become more receptive to using P3s, they are often hesitant in adjusting their traditional project oversight and management role for several reasons. First, public owners are mindful of their duty to protect the public's interests and are reluctant to reduce its role in project management for fear of being viewed as abdicating their responsibilities to the private sector. Also, there may be a concern among public owners whether the private sector partner will ultimately deliver a quality project if they scale back their involvement. However, inherent incentives, checks and balances exist in P3 projects to ensure a quality project, enabling the public sector partner to justifiably give greater project management responsibility commensurate with the increased role and risks assumed by the private sector partner.

For example, under a P3 concession contract where the private sector partner is responsible for operation and maintenance and is compensated after project completion through user fees or availability payments, the private sector partner has an incentive to ensure that the project is constructed in a way that minimizes costs and service interruptions during operation and maintenance. Specifically, a poorly constructed project will lead to increased repairs during the operating phase, requiring disruptions to service to complete these repairs. Therefore, in addition to the costs of the repairs, the private sector partner faces a potential loss of revenue to the extent that use of the infrastructure asset is impaired or disrupted. Investors and lenders also have an interest in ensuring the optimal availability and use of the project and therefore will likely require that the public sector partner have a robust quality assurance and quality control program during construction. In any event, the public sector partner must still comply with its contractual requirements and noncompliance may lead to liquidated damages, default, termination and the exercise of other remedies available to the public sector owner under the P3 contract.

12.9   Conclusion

P3s provide a valuable tool for the procurement and delivery of various types of projects that lack adequate public financing. The advent of P3s has created new opportunities for public owners to strategically partner with the private sector to finance and deliver vital infrastructure projects. With this new opportunity comes unique issues and risks that must be assessed, allocated and managed through P3 legislation and/or contractually by the parties.

[1] American Society of Civil Engineers, *2005 Report Card for America's Infrastructure*, at http://www.asce.org/reportcard/2009/index.html.

[2] NGA Center for Best Practices, *Issue Brief: State Policy Options for Funding Transportation*, Feb. 2007, at 1.

[3] Robert T. Lalka, *Improving American Infrastructure through PPPs*, INFRASTRUCTURE JOURNAL (Sept. 2, 2008), at http://www.ijonline.com.

[4] Robert N. Palter et al., *How Investors Get More Out of Infrastructure*, THE MCKINSEY QUARTERLY, Feb. 2008, at 1.

[5] *A $400 Billion Solution?*, INNOVATION NEWSBRIEFS (Ken Orski ed. March 10, 2008), *at* http://www.innobriefs.com.

[6] The National Council for Public-Private Partnerships, *How Partnerships Work*, at http://www.ncppp.org/howpart/index.shtml#define.

[7] UNITED STATES DEPARTMENT OF TRANSPORTATION, REPORT TO CONGRESS ON PUBLIC-PRIVATE PARTNERSHIPS 10 (Dec. 2004).

[8] *See* Lalka, *supra* note 6, at 42 (defining P3s as "an organizational structure by which the private sector finances, builds, rehabilitates, maintains, and/or operates specific public sector activities in exchange for contractually specified, but uncertain, stream of future returns").

[9] UNITED STATES DEPARTMENT OF TRANSPORTATION, INNOVATIVE WAVE: AN UPDATE ON THE BURGEONING PRIVATE SECTOR ROLE IN U.S. HIGHWAY AND TRANSIT INFRASTRUCTURE 7 (July 18, 2008).

[10] Rick Norment, *Fundamentals of Public Private Partnerships*, NATIONAL LEAGUE OF CITIES (Nov. 13, 2007).

[11] Yvette Shields, *Chicago Eyes Lease for Midway*, THE BOND BUYER, Oct. 1, 2008.

[12] UNITED STATES GOVERNMENT ACCOUNTABILITY OFFICE, HIGHWAY PUBLIC-PRIVATE PARTNERSHIPS: MORE RIGOROUS UP-FRONT ANALYSIS COULD BETTER SECURE POTENTIAL BENEFITS AND PROTECT THE PUBLIC INTEREST 21-22 (Feb. 2008) [hereinafter "GAO PPP REPORT"].

[13] *Id.* at 20.

[14] *Id.* at 32.

[15] *Id.* at 34.

[16] Press Release, T&I Leaders Outline Concerns over Public-Private Partnerships: Position paper expands on earlier letter to governors on PPP transportation deals

(June 4, 2007), *available at* http://transportation.house.gov/news/prarticle.aspx?newsid=219.

[17] *See* Robert J. Gibbons & Michael P. McGuigan, *The Challenges of Change,* PROJECT FINANCE, June 2008, at 42-43.

[18] Letter from Katherine A. Siggerud, Managing Director, Physical Infrastructure Issues, United States Governmental Accountability Office, to the Committee on Transportation of the Pennsylvania House of Representatives 4 (Sept. 8, 2008).

[19] *Id.* at 7.

[20] *See* MINN. STAT. § 160.85.

[21] *See* ARIZ. REV. STAT. § 7001(E); CAL. STS. & HIGH. CODE § 143(b)(3).

[22] GAO PPP REPORT, *supra* note 12, at 32.

[23] *Id.* at 34.

[24] *See* FL. STAT. ANN. §§ 334.30(2)(e); MISS. CODE ANN. § 65-43-3(4).

Chapter 13

Mitigating the Design Professional's Risk on International Construction Projects

John M. Wilson, Esq.

13.1 Introduction

International construction projects may be confronted by a host of risks, from natural disasters like fire and severe weather, to damage caused to third-parties stemming from professional negligence or accidental injuries, to uncontrollable country-specific risks that may be occasioned by unanticipated political or social developments. There are many ways that international contractors may mitigate against these general risks. In this chapter, we discuss the variety of insurance products available to provide coverage against some of the most prevalent risks on international projects. In particular, this chapter will discuss both widely-available and specialized insurance products that international contractors may consider as risk mitigation measures, including Political Risk, Builder's Risk, Professional Liability, and Commercial General Liability policies.

13.2 Political Risk Insurance

Overview of Political Risks

International construction projects are particularly vulnerable to political risks. Although the line between political and commercial risks is not always clear, political risks are generally considered to be those arising from adverse legislative or administrative action by the host government, or instability within a political or social system.[1] These risks assume many forms and are more prevalent in developing countries, which more often sacrifice foreign investors' property rights in the name of the common good.

In gauging political risk, project managers should be sensitive to many factors, including whether the host country has: (1) established an independent judicial system; (2) a government that is, or may become, hostile to foreign investment; (3) known terrorist networks; (4) an authoritative or populist leader contributing to an unstable political environment; or (5) onerous foreign exchange controls.[2] Political risk is not limited to well-known hotspots. International contractors and developers face similar challenges in countries such as Argentina, Peru, Nigeria, India, Russia, China, and other more seemingly hospitable regions.[3] Although some political risks are country-specific, others could impact virtually any international construction project and must be considered in evaluating the project's viability.[4]

Country-specific risks range from broad nationalization programs to more subtle confiscatory regulations that threaten the integrity of a particular industry. Once welcomed with open arms, foreign investors in the energy and natural resources sectors are often scapegoats for populist leaders aiming to reclaim the "people's resources," and all participants in such projects can be caught in the cross-fire.

Even in areas where the country-specific risks may be low, international construction projects are commonly susceptible to a host of project-specific political risks. These include special taxes, environmental controls, labor or wage restrictions, and other discriminatory measures directed at the project. Large-scale construction projects can also become targets for labor strikes, sabotage, and kidnappings.

Experienced international contractors understand that political risk is a double-edged sword. On the one hand, it represents uncertainty and the potential for loss, including disruption or destruction of the project. On the other, political risk can discourage competition, creating great opportunity for those who can effectively hedge against it.[5] While political risk can be mitigated in many ways, international contractors and developers are increasingly considering political risk insurance ("PRI") to help control the uncertainty associated with these potential losses.

Mitigating Risk with PRI Coverages

PRI can be tailored to cover expropriation, selective discrimination, political violence, currency inconvertibility, and many other types of political risks. Prospective policyholders should consult an experienced broker or legal adviser when evaluating these sophisticated products to learn how they can address the more salient risks. Some of the most common political risks affecting international construction projects are further discussed below.

13.3   Expropriation

Expropriation represents one of the most significant political risks that can threaten an international construction project. Expropriation occurs not only when "the government formally takes title to property, but also to other actions of the government that have the effect of 'taking' the property, in whole or in large part, outright or in stages."[6]   The host government is responsible "for an expropriation of property . . . when it subjects alien property to taxation, regulation, or other action that is confiscatory, or that prevents, unreasonably interferes with, or unduly delays, effective enjoyment of an alien's property or its removal from the state's territory."[7]

Expropriation may arise through law, order, or administrative action, and may be a discrete event or part of a broader confiscatory scheme. Types of projects that tend to be particularly susceptible to expropriation include those that: (1) involve the extraction of natural resources, (2) provide essential goods or services to the public, or (3) require transactions with, or special permits from, the local government.[8]

Typical forms of expropriation coverage require the insurer to indemnify the policyholder for the diminished value of the asset, investment, or property right that has been expropriated by the host government. Although the language varies depending on the carrier, most policies will insure against the deprivation, interference, or impairment of the fundamental assets or property rights affecting the project's long-term viability. In addition to coverage for direct seizures and other confiscatory acts, political risk policies can help mitigate losses stemming from more subtle takings. For example, a hostile government may arbitrarily deny necessary permits or easements, restrict the import of required materials, or deny entry to critical personnel.[9] Alternately, a government could pass a law creating a steep tax that is tantamount to a seizure, force the sale of foreign-owned assets, or compel the renegotiation of its contracts with foreign entities.[10]   Each of these risks should fall within the basic insuring agreement of most expropriation policies.

Some countries may seek to disguise their expropriatory conduct as legitimate regulation. Relevant factors in determining whether a regulation is legitimate or expropriatory include the degree to which it interferes with the owner's property interest, deprives the owner of effective control, or impairs the project's profitability.[11]

Forms of expropriation involving government interference, impairment, and destruction of intangible property rights (often embodied in project contracts) have been more common than overt nationalizations. Recent events in Latin America, however, may signal a resurgence of direct expropriation and should serve as a caution to international contractors and developers to consider obtaining PRI for these risks as well.

13.4   Political Violence

Political violence insurance generally insures against losses resulting from a violent act perpetrated for a political purpose.[12]

Political violence insurance can be purchased to insure the project property, reimburse income lost from construction interruption, or even pay ransom in the case of kidnapping. While many insurers previously offered terrorism coverage only as part of a broader political violence policy, many policyholders elect to purchase stand-alone terrorism coverage in certain high risk areas.[13] Contractors and project developers may be able to reduce the cost of political violence insurance by taking appropriate security measures to protect the project, such as hiring security personnel and training employees in escape and evasion.[14]

13.5   Currency Risk

Currency risk includes the possibility that the local currency: 1) will fluctuate unfavorably; 2) may not be convertible into another currency; or 3) may not be transferable from the host country. While unfavorable currency fluctuation is perhaps the most common risk affecting international contractors,[15] it is generally considered a commercial risk that cannot be insured through PRI.[16] However, unlike general currency fluctuations, the risks of currency inconvertibility and non-transferability are readily insurable.

Currency inconvertibility is one of the oldest and most common risks covered by PRI.   Before filing a claim under a currency inconvertibility policy, the insured must exhaust all legal channels to convert and remit the funds, including those which may be unofficial or inconvenient.[17] Once the insurer pays the claim, it becomes subrogated to the policyholder's right to the underlying payment obligation and to ownership of the blocked funds.[18]

13.6   PRI Providers

Various Forms of PRI

Several public and private insurers offer various forms of PRI, which may be purchased either as stand-alone coverage or as part of a more comprehensive policy.[19] The most active public entities offering PRI include the Overseas Private Investment Corporation (OPIC), which is wholly owned by the United States government, and the Multilateral Investment Guarantee Agency (MIGA), a part of the World Bank. The primary private carriers include Lloyd's, AIG, Chubb, Zurich, and Sovereign. Once dominated by the public insurers, the total market for PRI is now roughly evenly divided between public and private insurers.[20]

Public insurers are often subject to a number of constraints regarding the kinds of projects and investors they insure. For example, OPIC is bound by its mandate to "mobilize and facilitate the participation of United States private capital and skills in the economic and social development of less developed countries and areas, and countries in transition from nonmarket to market economies." Likewise, MIGA serves to "promote foreign direct investment into developing countries to help support economic growth, reduce poverty, and improve people's lives."[21] Private insurers are not restricted in this same manner.

Scope of Coverage

As a general rule, private insurers can offer broader coverage in some instances than their public competitors, and can insure a larger percentage of the project's value. For example, private insurers will routinely insure 100% of losses from an expropriation, whereas public insurers will generally insure no more than 90% of the total value of the assets or property rights expropriated.[22]

Term

Public providers tend to offer longer-term coverage than their private counterparts, sometimes for up to 20 years.[23] By contrast, private providers rarely offer cover for a term greater than 15 years.[24]

Stability

Private providers are typically more vulnerable to market forces than public insurers.[25] OPIC policies are supported by the full faith and credit of the United States government, and MIGA policies are backed by the World Bank.[26]

Responsiveness

Because of the often complex nature of claims involving foreign investments, both private and public insurers tend to invest significant periods of time in evaluating and responding to claims made against the policy.

Loss prevention

Public providers benefit from being backed by a government or multilateral entity. Tactful negotiation by government or multilateral entities, as well as the threat of retaliation, can help to deter hostile government actions and resolve brewing disputes.[27] In an effort to emulate the public insurers, some private insurers have hired politically connected consultants to help avert potential losses.[28]

Conclusion

PRI can be an important tool in mitigating certain political risks associated with international construction projects. Contractors and developers should evaluate the most salient risks threatening their project and take appropriate preventative measures. In addition to PRI, contractors can implement a variety of methods to mitigate political risk, including forming joint ventures with local partners and taking other steps to strengthen ties with the local community and government. Local partners may be an important asset in navigating the political environment and enhancing the project's benefits in the eyes of the host government.

13.7   Builder's Risk Insurance

Overview of Builder's Risk Coverage

Like any building, bridge, plant, or refinery built in the United States, international projects are vulnerable to accidental damage during the course of construction. However, damage or loss during construction can be mitigated through builder's risk insurance, which generally provides project-specific coverage from the date construction begins until the project is completed.[29]

Typical Policy Language

Builder's risk coverage is "all-risk" insurance, meaning it can be tailored to cover loss resulting from any cause. Typical policies often insure "against all risks of physical loss or . . . damage" to buildings or structures incurred during construction, unless such perils are expressly excluded. Therefore, the purchaser must pay careful attention to the exclusions in the policy, as these essentially define the scope of coverage.

International contractors should confirm that the project is clearly and accurately defined in the policy. This is important because builder's risk insurance covers not only damage to the actual structure, materials, and equipment to be installed at the project, but also damage to foundations, underground pipes and drains, and temporary structures used in construction, such as scaffolding.

Special Builder's Risk Considerations for International Construction Projects

International construction projects give rise to unique risks that have particular relevance in evaluating whether to purchase a builder's risk policy. For example, many builder's risk policies exclude damage resulting from extreme weather conditions, including earthquakes, hurricanes, or floods. Because the contractor might not be familiar with the weather patterns in a particular region, local experts should be consulted to evaluate this often overlooked exclusion.

Additionally, some builder's risk policies contain exclusions for damage caused by insects, vermin, rodents, fungus, mold, or mildew. While these risks may seem modest, they can cause significant damage to a project, and in certain locales may present a major risk.[30] Accordingly, the contractor should carefully evaluate these threats and implement appropriate safeguards to protect the project.

Because the coverage term of most builder's risk policies is closely tied to the estimated construction schedule, international contractors should carefully consider the various factors that might delay the project's completion. Weather delays, skilled labor shortages, and disputes with the local government often wreak havoc with the construction schedule.

Finally, the contractor must be mindful of local customs and project delivery methods when obtaining builder's risk insurance. For example, while many public projects in the United States are awarded under a design-bid-build or a design-build method, large international projects are often awarded utilizing other delivery methods, including design-build-maintain, build-operate-transfer, build-own-operate, and build-transfer-operate. Because project owners (particularly foreign governments) commonly attempt to shift delay and performance risks to the contractor, policyholders should understand that typical builder's risk policies will likely not insure the added commercial perils associated with obligations extending beyond construction, and seek to mitigate the potential for resulting losses from such perils through other means.

13.8   Overview of Professional Liability Coverage

Professional liability insurance, commonly referred to in the context of construction professionals as "errors and omissions" ("professional liability") coverage, is "designed to insure members of a particular professional group from liability arising out of the performance of their professional services as that term is defined by the policy.   In general, professional liability policies may be purchased by contractors, as well as design or engineering professionals, to insure against the risk that their negligent performance of professional services (as defined by the policy) may damage the project or otherwise cause a loss for their client. Contractors, design professionals, and consultants need to be mindful of the policy's purpose, scope, and limitations, which are discussed in more detail below.

13.9   Definition of "Professional Services"

The policy's scope of coverage is perhaps the most important consideration that must be weighed in evaluating whether to purchase Professional liability insurance.   Professional liability policies generally insure against damages caused by a policyholder's negligence in providing "professional services," as defined by the policy.

Recent trends indicate a recognition that many of the construction and design services typically provided by design/build contractors fall within the broad contours of the term "professional services."[31]   Indeed, the term "professional services" is often construed to embrace not only "mental or intellectual" work, but any services provided in exchange for a fee in the normal course of business.[32]   While much of the work of design professionals will be deemed to fall within this overarching definition, some services may not fit within the definition, or may be excluded either as part of the insurance application process or as an actual exclusion to the policy. Before deciding on any particular professional liability product, contractors and design professionals should verify that the policy's definition of "professional services" embraces the range of activities that they will perform on the international construction projects they undertake.

Some insurance policies define "professional services" narrowly to reference on specifically stated services, while others contain a broad but potentially ambiguous definition. Contractors and design professionals involved in complex international construction projects should attempt to negotiate as broad a definition of "professional services" as possible for their professional liability policies. Some professional liability insurers may agree to define as "professional services" those services customarily rendered by a policyholder to its clients in exchange for a fee, thereby adopting a more expansive interpretation. Under this expansive method for defining the scope of coverage, the purchaser may be able to encompass within the scope of its professional liability policy all manner of services of a professional nature that it is hired to perform by its client on an international project.

Another method for ensuring broad coverage under a professional liability policy is to include in the application for coverage a comprehensive listing of the variety of services that the prospective insured may be called upon to perform on international construction projects. Assuming the insured provides accurate and complete information regarding the scope of its services, this information can lay the foundation for establishing the "services" its professional liability policy is intended to cover.

Ultimately, the scope of a professional liability policy's coverage often depends on its definition of "professional services." Given the uncertainty that may arise over whether a particular service is embraced within the policy's coverage grant, firms engaged in international construction projects should attempt to match the policy's definition of "professional services" with the services they typically provide.

13.10   Typical Exclusions in Professional Liability Policy

Professional liability policies are primarily intended to insure policyholders against damages caused by their professional negligence. Absent policy language to the contrary, these professional liability policies will *not* typically insure policyholders against liabilities assumed under contractual guaranties and warranties. While a contractor, for example, may be entitled to professional liability coverage where damages have resulted from its failure to comply with the relevant design and engineering standards, it may not be entitled to coverage where it guarantees that this same work will achieve a specified result or be completed by a particular time.[33] This basic distinction between professional negligence and contractual guaranty may be more difficult to ascertain, however, in the case of international construction projects where the contractor's responsibilities include the entire spectrum of design, engineering, and construction services necessary for the project to be fully functional.

Many professional liability policies exclude liability for punitive damages on the theory that these damages are not typically awarded for negligent conduct. However, because of the differing legal frameworks that an insured may confront in the context of international construction projects, it is important to clarify the scope of any such exclusion in light of the governing law.

13.11   Coverage Triggers for Professional Liability

Professional liability insurance is available almost exclusively on a "claims-made" basis. In "claims-made" policies, coverage is generally triggered when a third-party asserts a claim against the insured during the policy period for damages arising out of its provision of professional services. Because contractors and other professionals engaged in international construction may be subject to unfamiliar legal structures and rules governing projects in the host country, it is especially important for these policyholders to carefully examine the professional liability policy's definition of "claim," as well as its accompanying notice requirements. Failure to properly understand and adhere to these policy provisions can, in certain circumstances, undermine coverage.

13.12   Application of Coverage Limits/Deductibles

A critical consideration in evaluating potential professional liability coverage is the policy's treatment of multiple acts of negligence. Because professional liability policies are written almost exclusively on a "claims-made" basis, the question of whether multiple errors will be construed as one or more "claims" can affect coverage limits and the application of deductibles. This concern is especially important to companies engaged in international construction projects, insofar as multiple disciplines may be involved on a single project, or a single discipline may extend to projects on a worldwide basis.

In light of the obvious interest the insured has in limiting coverage disputes and minimizing the deductible amounts applicable to its insurance claims, it is crucial that insureds engaged in international construction projects carefully tailor their insurance programs in accordance with the nature of their typical services.

13.13   Interplay With Other Types of Insurance

As discussed above, professional liability insurance serves to insure against liability that may not be covered by typical commercial general liability policies.   Accordingly, it is important in evaluating the coverage needs associated with work on international construction projects that insureds purchase an insurance package that will protect them against both the risks of bodily injury and property damage typically insured through general liability policies, as well as the risks they face as a consequence of the professional services they are hired to render.

13.14   Duty of Insurer to Defend in a Foreign Forum

The insurer owes two primary duties to the policyholder: (1) the duty to defend, and (2) the duty to indemnify. Generally, the duty to defend requires the insurer to provide the policyholder with a full and complete defense against any action that may result in liability under the policy. Therefore, unless the insurer can establish "as a matter of law, that there is no possible factual or legal basis on which the insurer might eventually be obligated to indemnify," the insurer must provide a defense as soon as the policyholder tenders the claim to the insurer.

Given the risk that an international project participant may be sued in a foreign court with far different rules and procedures than the insured has previously experienced, the right to an insurer-provided defense is an important factor for many policyholders. Large insurers with international resources are generally in a better position to navigate foreign legal systems and to identify competent local counsel to defend the claim. On the other hand, some project participants may desire more control over the claim defense and selection of foreign counsel, and seek to negotiate broader rights under their policies. In general, however, the right to call upon the insurer's resources to fund the defense of a third party property or bodily injury claim in a foreign jurisdiction is a key benefit of coverage for any international project participant.

International construction project participants who purchase policies with significant Self Insured Retentions (SIRs) must be cognizant of many more factors than the policy's attachment point and associated cost. Careful consideration should be given to how the SIR will be exhausted, to the policyholder's rights to control and settle claims within the SIR, and to reporting obligations for claims that are expected to resolve within the SIR. Policyholders who lack the resources and expertise to effectively defend and resolve claims brought in foreign jurisdictions should be wary of structuring their policies to have an attachment point above a substantial SIR, despite the higher premium cost that is associated with more comprehensive coverage.

Acknowledgement: This chapter is based on a paper by the author presented to the ABA Forum on the Construction Industry program, "Coverage, Disputes, and Tactics for Survival: Critical Insurance and Litigation Issues and Insights," January 15, 2009, Bonita Springs, Florida.

---

[1] John D. Finnerty, *Securitizing Political Risk Investment Insurance: Lessons from Past Securitizations*, in INTERNATIONAL POLITICAL RISK MANAGEMENT: EXPLORING NEW FRONTIERS 80 (Theodore H. Moran ed., 2001).

[2] *See* John Minor, *Mapping the New Political Risk*, RISK MGMT., Mar. 1, 2003, at 16; Daniel Wagner, *Defining "Political Risk,"* Oct. 2000, http://www.irmi.com/irmicom/expert/articles/2000/wagner10.aspx (last visited June 27, 2007).

[3] *Of Coups and Coverage*, Economist, April 7, 2007, at 71.

[4] *See* Wagner, *Defining "Political Risk," supra* n.2.

[5] *See* Ian Bremmer, *How to Calculate Political Risk*, INC., Apr. 2007, at 99.

[6] RESTATEMENT (THIRD) OF THE FOREIGN RELATIONS LAW OF THE UNITED STATES § 712, comment g.

[7] *Id.*

[8] *See* THEODORE H. MORAN, FOREIGN DIRECT INVESTMENT AND DEVELOPMENT: THE NEW POLICY AGENDA FOR DEVELOPING COUNTRIES AND ECONOMIES IN TRANSITION 141 (1998); Robert T. Wray, *PRI Pricing: Understanding the Basics of a Non-Traditional Market*, Political Risk Insurance Newsletter, April 2006, at 1, 5, *available at* http://www.robertwraypllc.com/documents/robertwraypllc-PRINewsletter-Volume2Issue1.pdf; Nick Robson & Elizabeth Stephens, Jardine Lloyd Thompson, *Managing Country Risk in an Era of Resource Nationalism* (2007), *available at* www.jltasia.com/media/publications/pdf/ResourceNationalisation0701.pdf.

[9] *See* PHILIP LANE BRUNER & PATRICK J. O'CONNOR, BRUNER & O'CONNOR ON CONSTRUCTION LAW §§ 7:238-41 (2002).

[10] *See, e.g.*, Paulo Prada, "Bolivia Nationalizes the Oil and Gas Sector," N.Y. Times, May 2, 2006, at A9; Alvaro Zuazo, "Bolivia Moves to Nationalize Gas Industry," A.P., May 1, 2006.

[11] *See* Frederick E. Jenney, *The Future of Political Risk Insurance in International Project Finance: Clarifying the Role of Expropriation Coverage*, in INTERNATIONAL POLITICAL RISK MANAGEMENT: LOOKING TO THE FUTURE 113 (Theodore H. Moran & Gerald T. West eds., 2005) at 113.

[12] However, private sector providers will in some instances cover losses even from violence not perpetrated for a political purpose.

[13] Vivian Brown, *Political Risk Insurance After September 11 and the Argentine Crisis: A Public Provider's Perspective*, in INTERNATIONAL POLITICAL RISK MANAGEMENT: THE BRAVE NEW WORLD 20 (Theodore H. Moran ed., 2004); Julie A. Martin, *Commentary on Political Risk Insurance After September 11 and the Argentine Crisis: A Public Provider's Perspective*, in INTERNATIONAL POLITICAL RISK MANAGEMENT: THE BRAVE NEW WORLD 58 (Theodore H. Moran ed., 2004).

[14] *See* Carolyn Aldred & Michael Bradford, Despite Security Concerns, "Coverage Available for Iraq: More Buyers Seeking Policies for Iraq Risks," Bus. Ins., Feb. 2, 2004, at 1; William Atkinson & Bill Coffin, "Opportunities or Liabilities? Construction Projects in the Middle East," Risk Mgmt., Nov. 1, 2003, at 12.

[15] *See, e.g.*, *ITT Arctic Servs., Inc. v. United States*, 524 F.2d 680 (Ct. Cl. 1975) (American contractor operating in Canada held liable for increased labor costs after Canadian Dollar is uncoupled from U.S. dollar and rises in relative value).

[16] *See* Daniel W. Riordan & Edward A. Coppola, *Currency Transfer and Convertibility Coverage: An Old Reliable Product or Just an Old Product?*, in INTERNATIONAL POLITICAL RISK MANAGEMENT: LOOKING TO THE FUTURE 191 (Theodore H. Moran & Gerald T. West eds., 2005); OVERSEAS PRIVATE INVESTMENT CORPORATION, OPIC CLAIMS: THE PICTURE TO DATE (2007), http://www.pri-center.com/documents/OPICClaims.pdf (last visited June 27, 2007).

[17] Riordan & Coppola, *Currency Transfer and Convertibility Coverage: An Old Reliable Product or Just an Old Product?*, *supra* n.16 at 191.

[18] *Id.* at 183.

[19] Theodore H. Moran & Gerald T. West, *Overview: The Evolution of Private-Public Relationships in the Political Risk Insurance Industry*, in INTERNATIONAL POLITICAL RISK MANAGEMENT: LOOKING TO THE FUTURE 123 (Theodore H. Moran & Gerald T. West eds., 2005). *See, e.g.*, Felton (Mac) Johnston & Robert T. Wray, *Insuring the West Africa Pipeline*, POLITICAL RISK INSURANCE NEWSLETTER, Oct. 2005, at 1, 4, *available at* www.robertwraypllc.com/documents/robertwraypllc-Newsletter-Volume1Issue2.pdf.

[20] *See Of Coups and Coverage, supra* n.16.

[21] WORLD BANK GROUP, MULTILATERAL INVESTMENT GUARANTEE AGENCY, ABOUT MIGA, *available at* http://www.miga.org/sitelevel2/level2.cfm?id=1069.

[22] DANIEL WAGNER, IRMI'S POLITICAL RISK INSURANCE GUIDE 44 (2001) at 12.

[23] *See Of Coups and Coverage, supra* n.16.

[24] Rod Morris, *Political Risk Insurance Realities*, RISK REPORT, Aug. 2005.

[25] *Id.*

[26] *See* WAGNER, *supra* n.22 at 40.

[27] *See, e.g.*, WORLD BANK GROUP, MULTILATERAL INVESTMENT GUARANTEE AGENCY, MANAGING POLITICAL RISKS WITH MIGA'S GUARANTEES, *available at* http://www.miga.org/sitelevel2/level2.cfm?id=1058 (last visited June 27, 2007).

[28] *See Discussion of Learning from Recent Losses, Claims, and Arbitrations, in* INTERNATIONAL POLITICAL RISK MANAGEMENT: LOOKING TO THE FUTURE 77-78 (Theodore H. Moran & Gerald T. West eds., 2005); WAGNER, *supra* n.22 at 26-27.

[29] *See* 43 AM. JUR. 2D *Insurance* § 518 (2007) ("A 'builder's risk policy' ordinarily indemnifies a builder or contractor against the loss of, or damage to, a building he or she is in the process of constructing.").

[30] *See, e.g.*, Philip L. Bruner, *Allocation of Risks in International Construction: Revisiting Murphy's Law, The F.I.D.I.C. Conditions and the Doctrine of Force Majeure*, 3 INT'L CONSTRUCTION L. REV. 259, 259 (1986) (listing as a risk of international construction the "unfamiliar forms of disease, plant, insect, and animal life"); *see also* BRUNER & O'CONNOR, *supra* n. 9, § 21:2 (same).

[31] *See, e.g., Stone v. Hartford Ins. Co.*, 470 F. Supp. 2d 1088, 1098-99 (C.D. Cal. 2006) (holding that because the insured contracted to provide as a "professional undertaking" specific tasks, including "to draft plans for room additions, construct and/or supervise construction of the additions, and install a driveway," the services provided, "including measuring and handling windows and shear wall, removing drywall and insulation, and working with electricians and plumbers," were "clearly related to the rendering of professional services.").

[32] *See Tradewinds Escrow, Inc. v. Truck Ins. Exch.*, 97 Cal. App. 4th 713 (2002) ("'Professional services' ... is a broader definition than 'profession' and encompasses services performed for remuneration.").

[33] *See generally* 4-13 MATTHEW BENDER, CONSTRUCTION LAW § 13.06 (2007).

Chapter 14

Insurance Challenges in the U.A.E.

Stephen C. Taylor

14.1   Introduction

Now more than ever many architects, engineers, and contractors are looking to expand their services on a global level. Projects in the United Arab Emirates (the UAE) present unique challenges for design firms, especially with respect to contractual insurance requirements.

14.2   Each and Every Occurrence

Contracts may require that an architect's or engineer's professional liability limits apply on an "each and every" basis, also known as "any one claim" or "unaggregated limits."

"Each and Every" professional liability limits are not available from insurers in the U.S. domestic marketplace; however, this coverage may be procured in the global marketplace. It may be purchased as a stand alone tower of coverage or placed as a layer of coverage excess of underlying aggregated coverage, known as Top & Drop.

14.3   Top & Drop Professional Liability Policy

Utilizing the professional liability program an architect or engineer currently has in place may be the most cost effective alternative when procuring "each and every" limits, particularly if the design firm has a strategic business plan that contemplates multiple projects in the UAE. A global practice program can be structured to include an "each and every" policy for non North American projects. This Top & Drop policy is a form of excess professional liability coverage. The term "Top" indicates this policy sits "on top" of a designer's global practice program. The term "Drop" indicates the policy will drop down on an each and every basis in the event the underlying policies have been eroded; however, this policy will only respond to claims brought in jurisdictions outside of North America. This policy is an annually renewing policy and is typically concurrent with the underlying professional liability policy (or policies).

14.4   Stand Alone Professional Liability Tower

This alternative is similar to the global practice program; however, the each and every professional liability policy is written as a separate primary program tower, not as an excess layer. Like Top & Drop, this separate tower can be written to cover all non-North American projects or for a particular non-North American project. It is an annually renewing policy and provides coverage only for claims brought in jurisdictions outside of North America. A separate program tower is typically more expensive than a Top & Drop program as it would not have the benefit of the underlying professional liability limits.

Both alternatives can be structured to cover claims only where required by written contract or only in countries where specified or applicable.

14.5   Local Insurance

In addition to requiring "each and every" limits, contracts may require that the design firm's professional liability policy be placed with a licensed, locally admitted insurer. The need for policies from a locally-licensed insurer may also be dictated by the UAE law. If the design firm's insurers are not licensed in the UAE, a local risk-bearing or fronting policy will be necessary.

14.6   Fronting Policies

A fronting policy is a policy that is procured from a local insurer and is backed up by reinsurance from the design firm's global practice program; ideally, following the same terms and conditions as that global program. The local insurer will charge a fronting charge which is based on several variables such as project type, design fee, construction values, etc.

14.7   Risk-Bearing Policy

An alternative to a fronting policy would be a risk-bearing insurance policy also known as a local risk transfer policy. This alternative is similar to a design firm's global practice program; however, this risk-bearing policy would be purchased directly from a local insurer and claims are paid by the local insurer on a primary basis.

Certain UAE insurers are licensed in both Abu Dhabi and Dubai and can therefore issue either a fronting policy or a risk-bearing policy evidencing local insurance for projects in both Emirates.

Local risk-bearing policies may not be available on an unaggregated basis. If not, the need for a Top & Drop or separate Each and Every tower professional liability policy will remain if unaggregated limits is also a contractual requirement.

There are a few things to consider when obtaining local insurance coverage:

14.8   AM Best Ratings

Many contracts will require that the firm's insurer maintain an AM Best rating of A- or better. Few local insurers can meet this requirement and most have not been assigned a Best's rating. The financial stability of the local insurer of a risk-bearing policy should be carefully evaluated by the design firm, particularly if a Best's rating is not available.

14.9   Reinsurance Agreements

When obtaining a local fronting policy, the insured will likely be required to sign an indemnity agreement in favor of the local insurer. In addition, the local insurer will execute a reinsurance agreement. A reinsurance agreement is an agreement between the local insurer and the reinsurance market, typically the architect's or engineer's global practice program insurer(s).

The challenges specific to reinsurance arrangements include:

    a. The firm's global practice program insurer may not be willing to agree to the requested reinsurance agreement.

    b. U.S. insurers may require that they arrange for the placement of the reinsurance, which adds cost to a layered professional liability program and increases the fronting policy fees.

    c. Some U.S. insurers are reluctant to provide fronting policies with no element of risk transfer and prefer that the architect or

254 Risk Management for Design Professionals

engineer obtain a risk-bearing policy with covered claims eroding their global practice program.

14.10   Typical Contract Requirements

Principal Interest Clause

This is specific cancellation wording in favor of owners that can be obtained from local insurance markets in the UAE. .If the architect or engineer obtains a local fronting policy, the local insurer will require the reinsurers of the global practice program to provide this coverage as well, to maintain consistent terms and conditions throughout the reinsurance arrangement. This could be problematic for the reinsurers, i.e. domestic carriers and London underwriters.

Waiver of Subrogation

This is a common requirement in construction contracts both domestically and worldwide. This coverage can be obtained from the local insurance market in the UAE; however, it remains a business decision of the architect or engineer to waive its rights of subrogation.

10 Year Post Completion Coverage

Many construction contracts within the UAE will require that the insurance be maintained for a period of no less than 10 years post completion. Design firms can meet this requirement in a couple of ways.

Maintain Through Annual Corporate Program

The design firm can agree to maintain its global practice program for a period of 10 years on an annually renewing basis; however, this can present a few challenges:

a.   If a fronting policy has been procured, the architect or engineer will need to renew the local fronting policy on an annual basis in addition to its global practice program, incurring its additional fronting fees each year. The fronting charges are not guaranteed in advance and must be estimated over the 10-year period to determine total cost attributable to the project.

b. The design firm runs the risk of the local insurer nonrenewing the local fronting policy and may be unable to find a replacement carrier.

Project Policies

Some owners may not accept the firm's offer to maintain coverage and will insist upon evidence of a 10-year ERP. Likewise, some design firms prefer certainty of coverage for the 10-year post-completion period. Both situations can be addressed through project insurance. As mentioned previously, there are few insurers who will write project professional liability insurance and even fewer who have expressed interested in providing this coverage in the UAE. Coverage terms, conditions, and pricing vary greatly. For instance, the insurer consistently providing the least expensive pricing offers a very narrow coverage form. One U.S. insurer offers typical U.S. terms and conditions, with coverage for claims brought anywhere in the world, but only for their own existing insureds.

It is important to be alert to contractual terms that allow the owner to change the insurance requirements in the event the owner requires the placement of project insurance. There have been situations in which owners have advised a design firm to bind project professional liability policies, only to later change their minds and refuse to pay for the policy when the premium was due. As the named insured, the design firm is still obligated to pay the premium and must appeal to the insurer to be released from the bound policy.

14.11   Non-Contract Risk: Decennial Liability

Insuring projects in the UAE has proven to be challenging for architects and engineers as local Civil Codes impose strict liability for structural defects for a period of 10 years after substantial completion of the project. Certain Civil Codes hold the designer and contractor jointly and severally liable for a period of 10 years for "any total or partial collapse of the building they have constructed or installation they have erected, and for any defect which threatens the stability or safety of the building, unless the contract specifies a longer period."

The architect and engineer cannot avoid the Civil Code liability even with favorable contract terms or an indemnification. For example, Article 882 of the Civil Code states "any agreement the purport of which is to exempt the contractor or the architect from liability, or to limit such liability, shall be void." This liability is also known as Decennial Liability.

Article 881 of the Civil Code indicates that if the designer's work is restricted to preparing the plans for a building or fixed installation and is not in any way involved in the supervision of the execution of those plans, then he or she is liable only for defects in the plans. Therefore, he or she would not be held jointly and/or severally liable with the contractor. Many design firms have elected to take on work in the UAE only on the basis of engaging in the conceptual phases of design in order to take advantage of this protection.

Decennial Liability remains a concern from both a liability aspect and an insurability aspect. Architects and engineers performing professional services throughout the world are faced with this exposure daily, particularly in the UAE, and few insurers offer a solution to this increased exposure.

14.12   Inherent Defect Insurance (IDI)

This coverage is only available in select markets outside the U.S.. These policies are typically written for the benefit of the owner and do not include coverage for the architect, engineer, or contractor without modification. These policies are expensive in nature, 1-2% of total contract value, and are written in the name of the owner - leaving the architect, engineer, or contractor (A/E/C) uninsured. The A/E/C should seek coverage as a Named Insured under the IDI policy as well as require a waiver of subrogation from the insurer in order to prevent the insurer from seeking recovery from the A/E/C once the claim has been paid under the policy. Without the waiver of subrogation from the insurer, the A/E/C may still be held liable for the loss but may not have insurance to respond to the loss.

There are several concerns that should be addressed when looking to procure IDI coverage. The insurer will hire an independent reviewer, the cost of which is not typically included within the premium quoted and must be borne by the policyholder(s). The independent reviewer will monitor the project throughout design and construction; and the insurer may at any time, up to substantial completion, withdraw the inherent defect coverage quote. This results in no coverage for all parties. The independent reviewer must be engaged at the time the design phase begins; however, the IDI insurer will require underwriting information about the contractor for the project – who most likely is not known at the time the design begins. The A/E/C should contractually require the owner to confirm and comply with the reviewer's recommendations to help ensure coverage will become effective at the time of substantial completion.

14.13   Alternative Approaches to Coverage

Insurance markets are unwilling to write professional liability policies that fully insure the joint and several liability exposure of design firms. However, there are approaches that are worthy of consideration in that they may provide significantly more protection than traditional policies.

One such insurer, Arch, through its managing general agent, DUAL, is willing to write an annual policy for design professionals with established offices in the UAE. The basis of coverage under this policy is "Civil Liability" arising from the breach of professional duty by the Insured. Discussions with the underwriter indicate that it is understood that this language may provide coverage for a decennial liability claim made against the designer; however, they are adamant that it is not their intent to provide coverage for the joint and several liability exposure of the designer arising from the contractor's operations.

Some insurers are willing to endorse their annual practice policies to offer an affirmative grant of coverage for "Strict Liability" imposed by a governmental authority. We believe this approach provides, in a different way, the same level of protection as the DUAL option, without the cost of an additional policy.

14.14   Countries with a History of Decennial Liability Exposure (IMIA Conference, 2001)

This list is not intended to be all-inclusive, but references a number of countries for which additional research into decennial liability exposures and coverage is recommended:

- Countries with compulsory decennial liability insurance: France, Spain, Italy, Finland, Australia (Victoria), Canada (British Columbia), Algeria, Saudi Arabia, Gabon, Cameroon, Congo Brazzaville, Mali, Morocco, Centrafrica, Tunisia, Egypt

- Countries without compulsory decennial liability insurance but with inherent defect insurance market: Belgium, Japan, Kuwait, Senegal

- Countries without compulsory decennial liability insurance and without significant inherent defect insurance market: Argentina, United Arab Emirates, Canada – Quebec, Netherlands, Iraq, Jordan, Philippines

14.15   Additional Points to Consider

Design firms providing a full scope of services in countries having a Civil Code with a Decennial Liability clause may have few viable insurance solutions to deal with the risks assumed.

Should the decision be made to proceed to seek work in the region, it would seem prudent to consider the following points:

- At the earliest stages, establish a working relationship with a reputable law firm practicing in the region.

- Give consideration to putting only the most skilled and seasoned professionals on these projects.

- Given the fact that simply notifying an owner of observed defects in the construction process is insufficient to relieve the architect of liability under the Code, one may want to consider requiring the right to stop the construction. This may be more effective than any other means in achieving a positive outcome.

- Attempt to obtain owner agreement to obtain a waiver of subrogation from its permanent property insurer(s) for a period of 10 years following completion of the project.

- Give consideration to requiring that dispute resolution in all contracts be governed under the rules of the DIFC-LCIA Arbitration Centre. According to Michael Gross of Clyde & Co., the Civil Code and the Commercial Code are the twin pillars of law in the UAE. The Commercial Code governs contracts. Usual contract terms will be upheld, including standard of care. Arbitration is upheld by the Commercial Code; however, most arbitration awards must be ratified by the local courts in order to be final. These courts can be capricious and are not guaranteed to rubber stamp arbitration awards. The new DIFC Arbitration Law gives more finality to awards reached using the DIFC–LCIA Arbitration Centre. These awards can be routinely converted into a DIFC court judgment.

- Explore the potential for use of the DIFC as the basis for determining liability under the Decennial provisions of the Civil Code.

Chapter 15

Continuing Education Courses

Course 1: Green Design and Construction Risk Management
Course 2: IPD and BIM Risk Management
Course 3: New Contract Documents
Course 4: International and P3 Risk Management

These courses may be taken through the end of 2012. After that, please contact a/e ProNet before submitting answers and payment.

Continuing Education: Course 1
(3 Learning Units; $39.95)

Green Design and Construction Risk Management

This course has been submitted to the American Institute of Architects (AIA) Continuing Education System (CES) as a three (3) learning unit course by a/e ProNet, an AIA registered provider of continuing education. To obtain credit, you must read the text of the chapters referenced in the questions below and submit your answers to the quiz, along with the self certification statement indicated at the conclusion of the quiz, together with your payment. Register at www.aeProNet.org. or contact info@aepronet.org for additional information.

Learning Objectives:
- To become familiar with green certification systems
- To learn key legal risks arising out of green design and how to manage them
- To learn key insurance risks arising out of green design
- To learn issues and strategies for insuring green design risks

These questions are based on the chapter by John Binder.

1.   In what year was the first LEED certified apartment building certified?
a) 2002   b) 2004   c) 2006   d) 2008

2.   The first LEED certified chapter is described by the project architect, John Binder, as a collaborative effort with the general contractor who committed to higher standards and more intensive recordkeeping.
a) True   b) False

These questions are based on the chapter by Frank Musica.

3.   What organization defines sustainability in part as follows: "The concept of meeting present needs without compromising the ability of future generations to meet their own needs?"
a) EJCDC   b) AGC   c) ABC   d) AIA

4.   Contractually committing to obtain third-party certification can lead to obligations beyond the ordinary standard of care for architects and consequently lead to contractual liability that is excluded from coverage under the professional liability policy.
a) True   b) False

5.   What are two key sections of the new AIA B101 document that create environmentally responsible design obligations?
a) Sections 2.3 and 3.3
b) Sections 3.2.3 and 3.2.5.1.
c) Sections 3.6.1 and 3.7.2.

6.   Efforts to use publications, such as codes of professional conduct, have been attempted in the past as a bases for filing a complaint alleging that a professional failed to meet the required standard of care.
a) True   b) False

7. What does the acronym LEED stand for?
a) Leading Energy Efficiency Details.
b) Leadership in Energy and Environmental Design.
c) Leadership in Environmentally Efficient Design.
d) Leading with Environment and Energy Documentation.

8. What organization created the LEED program?
a) U.S. Green Building Council
b) Green Globes
c) United Nations
d) U.S. Environmental Protection Agency

9. What organization created the Green Globes program?
a) USGBC   b) GBI   c) EPA   d) Department of Energy

The next questions are based on the chapter by Ujjval Vyas.

10. When was the U.S. Green Building Council (USGBC) formed?
a) early eighties   b) early nineties   c) early 21st century

11. With a broad-based definition of green and the relative lack of specific performance standards or specifications, the possibility of litigation as a result of failed expectations is greatly enhanced.
a) True   b) False

12. Building a project in conformance to the LEED certification process assures an "environmentally sound" building.
a) True   b) False

13. Certification and final affirmation of a rating level can be achieved during the planning stage of a building and does not have to await project completion.
a) True   b) False

14. One provision a design firm or contractor could use in its contract with a project owner to manage the extent of its risk and liability arising out of economic losses sustained by the owner due to failure to achieve a specified LEED certification is a waiver of consequential damages clause.
a) True   b) False

15. A general contractor and its subcontractors have a major role to play in the actual acquisition of a LEED certification that a design firm should not take full responsibility for the building achieving LEED certification.
a) True   b) False

16. A risk unique to green construction includes checking warranty and guaranty language to confirm that new green construction procedures and installation materials and/or techniques do not void the warranty or guaranty for products.
a) True   b) False

The next questions are based on the chapter by Kent Holland on Green Design Risks.

17. LEED certification by third party evaluators is granted only after construction of a building has been completed.
a) True   b) False

18. Specifying the use of innovative new green products has the potential to create an increased risk of product or even project failure than would occur using traditional, tried and tested products.
a) True   b) False

19. The fact that an individual is LEED certified qualifies them legally and professionally to design a project specifying the use of green products.
a) True   b) False

20. If an architect commits that LEED certification will be achieved, but for reasons beyond its responsibility LEED is not granted, the professional liability policy will probably cover a claim for damages for breach of contract.
a) True   b) False

I hereby certify that I have read the chapters referenced in the quiz for Course 1, Green Design and Construction Management, out of the book, *Risk Management for Design Professionals in a World of Change*, and personally read and answered each of the quiz questions.

Signature:_____ Date: _____

Individual Name: _____

Firm Name: _____

Address: _____

City: _____ State: _____ ZIP: _____

Phone: _____

E-mail Address: _____

AIA Member Number (if applicable): _____

Continuing Education: Course 2
(3 learning units; $39.95)

Integrated Project Delivery and Building Information Modeling

This course has been submitted to the American Institute of Architects (AIA) Continuing Education System (CES) as a three (3) learning unit course by a/e ProNet, an AIA registered provider of continuing education. To obtain credit, you must read the text of the chapters referenced in the questions below and submit your answers to the quiz, along with the self certification statement indicated at the conclusion of the quiz, together with your payment. Register at www.aeProNet.org or contact info@aepronet.org for additional information.

Learning Objectives:
- Learn key legal risks arising out of Integrated Project Delivery
- Learn key legal risks arising out of building information modeling
- Learn issues and strategies for insuring risks from IPD and BIM
- Become familiar with new contract documents for addressing IPD and BIM
- Learn contracting clauses and techniques to addressing risks of IPD and BIM

The first questions are based on the chapter by Howard Ashcraft.

1. BIM collides with traditional professional responsibility principles because although virtually all professional licensing regulations require that designs be prepared by a person 'in responsible charge', much in a collaborative design is not supervised or directed by a single person or entity.
a) True   b) False

2. BIM is not intended to be used as tool to identify and resolve conflicts between systems in the project such as HVAC, electrical and plumbing.
a) True   b) False

3. What organization is responsible for the National BIM Standard?
a) AIA   b) AGC   c) NIBS

4. A typical BIM model contains information, or can link to information, necessary to generate bills of quantity, size and area estimates, productivity, materials cost, and related estimating information
a) True   b) False

5. The information in most BIM models cannot be used to directly create fabrication drawings.
a) True   b) False

6. Because BIM can increase the designer's potential liability, there is a significant disincentive for the designer to adopt BIM, especially since the project owner and the general contractor are the most obvious beneficiaries of BIM.
a) True   b) False

7. A consensus business model for BIM now has emerged and been incorporated into a standard BIM contract document in the form of an AGC contract.
a) True   b) False

8. There will rarely be a single BIM on a complex project. The architect may have its design model, the structural engineer its analysis model, the contractor its construction model, and the fabricator its shop drawing or fabrication model.
a) True   b) False

9. Current BIM practice uses a series of interlocking models to communicate the design and construction intent for a project. In many instances, the complete design is only visualized when imported into a viewing program, such as NavisWorks JetStream.
a) True   b) False

10. With regard to design delegation issues under BIM, it can safely be concluded that BIM creates no potential new issues concerning licensing and responsible charge, especially since the model can never change details in response to changes in the design.
a) True   b) False

11. There will be a tension between historic concepts of legal liability with insurance for individual responsibility in contrast to BIM which is essentially collaborative involving joint involvement by project participants with a blurring of the lines of responsibility.
a) True   b) False

12. Extensive contractor and subcontractor involvement in the BIM is not likely to have any impact on the implied warranties of design that they might otherwise have in relying upon the design provided by the design professional pursuant to what is known as the Spearin doctrine.
a) True   b) False

13. The American Institute of Architects has issued two very different contract sets. The most innovative uses a special purpose limited liability company that is owned by the project owner, architect and contractor.
a) True   b) False

These next questions are based on the IPD/BIM chapter by Kent Holland.

14. BIM is a new project delivery system.
a) True   b) False

15. Depending upon the terms and conditions of the IDP contract, liability for design errors and construction defects could be assigned to the entire project team on some basis of shared responsibility even if a particular participant had nothing to do with causing the problem.
(a) True   b) False

16. Due to the collaborative nature of BIM, it is likely to be used on most if not all IPD projects.
a) True   b) False

17. The collaboration of contractors and subcontractors in a BIM design model has the potential to create professional liability risks for them that are not insured under their commercial general liability policy.
a) True   b) False

18. Which of the following may be of concern to the insurance underwriter when considering writing coverage for a design firm involved in an IPD/BIM project?
a) unreasonable expectations of the project owner.
b) design accepting responsibility for contractor means and methods.
c) unskilled participants involved in the project.
d) all of the above.

19. Current professional liability policies that are standard in the marketplace today for design professionals generally exclude liability arising under projects that use BIM.
a) True   b) False

These next questions are based on the AIA Documents Chapter on IPD/BIM by Suzanne Harness.

20. The AIA integrated project delivery guide (IPD Guide) was prepared jointly by the AIA's Documents Committee and AIA Wyoming Council.
a) True   b) False

21. IPD is a rigid formula that project participants must follow in a very specific manner because IPD principles can be applied to only a single type of contractual arrangement.
a) True   b) False

22. AIA C106–2007 does not forbid reliance on the data or disclaim responsibility for errors or omissions in the content; however, under certain circumstances parties may limit uses of the data by insertions in the Permitted Uses column of E201–2007, or in Article 3 of C106–2007.
a) True   b) False

23. Design professionals may consider using C106–2007 if a new building owner wishes to use the original architect's, or a consultant's, instruments of service to modify the building.
a) True   b) False

24. AIA's IPD agreements, released in 2008, all require the use of BIM to the fullest extent possible.
a) True   b) False

25. Using C195, the owner, architect, construction manager, and perhaps other key project participants, each becomes a member of a single purpose entity (SPE).
a) True   b) False

I hereby certify that I have read the chapters referenced in the quiz for Course 2, Integrated Project Delivery and Building Information Modeling, out of the book, *Risk Management for Design Professionals in a World of Change*, and personally read and answered each of the quiz questions.

Signature:_____ Date: _____

Individual Name: _____

Firm Name: _____

Address: _____

City: _____ State: _____ ZIP: _____

Phone: _____

E-mail Address: _____

AIA Member Number (if applicable): _____

Continuing Education: Course 3
(4 learning units; $49.95)

New Contract Documents

This course has been submitted to the American Institute of Architects (AIA) Continuing Education System (CES) as a four (4) learning unit course by a/e ProNet, an AIA registered provider of continuing education. To obtain credit, you must read the text of the chapters referenced in the questions below and submit your answers to the quiz, along with the self certification statement indicated at the conclusion of the quiz, together with your payment. Register at www.aeProNet.org or contact info@aepronet.org for additional information.

Learning Objectives:
- Become familiar with ConsensusDOCS
- Become familiar with new AIA B101-2007
- Become familiar with new EJCDC documents
- Learn key new and controversial issues of AIA B101 impacting risks
- Learn to revise contract clauses to manage risks

The first questions are based on the AIA documents chapter by Suzanne Harness.

1. The AIA's 2008 BIM exhibit may be used with any project delivery method, including design-bid build, construction management, design-build, and IPD.
a) True   b) False

2. The AIA's IPD agreements all require the use of BIM.
a) True   b) False

3. Which of the following is for use on IPD projects?
a) B 141   b) C 141   c) B-195   d) None of the above

4. For single purpose entity (SPE) the AIA provides from C-195-2008.
a) True   b) False

The next questions are based on the chapter by Mark Friedlander.

5. In the new AIA B101 document, there is for the first time an express standard of care to which the architect is to perform.
a) True   b) False

6. The new AIA B101 form provides a detailed description of the insurance, including amounts, terms and conditions, to be maintained by the architect.
a) True   b) False

7. Under the new AIA B101, the architect is not responsible for an owner's directive or substitution made without the architect's knowledge or evaluation.
a) True   b) False

8. B101, Section 3.2.3 requires the architect to contact the permit-issuing governmental authority and any utility servicing the project.
a) True   b) False

9. The language of B101, section 3.4.2 requires the Architect to comply with governmental requirements by incorporating these requirements into the design.
a) True   b) False

10. Under section 3.6.1.2 of B101, the Architect is given greater responsibility for the contractor's means, methods, and procedures.
a) True   b) False

11. In the new B101 document, the Architect's time for reviewing shop drawings and other submittals is linked to a submittal schedule to be prepared by the contractor.
a) True   b) False

12. Under section 5.2 of B101, the architect is given veto power over budget changes to the project by the owner.
a) True   b) False

13. Under section 5.10 of B101, the owner is forbidden from having any direct communications with the contractor or architect's consultants without going through the Architect.
a) True   b) False

14. Section 10.8 "Confidential Information," makes confidentiality a mutual obligation of the owner and the architect.
a) True   b) False

The next questions are based on the EJCDC chapter by Hugh Anderson.

15. The EJCDC Construction Series (C-series is comprised (as of 2007) of twenty-one documents for use in establishing and administering the contractual relationships.
a) True   b) False

16. EJCDC takes the position that owners should not typically require bidders to conduct their own subsurface testing.
a) True   b) False

17. Under the general conditions of the EJCDC construction contract documents, the rights of the contractor to an adjustment in price because of differing site conditions are similar in most situations to that provided in the Federal Acquisition Regulations.
a) True   b) False

18. Written notice of a claim by the contractor must be provided to the engineer no later than 20 days after the start of the event giving rise to the claim.
a) True   b) False

The next questions are based on the chapter by Brian Perlberg.

19. Thirty-two leading construction associations representing a diverse coalition of owners, contractors, sureties, and design professionals joined together to develop the first consensus standard contracts based on best practices and fair risk allocation for all parties.
a) True   b) False

20. The participating organizations built consensus from the foundation of the previous AGC as well as the COAA contracts.
a) True   b) False

21. The "DOCS" in ConsensusDOCS stands for designers, owners, contractors, subcontractors and sureties.
a) True   b) False

22. The ConsensusDOCS have a "check the box" provision by which the parties select litigation or arbitration for claims elevated to binding dispute resolution.
a) True   b) False

23. ConsensusDOCS adopts an innovative approach that permits the owner to release retainage applicable to the work of early finishing trades and other subcontractors once their work has been accepted. Once the overall work of the project is 50 percent complete, then the Owner is not permitted to withhold any additional retainage.
a) True   b) False

24. The ConsensusDOCS 301 BIM Addendum gives Parties five options to determine their reliance on the model that range from full reliance for dimensional accuracy to using BIM for informational purposes only in Section 4.3.11.
a) True   b) False

The next questions are based on the chapter by Jerry Bales.

25. ConsensusDOCS 240 differs from the AIA documents in that it grants the project owner with a property interest in the architect's instruments of service whereas the AIA documents (B141 and B101) give property ownership and copyright interest exclusively to the architect.
a) True   b) False

26. It must be noted that ConsensusDOCS 245, Short Form Agreement defines the standard of care in a manner that is similar to the AIA definition, whereas in contrast to ConsensusDOCS 240 states that the architect has a position of trust and confidence – and this could create a fiduciary duty with uninsurable liability.
a) True   b) False

27. ConsensusDOCS 240 requires these Documents to *"completely describe all work necessary to bid and construct the Project."* This sentence is not contained in ConsensusDOCS 245, Short Form Agreement, and is not a practical obligation to be agreed to by the design professional.
a) True   b) False

28. In its 2007 documents, the AIA requires the Architect to discuss with the Owner the feasibility of incorporating *"environmentally responsible"* design alternatives. By comparison, ConsensusDOCS 240 and ConsensusDOCS 245, Short Form Agreement, do not require the Architect/Engineer to consider sustainability issues.
a) True   b) False

I hereby certify that I have read the chapters referenced in the quiz for Course 3, New Contract Documents, out of the book, *Risk Management for Design Professionals in a World of Change*, and personally read and answered each of the quiz questions.

Signature:_____ Date: _____

Individual Name: _____

Firm Name: _____

Address: _____

City: _____ State: _____ ZIP: _____

Phone: _____

E-mail Address: _____

AIA Member Number (if applicable): _____

Continuing Education: Course 4
(2 learning units; $29.95)

International Risk Management and Public Private Partnership Risk Management

This course has been submitted to the American Institute of Architects (AIA) Continuing Education System (CES) as a two (2) learning unit course by a/e ProNet, an AIA registered provider of continuing education. To obtain credit, you must read the text of the chapters referenced in the questions below and submit your answers to the quiz, along with the self certification statement indicated at the conclusion of the quiz, together with your payment. Register at www.aeProNet.org or contact info@aepronet.org for additional information.

Learning Objectives:
- Become familiar with legal risks unique to international projects
- Become familiar with insurance issues unique to international projects
- Learn key risk management strategies for international projects
- Learn key insurance strategies for addressing international projects

The first questions are based on the chapter by John Wilson.

1. International construction projects are commonly susceptible to a host of project-specific political risks. These include special taxes, environmental controls, labor or wage restrictions.
a) True   b) False

2. Political Risk Insurance (PRI) can be tailored to cover expropriation, selective discrimination, political violence, currency inconvertibility, and many other types of political risks.
a) True   b) False

3. Typical forms of expropriation coverage require the insurer to indemnify the policyholder for the diminished value of the asset, investment or property right that has been expropriated by the host government.
a) True   b) False

4. Stand-alone terrorism in high risk areas is never available.
a) True   b) False

5. Unfavorable currency fluctuation is perhaps the most common risk affecting international contractors, and this can easily be insured through a political risk policy.
a) True   b) False

6. Professional liability policies are primarily intended to insure policyholders against damages caused by their professional negligence. Absent policy language to the contrary, these policies will *not* typically insure policyholders against liabilities assumed under contractual guaranties and warranties.
a) True   b) False

7. Given the risk that an international project participant may be sued in a foreign court with far different rules and procedures than the insured has previously experienced, the right to an insurer-provided defense is an important factor for many policyholders.
a) True   b) False

The next questions are based on the chapter by Steve Taylor.

8. Contracts may require that the design firm's professional liability policy be placed with a licensed, locally admitted insurer. The need for policies from a locally-licensed insurer may also be dictated by the UAE law. If the design firm's insurers are not licensed in the UAE, a local risk-bearing or fronting policy will be necessary.
a) True   b) False

9. It is easy to obtain insurance coverage for decennial liability in the UAE under a standard professional liability insurance policy issued by an American based insurance carrier.
a) True   b) False

10. Inherent Defect Insurance (IDI) is available in select markets outside the US. These policies are typically written for the benefit of the owner and do not include coverage for the architect, engineer or contractor without modification.
a) True   b) False

The next questions are based on the P3 chapter by Simon Santiago

11. In a 2009 assessment, the ASCE assessed the condition of the nation's aging pubic infrastructure as equal to:
a) A   b) B   c) C   d) D

12. The guiding principles of assessing, allocating, and managing risks on a P3 project are similar for the private and public partners.
a) True   b) False

13. One concept of P3 is that greater risks are able to be transferred to the private sector because P3 contracts generally are "performance based" and give more control to the private sector than is customary with traditional contracting methods.
a) True   b) False

14. Under a typical P3 concessionaire arrangement, the private sector partner is responsible for developing the plans, making the assumptions in the design, and operating and maintaining the project after construction is complete.
a) True   b) False

15. One key method for maintaining and managing the parties' predetermined responsibilities and risk allocation to the contractor on P3 projects is the use of performance specifications as opposed to prescriptive design specifications.
a) True   b) False

16. Prescriptive design specifications give the private sector partner greater ability to innovate and pursue alternative design solutions than do performance specifications.
a) True   b) False

17. On P3 projects, the public owner, by imposing its own preferences and design details, can generally shift greater risk to the private sector partner in the event of a design defect or failure.
a) True   b) False

I hereby certify that I have read the chapters referenced in the quiz for Course 4, International Risk Management and Public Private Partnership Risk Management, out of the book, *Risk Management for Design Professionals in a World of Change*, and personally read and answered each of the quiz questions.

Signature:_____ Date: _____

Individual Name: _____

Firm Name: _____

Address: _____

City: _____ State: _____ ZIP: _____

Phone: _____

E-mail Address: _____

AIA Member Number (if applicable): _____